Energy Problems& Future Perspective

About commodities, the environment and financial markets

A global view from a Dutch perspective

Publisher:
Mercurious
WTC (B Tower), 8th floor
Strawinskylaan 829
1077 XX Amsterdam
The Netherlands

Printer:
Drukkerij De Steegh
Snoekbaarsweg 4
3751 BK Bunschoten-Spakenburg
The Netherlands

First published in Dutch, December 2007;
1st English print, December 2008

ISBN: 978-90-811109-5-2

This book was written by Jerry de Leeuw. English translation by Rosalyn Gingell.
Final edit by Rosalyn Gingell and Jerry de Leeuw. The cover was designed by Eric Janson.

The information in this book is not intended as investment advice or as a recommendation for making particular investments or performing certain activities.

CONTENTS

ABOUT THE AUTHOR

After completing his studies in Economics at the Vrije Universiteit in Amsterdam, author Jerry de Leeuw became a market maker (a professional option trader) on the floor of the Option Exchange in Amsterdam.
Jerry is still active in the financial world: his company, Mercurious (www.mercurious.nl), delivers training and consultancy for the financial sector and the energy branch. His competences lie in the areas of energy markets, risk management and derivatives. In this capacity, he is a regular speaker at seminars and meetings at home and abroad.

He is also a columnist for the Dutch financial websites of Het Financieele Dagblad and IEX, and he fulfils a similar role in the Middle East for AMEinfo.com, for which he writes the Futures & Commodities column.

At the Anglo-Dutch energy exchange, the APX Group, Jerry was responsible on ad interim basis for developing the continental gas markets of the Netherlands and Belgium. He is further associated with Nyenrode Business University where he is project leader for the development of a new oil index. He presented the underlying

scientific report for the first time at the 2007 Energy & Value symposium organized by the Rijks Universiteit Groningen and the Energy Delta Institute, under the auspices of the Multinational Finance Society.

Other books published by the author: *Milkshakes & Butterflies* (2006) and *Hit & Lift* (2007).

INTRODUCTION

In 2006, George Bush spoke those legendary words: *"We have a serious problem. We are addicted to oil".* The truth is, the whole world is addicted to oil, just as it is to many other commodities. The human race is increasing fast and is also becoming more prosperous, which is resulting in all of us consuming far more, in both an absolute and a relative sense. The combination of population growth and the increase of per capita income is creating enormous growth of the commodity sector.

The United Nations (UN) expects that in 2050 there will be about 9.2 billion people living on Earth. At the moment there are 6.5 billion, compared to 1.7 billion at the beginning of the 20th century. As a result of prosperity and progress in medical science, people are also living longer. Because of this, the UN's prognosis could possibly even be amended upwards in the (near) future.

The average income of more than half of the world's population is at the moment two euros per person per day. In total, 1.2 billion people have to manage on less than one euro per day. The average annual income of an African family in 2007 was even lower than in 1970. However, when economic prosperity takes a grip of that continent, it is expected that even there demand for elementary goods will rocket.

In 2007, almost 1 billion people had an annual income of more than 10,000 dollars. This number will rise to 2.5 billion by 2030. The middle-income group today consists of 1.5 billion people; by 2030 this number is expected to have risen to 5 billion.

Commodity consumption is closely linked to the level of prosperity. In absolute quantities, the Americans use far and away the most oil. In 2006, the United States got through a total of 21 billion barrels, compared to 15 billion in Europe, 7 billion in China and 2.5 billion in India. Even in regard to relative use of oil, the US is a clear leader. An average American gets through 25 barrels a year; Europeans get through half that amount and the average use in China and India in 2007 was less than 2 barrels per person. The current strain on the world market for commodities comes from, among other things, the high economic growth of both of the last-mentioned countries. China and India are home to 2.5 billion people, which equates to almost 40% of the world's population. In 2030, global consumption of primary commodities will be three-and-a-half times more than it is now. At the moment, 20% of the world's population (Europe and the US together) is responsible for 86% of total oil consumption.

There will be new customers for scarce goods in the future. The availability of commodities, like a variety of energy forms, is already surpassing national interests. China, for instance, is so desperately searching for all sorts of commodities that it is intensifying contact with African countries and offering them more economic aid in exchange for commodities. China is also strengthening contact with the Middle East and with Russia. Many countries are trying to manoeuvre themselves into positions that will ensure them a supply of basic products in the future. The largest economic powers (US, Europe, Japan, China and India) are all dependent on the import of energy sources.

That securing own interests is paramount was proven in January 2006 when, without warning, Russia temporarily cut the gas supply to Europe because of a conflict Russia had with the Ukraine. Partly because of that, importing countries do not want to be dependent on unstable regions, preferring instead to pursue an independent policy with the 'energy supply security policy'. Unfortunately, such wishes are not always easy to realize. Demand for energy continues to increase while supplies decrease. Dependence on countries like Russia will, therefore, only continue to increase. Europe is already getting 25% of its gas supply from Russia, and that percentage will have risen to 60% by 2025. The Kremlin tries to use the position of power that it has, whereby (geo) politics and prestige sometimes play a more prominent role than pure economic interests.

In that sense, it can be said that it is not so much a question of an energy problem, but more a stability problem concerning supply security. There is still sufficient energy in various forms, it is just that people have to be capable of getting their hands on it. Environmental pollution and the climate changes linked to it are huge problems that are receiving a great deal of attention at the moment. In 2006, former Dutch Secretary of State Van Geel quite rightly said: "We can deny it no longer".

The energy problem is not only a supply problem; it seems to be chiefly a political matter and a matter of environmental-sensitivity, technology and costs. There is still plenty of oil in the world, but it is becoming increasingly more difficult to extract. Sources on the surface are the first to be exploited and are now clearly scarcer. Deepwater drilling can open up sources that lie far below sea level, but complicated production tools are needed and accompanying costs can be exorbitant.

Techniques are advancing rapidly, but with current technology only 30% of the available oil is being extracted from regular sources. Complex processes and operations needed to extract all the oil from a source or to exploit difficult-to-access sources demand huge investments. The rise in commodity prices over the last few years is proof of that. Effects that force prices up stimulate the development of alternatives. The search for such alternatives is now well under way. Enterprises like Royal Dutch Shell are increasingly concentrating on highly technologically activities; activities such as oil extraction oil in deep water, liquefied natural gas and unconventional oil, including oil from tar sands. But it doesn't end with these new forms of fossil fuels because the climate is also changing. Most theories assume that man is the major cause of this. Many scientific experiments show with significant certainty that excessive carbon dioxide emissions are to blame for the drastically-changing weather conditions. That is why the Kyoto Protocol was drawn up with the intention of avoiding further global warming by reducing greenhouse gas emissions. On the basis of this protocol a trading system with CO_2 emission rights has been implemented in various countries. CO_2-emitting enterprises in countries that ratify the protocol must now have these contracts.

The primary objectives of energy policy are in respect of issues like sustainability, competitive positions and supply security. This will lead, among other things, to a change in the sorts of products used. Energy transition plays a major role in this process and includes, among other things, replacing classic fossil fuels with alternative sources. In addition to achieving environmental advantage, durable energy must also make the supply to Western countries less vulnerable.

Energy transition has become irrevocable and no-one knows where this will eventually lead. The adjustment process is extraordinarily difficult because the habits of the general public have to undergo a change. Willingness to change must be increased, and that doesn't happen by itself. The government will have to offer support in order to create a basis for the necessary alterations. It should create the right conditions under which people will actively adjust their standards and values *and* their behaviour. The need for energy transition must be clear and evident, otherwise any attempt at it is doomed to failure and clever words will become empty promises. For the Netherlands, the role of the government in this process has diminished as energy markets are liberalized. Consumers can now choose for themselves which form of energy, energy system and energy supplier they want. The government attends to the duty and collection of tax for pollution issues and gives, where necessary, subsidies for sustainability as a stimulant for the transition.

Sustainability, re-cycling and savings offer a solution for the energy and environment problem. The search for alternatives and the optimization of their efficiency is now in full swing. The European Union (EU) has translated this view into policy and set itself the goal that in 2020 20% of all energy used must come from durable solutions. By that time, CO2 emissions must be 20% lower than in 1990 and energy-saving must be increased by the same amount, which will mean an annual reduction of about 2%.

The energy sector is totally active. The developments in this branch are particularly interesting because of the many areas of knowledge that are involved. A good understanding of the energy markets is a decisive factor for all involved. Knowledge of technology and physics and chemistry is required, as is knowledge of geography and politics. In addition, environmentology, climatology and even meteorology require our attention. Fortunately, we do not need to know everything; that is, after all, virtually impossible. No-one knows exactly how much extractable fossil fuel is still available. Furthermore, many alternatives still have to be crystallized or even discovered, and nothing is yet known about that. The subject of energy is so comprehensive that the search for answers to all the accompanying problems seems endless. Striving for complete knowledge is, however, not unique. We can consider ourselves fortunate with the knowledge that Johann Heinrich Zedler began to write in 1731 in his book *"Universal-Lexicon aller Wissenschaften und Künste"*, a book that tried to describe all the knowledge in the world. When the German finished this mega project 23 years later, it appeared that all this knowledge was contained in 64 volumes. A reprint of this lexicon is still available at better bookshops. The whole series costs just 16,200 euros, including VAT. Not much for anyone wishing to know everything.

This book is alternatively aimed at the global energy market and, more specifically, at the European and Dutch market. National developments and policy in the field of energy are now largely determined by international politics. The wider picture therefore has to be reviewed. This book, just as the bud of a rose, is built up of various layers and separate parts. The total gives a clear view of today's most important energy problems and (potential) solutions. This book deals with controversial issues such as the fight against climate change, durable energy, more efficient use of energy, improvement of supervision in the energy sector, division of energy companies and diversification of energy acquisition. At the moment, energy markets are in dire need of concrete decisions; the pitch is strewn with uncertainty. There are various risks in several areas: how secure is CO2 capture? How easy will it be? Will the European emission trading system (ETS) work? Is a reduction of 30% actually achievable? Are the cabinet's objectives actually reasonable? Are enough measures being taken to motivate all parties to sustainability? Will we still be forced to choose power plants and nuclear energy? Is enough space being created for decentralized generation of energy?

Chapter 1 deals with commodities in general. Various categories are described and per group more light is shed on a number of products. Moreover, the basis is formed in this section for understanding the factors that are important for pricing commodities. Important energy products, like oil, gas, coal and electricity, are dealt with in Chapter 2. Chapters 3 to 6 deal with the problems that crop up on the energy markets, and a number of possible solutions are set out in Chapters 7 to 9. In Chapter 10, all these issues are tested for feasibility and therefore subjected to common-sense and reality. Chapter 11 deals with the liberalization of energy markets and everything that involves, like pricing, market power and division. Then more light is shed on the financial markets in Chapter 12. This involves the integration of the energy markets in the financial circuit being dealt with, and a close look being taken at issues like transparency, regulation and benchmarks. Chapters 13 and 14 give insight into the way in which attention can be given to risk control.

Note:
Unless otherwise expressly stated, the figures and amounts in this book relate to 2006 as a whole year, or to 1 January 2007 as a specific date. Some amounts have been converted from dollars to euros, or vice versa. On 1 January 2007, 1 euro cost 1.32 dollars.

CHAPTER 1:
Commodities

1.1   Introduction

All material is made up of atoms. Practically all physical and chemical characteristics of materials found on Earth are linked to the characteristics of atoms. For their part, chemical elements are the jigsaw pieces of atoms. Mother Earth is made up of numerous elements and contains many different materials. Most of these are found deep underground; we call them commodities or base products that can be used for the manufacture of end products. The Earth is actually one great collection of commodities, but because of excessive use, this supply of raw materials will one day run out. In other words, Earth is being exhausted. Because of exploitation, underground supplies of, for example, oil, gas, gold, copper, nickel, zinc and iron ore are decreasing. Wood will remain available only as long as man continues to plant sufficient trees.

The Earth's core has a diameter of almost 7000 kilometres (4350 miles) and consists primarily of iron and nickel. These elements are therefore present in abundance. The question regarding every commodity is whether it can be found on the surface or only in the depths of the Earth. In the case of the latter, it is virtually impossible to mine these materials with current techniques. According to geologist Bernard Wood of Macquarie University in Australia, 1% of Mother Earth, including her core, is even made up of gold. If this is correct and if this gold were to be smeared over the Earth's surface, we would be up to our knees in this precious metal and the price of gold would almost certainly undergo drastic alteration.

1.2 Applications

Commodities are, therefore, used to make end products. Just like a *black-box*, commodities go in one end of the factory and then roll off the production line at the other end as ready-to-use products. A computer, for example, is made up of about 30% ferrous metals, 23% plastics, 18% non-ferrous metals (like lead, cadmium and mercury), 15% glass and 12% precious metals (gold, silver, palladium and platinum). In addition, a lot of energy is needed for the end production or the assembly of semi-manufactured products. This can be supplied in different forms; the most usual are electricity, gas, oil and coal. The manufacture of steel actually requires so much energy that, at the price level of 2007, about a third of the total cost comes from energy consumption.

Commodities are necessary for the manufacture of all products. While drinking beer, very few people stop to think about how it is made. The packaging is made of aluminium, glass or plastic. Hops, malt and barley are the specific ingredients in the brew. In addition, a great deal of pure water is needed and the whole process requires a lot of energy. Those who have ever taken a car to pieces know how many different parts this form of transport is made up of. Any random car is made up, on average, of 70% of all sorts of steel and iron and 12% synthetic material or plastic. Then there is rubber (5%) and glass (3%). Oils, grease and gasses account for 4% of the total. Aluminium (2%), non-ferrous metals (2%) and lead (1%) complete the whole thing.

1.3 Categories

Commodities can be divided into various groups; and each category has its own specific characteristics. Broadly speaking, there are the following divisions: metals, agricultural products, energy, base products, fibres, emissions and freight. The last one does not involve (raw) materials but does involve the transport of them. In financial markets this group is nevertheless often included in the asset class "commodities" because freight is closely linked to developments within the commodity sector.

The division of commodity classes can be refined by use of sub-categories. Metals are generally sub-divided into precious metals and industrial metals. Agricultural products (or soft commodities) include stock breeding and grown (rather than mined) products. This last group, in turn, is further divided into crops such as those grown in the West, and products from exotic regions. This division can be seen in Figure 1.

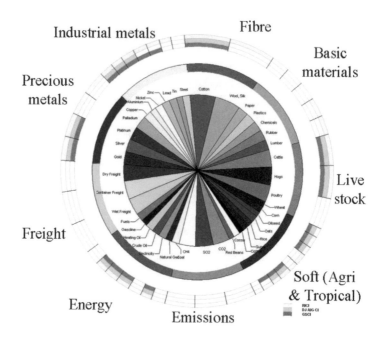

Figure 1: Individual commodities and categories

In this book, the emphasis is on energy and everything that entails (especially emissions, freight and agricultural products). Some attention is given to metals and agricultural products below. The large demand for metals (and other non-energy products) is keeping pace with the demand for energy. They basically both have the same source: population growth in combination with rising prosperity. The fundamental factors that influence price are largely the same as, or at least similar to, the factors that apply to fuels. Moreover, a lot of energy is often needed for the extraction of commodities, as it is for the manufacture of end products. This is yet another reason to take a closer look at developing commodities other than fuels. In the following paragraphs, the handling of questions concerning the last-mentioned category aims at contributing to the increase of general insight in the energy sector.

The agricultural crops category is not only important for the production of food; some products can even serve as a source for the production of environment-friendly bio-energy.

(More about that in Chapter 8, section 8.6 of this book. The freight category is very closely linked to the transportation of energy and is discussed at length in Chapter 4. The emission class is thoroughly covered in Chapter 6.)

1.3.1 Industrial metals

Industrial metals are, among other things, used for building houses, offices, factories and infrastructure: solid constructions, but even the preparatory logistic processes require a lot of commodities.

Iron

Steel is an alloy of iron and carbon and is used a lot in building structures. Iron is the most used metal worldwide, with aluminium a close second. The largest iron ore mine in the world is in Casa de Pedra. This Brazilian quarry has a reserve of 8.4 billion tons and the quality of the iron ore is extremely high-grade; it has an iron content of 65%, which denotes a very attractive (high) grade of purity.

The Brazilians have launched plans to strengthen their position on the iron ore market. The country is investing 1.5 billion dollars to boost the present production of 16 million tons of iron to 40 million tons in 2009, and to 55 million tons in 2011.

The Brazilian CVRD and the Australian Rio Tinto and BHP Billiton are together good for 75% of all globally shipped iron ore. These enterprises enter into agreements with customers in which particular conditions are set down, such as the price. This 'tripartite oligopoly' price is used as the reference in the steel market and is the benchmark for this product. There is no real Futures market for iron ore, and because of this there is a lack of transparency. This means in practice that market parties keep a close eye on the big players so they can determine what the current prices are.

	Iron ore production
China	420
Brazil	281
Australia	262
India	154
Russia	97
Ukraine	69
United States	55
South Africa	40
Canada	28
Sweden	23

Figure 2: Countries with the largest production of iron ore (in million tons) (FD Research, 2007).

Aluminium

At 8%, aluminium is the most common metal in the Earth's crust, yet it was only discovered in 1807. The metal is found mixed with oxygen in bauxite (aluminium ore). About 90,000 tons of aluminium comes onto the market every day. A great deal of treatment is required to obtain aluminium in pure form. Energy-wasting processes demand, dependent on the price level, 20 to 40% of total production costs. Because of this, the demand for aluminium often equals the demand for coal, or vice versa. Various aluminium producers set up their production systems in areas where energy is also produced. The Russian Rusal, that was set up by, among others, the owner of Chelsea Football Club, Roman Abramovic, wants to establish an aluminium forge in Papua, New Guinea, chiefly because this country is so rich in natural gas.

New Guinea in West Africa is the largest exporter of bauxite. Alcao is the largest aluminium producer in the world. The five largest suppliers together hold a 51% share of the market. This percentage has increased over the last few years, which is also the case with many other commodity sectors. Consolidation processes lead to the power of parties such as these increasing, which could result in commodity prices being driven up artificially. This could lead to the forming of cartels and abuse of power.

	Bauxite production
Brazil	22.03
Guinea	19.24
China	18.00
Jamaica	14.12
India	12.34
Russia	6.41
Venezuela	5.90
Kazakhstan	4.82
Suriname	4.76
Greece	2.44

Figure 3: Countries with the largest production of bauxite (in million tons) (FD Research, 2007).

Copper

In 1856, mine workers in Michigan (USA) encountered a block of pure copper that weighed 500 tons. At the end of 2006, this lump of copper was worth more than 3 million dollars as the price per ton was then 6,300 dollars. During the period from the beginning of 2004 to May 2006, the price of copper rose by 400%. This wild growth got even more out of hand because of strikes in the mining industry. The risen prices were the cause of all sorts of strange activities. In 2006, an attempt was made to steal 2,000 kilos of copper from a depot of a recycling company in Utrecht. The Dutch Railway Police (Nederlandse Spoorwegpolitie) further reported almost a hundred cases of copper theft from pipes along the lines. Furthermore, seven statues were stolen from the garden of the Singer Museum in Laren. These art treasures were actually not made of copper but of bronze, a copper alloy.

There's a lot of copper present in the environment; it can even be found in food, in the air and in drinking water, which is why people daily consume a considerable amount of copper particles. Copper is actually a necessary micro-nutrient, but that doesn't alter the fact that consumption of large amounts can cause health problems. Copper is primarily employed in industry and house-building where the material is used, among other things, in making electricity cables and telephone cables. An average American newly-built house contains about 200 kilos of copper.

Copper is quite simple to work and to extract. Archaeological research has taught us that man was already using copper 11,000 years ago. Together with other metals, it forms alloys. Copper (75%) and tin (25%) together form bronze, while the combination of copper and zinc is called brass.

Chile, with 4.5 million tons, is the largest copper producer (33%). Peru and the US, some way behind, are numbers two and three respectively. These three countries together are good for half of the world's total copper production. Australia, Indonesia, Poland, Zambia, Zaire and Canada each also have a considerable finger in the pie in the copper market. Phelps Dodge is the largest exchange-listed copper producer. The performance of this mining-industry share is highly dependent on the price development of copper. Prices of commodities are sometimes kept artificially high; in 2005, a third of the capacity of the copper sector was even deliberately immobilized.

At the end of 2005, China, via the Chinese agency that watches over trading in commodities, claimed to have a reserve of 1.3 million tons of copper. The rest of the world doubted the accuracy of this amount, but control is almost impossible. Chinese copper production rose in 2006 to 2 million tons per year. Annual consumption, however, was 3.7 million tons, as a result of which China imported 1.7 million tons in 2006. About 18 million tons of copper are put on the market worldwide, and of that China therefore uses up 20%.

Lead

Pure lead, which is generally present in zinc, silver and copper ores, is seldom found. It seems to be harmful to the environment and to health. Prolonged exposure to lead and lead alloys can cause brain damage and can lead, among other things, to dementia.

Pure lead used to be added to gasoline as a stabilizer. By adding it to paint, paint became more resistant to the influences of weather. Nowadays, lead-free gasoline has become a general concept, paint is also made differently, and batteries are generally lead-free.

Lead is found in a great many countries, including Australia. The country 'down under' is one of the most important commodity suppliers in the world. Not taking oil and gas into account, about 38% of all exchange-listed raw-material enterprises are of Australian origin. The Australian BHP Billiton is the largest mining enterprise in the world and at the end of 2006, 18% of the Australian exchange was even defined by developments in the mining sector. Australia profits greatly from its raw material sources. In 2006, the country deposited 140 billion Australian dollars (84 billion euros) worth of commodities on foreign soil, which was 60% of Australia's total export.

The Magellan Mine in Australia was opened in 2005 and is the most promising lead mine in the world. Because of the mass death of birds and other animals, Esperance Harbour in Western Australia was closed to the transport (export) of lead in 2007. Because of this, production was suspended for a few months.

Nickel

Nickel is chiefly used for forming stainless steel. The shortage of nickel on the market is so great that the price has risen drastically, and it is not inconceivable that soon even nickel will be classified in the sub-category 'precious metals'. Chrome and manganese can serve the same objective as nickel and are therefore both seen as substitutes. Substitution takes place when the price of a commodity has risen so much that alternative products are sought and used instead. This shift leads to price restraint of the initial commodity, and in some extreme cases it can even result in a severe drop in the value ('demand destruction').

At the end of January 2007, a container ship stranded off the coast of England in a mighty storm. The vessel, which came from South Africa, was laden with thousands of tons of nickel. Seeing as four thousand tons of nickel is used worldwide every day, this incident led to a hefty price movement on the nickel market. The load was later retrieved from the ship but it took a year before it could be traded on the market.

The Canadian nickel mine Sudbury, property of the Xstrata company, is good for 5% of global nickel production. The province of Ontario produces one-third of the worldwide total. Cuba commands 33% of the world's nickel reserve and has delivered exclusively to China since 2007. Russia, Australia and Indonesia are also large suppliers to the world's bulk consumers.

	Country	Turnover
BHP Billiton	UK / Australia	39
Anglo American	UK / South Africa	33
Alcoa	United States	30
Rio Tinto	UK / Australia	25
Alcan	Canada	24
Comp. Vale do Rio Doce	Brazil	20
Xstrata	UK / Switzerland	18
Codelco	China	17
Phelps Dodge	United States	12
Norilsk Nickel	Russia	11

Figure 4: The largest mining producers in the world, measured by turnover (in billion dollars) (2006).

The position these large mining companies hold on the commodity market is especially important because it provides an insight into the developments of commodities. The mining sector has been characterised by mergers and take-overs over the last few years; in total, 157 billion dollars were committed to mergers and company take-overs in 2006 and 2007. Mine companies also buy interests in energy companies. The Russian Norilsk Nickel made a bid for the Russian electricity producer OGK. Production of energy and industrial materials are closely linked because melting processes are extremely energy-intense; that is why mining companies increasingly establish themselves near energy sources.

Tin

Tin adheres easily to iron and is therefore often used as an anti-rust coating for tin cans. The application of tin in batteries is generally known. The metal is found on almost every continent, but Indonesia is one of the largest producers. The Indonesian government launched plans at the end of 2006 to curb the export of tin and to tackle illegal extraction of the hard metal. Moreover, the country threatened to impose a tin export ban on a few companies. This political action led to panic on the tin market, which came under even more pressure than it been until then.

In the middle of 2007, the harbour of the Australian town Esperance closed its ports because of the mass death of birds due to lead poisoning. Because of the closing of one of the most important tin export ports, the price of tin rose to new records.

Zinc

Just like tin, zinc is also used as a protective component against rust. China used to be an important exporter of this metal, but now this Asian country is one of the largest importers. But China is now also a large zinc producer (25% of the world market). Russia needs increasingly more zinc for its own use, which makes the Russian role of exporter less considerable. Peru has large reserves of zinc, but this country wrestles with the problem of being able to increase capacity. Finally, the US and Canada are also two important zinc producers.

1.3.2 Precious metals

Precious metals are not only used in the manufacture of coins and jewellery, they also have application possibilities in electronics and medicine. High-quality metals are often used by investors as a safe haven in the event of political instability and/or inflation.

Gold

Only a handful of metals are extracted from the ground in pure and polished form. Usually metals are mixed with oxygen, sulphur or carbon and formed into ores. Occasionally, nuggets of gold are still found. In 1869, one lucky devil came upon a lump of pure gold weighing 69.92 kilos, the equivalent of 2248 troy ounces. At the end of 2007, one troy ounce was worth about 800 dollars. At that time the value of that lump of gold was almost 2 million dollars. Unfortunately such finds don't happen very often. One ton of ore containing gold particles usually yields only ten grams of gold in total. Gold used to be used as a method of payment, later it became a hedge for paper money brought into circulation. Gold has always been regarded as the ultimate method of payment. It is the property of no-one and always represents a certain value. Even under awful economic circumstances, gold still has value, although this does, of course, fluctuate. Gold is a useful instrument for overcoming rising inflation. Even now, the title 'safe haven' is still always justified. When restlessness prevails on financial markets, investors often exchange their shares for gold. It is important for everyone to realise that gold is priced in American dollars; a weakening in the dollar rate will therefore directly lead to relatively cheap gold in the eyes on non-Americans. It has to be said that this phenomenon stimulates extra demand, which facilitates the chance of a rise in the price of gold quickly arising.

Gold is traded per troy ounce (31.10348 grams) and, depending on the standard employed, in a particular purity. The Dubai Gold Delivery Standard uses a standard of 99.5%. Of all the prices of commodities that are traded worldwide, the gold price is the least influenced by fundamental forces. Supply and demand are less relevant for gold than for other commodities. It is mainly speculative money flows that send the gold rate in a particular direction. Because of this, gold is often regarded as 'directionless'. Making a thorough analysis of the future direction of the price is difficult, which is why gold is an especially interesting investment for investors who have strong views; investors with a long-term vision who are not deterred by interim price movements in the opposite direction. An investment in gold between 2002 and 2006 wouldn't have done anyone any harm. During this period, the value doubled. But it gets crazier still. In 1994, shares in the Canadian gold mine company Bre-X, rose from fifty dollar cents to 286 dollars in a short space of time. It was reported that miners had chanced upon a gold vein. When it was later discovered that there was no truth in the report, the share price directly plunged to its old level. Partly because of that, it is often jokingly said that a mine (read: commodity source) is nothing more than a hole in the ground beside which a liar stands.

Worldwide gold possession is concentrated particularly in the Eurozone (39%) and in America (26%). Asians own only 6% of the total world's stocks, but they have made an obvious resurgence over recent years in relation to the West. European central banks continually sell their supplies, while India, especially, is importing a lot of gold at the moment. India is the largest gold importer and uses the precious metal particularly in the manufacture of jewellery. Dentists have used gold from way back as a reconstruction agent, but they are now also using it as adornment. In addition, gold is used in industrial processes, especially because of its thermal characteristics and limited sensitivity to corrosion.

Of the total gold supply, 64% comes from gold mines. From these sources, 2,464 tons of gold were extracted in 2004. Recycling accounts for 21% of the supply: 828 tons per year. Re-use of gold is a phenomenon that leads to price pressure. The extraction of the precious metal from scrap has risen considerably over recent years. The remainder of the supply comes from sales by central banks.

	Gold production
South Africa	290
Australia	260
United States	260
China	220
Peru	210
Russia	160
Indonesia	140
Canada	120
Papua New Guinea	70
Ghana	70

Figure 5: Countries with the largest gold production (in thousand kilograms) (FD Research, 2007).

South Africa has many gold mines and is the largest producer at 14%. Production was down by 8% in 2006 compared to the year before. The US (11%), Australia (10%) and China (9%) are other important gold producers. A lot of gold is also mined in Indonesia, Peru, Russia and Canada. The Canadian company, Barrick Gold, is the largest gold-digger in the world, followed by Newmont Mining of the US. This last-named company has proven gold reserves of at least 60 billion dollars.

Many (Western) central banks are increasingly reducing their gold supplies because the function of gold as a stabilizer of national currency units is a much less important factor than it used to be. These sales transactions put enormous pressure on the price of gold. At the end of the 90s, excessive sales resulted in a sharp drop in the price of gold. Since September 1999, the sale of gold has been regulated via the Central Bank Gold Agreement (CBGA). At the end of 2006, the European Central Bank (ECB) finalized the sale of 23 tons of gold that then had a value of about half a billion dollars.

According to the European Gold Agreement, central banks within the Eurozone were together allowed to sell 2,500 tons of gold between 2004 and 2009. In 2006 they only sold 350 tons, while they had permission to get rid of up to 500 tons of gold, almost 15% of the worldwide supply. In 2007, The International Monetary Fund (IMF) made it known that it wanted to sell 400 tons of gold. The fund manages, in total, 3,200 tons of gold for its members.

Silver

The ten largest silver producers together account for 86% of world production. There is a lot of silver in the ground in Mexico (16%), Peru (15%) and China (10%). This threesome, together with Australia (11%), accounts for half of worldwide silver reserves. The Australian company BHP Billiton is the largest silver producer. Russia and China are probably the largest owners of silver, but the supply and quality figures are not public and are therefore based on estimations.

Only 30% of all silver is directly extracted out of special silver mines. The remaining 70% is retrieved from the ground as a by-product during extraction of other metals such as gold (12%), copper (26%), lead and zinc (32%). About three-quarters of the worldwide 900 million ounces or 25 million kilos of silver that are for sale on the market comes from the mining industry. Peru, Chile, Australia and China each supplies between 65 and 85 million ounces per year. The remaining market-supply comes from the sale of silver by central banks, and by recycling. Demand can be divided into manufacture of products (13,817,000 tons), industrial applications (4,974,000 tons), jewellery (7,313,000 tons), coins (1,545,000 tons) and direct investments (about 2,000,000 tons). The use of silver in photography is decreasing considerably; in 2004 this represented 18% of the total annual demand. Silver is further also used in solar cell panels, plasma screens and computer chips. In 2004, this industrial production accounted for 44% of the total silver demand.

Platinum

Platinum is used in catalytic converters for cars, which enable exhaust fumes to be thrust into the world cleaner. It is also used in the electronic sector, particularly in the making of computers. Platinum is chiefly extracted in South Africa; the country accounts for 75% of the total worldwide production. The largest platinum producer is the South-African Anglo company, Platinum. Russia also plays a creditable role in the quest for this specific metal, which in Russia is chiefly obtained as a by-product during the extraction of nickel.

Palladium

Just like platinum, palladium can also be used in converter systems. It is more resistant to heat than its counterpart. Car manufacturer Ford bought 1.8 million ounces of palladium for the manufacture of converter systems at the end of 2000. Unfortunately for Ford, the price dropped by more than 80% the following year. Palladium was discovered by William Hyde Wollaston in 1803 during research into crude platinum ore from South Africa. Palladium is named after the planet Pallas which had been discovered two years earlier. Palladium is usually extracted as pure metal as a by-product from copper and nickel ores. In addition, palladium is found in the ground in alloys with gold and platinum. Most finds are in Russia (50%), but large amounts of palladium also come from Australia, Ethiopia, Brazil, Canada and the US.

1.3.3 Agricultural products

Agro or soft commodities are the two collective terms for all produce that falls into the categories agriculture, cultivation of tropical products, and livestock and meat. Disease and the climate have a large influence on these categories of live (or formerly alive) products. Natural disasters and extreme weather conditions can easily throw a spanner in the works. The price of potatoes, for example, shoots up when the harvest is threatened by continued drought, excessive rainfall and/or plant or animal disease.

Rape seed

There were 33,000 hectares of rape in the Netherlands at the beginning of 2007. In Germany at the same time, 1.5 billion hectares of rape was planted. Each hectare produces about five tons of usable rape. The oil pressed from the seed, the rapeseed oil, is used as a source of energy in the form of bio-diesel.

Grains

Wheat, rye, barley, malt and oats are examples of grains. Maize is also included in grains, and it contains a lot of energy. Maize is not only nutritious for people and animals; it is now also used for generating bio-fuel. America produces half of all the maize in the world. It is virtually the only country in the world that exports maize; other countries produce almost exclusively for their own consumption. Half the maize production in the US is intended as livestock feed and a quarter is for human consumption. The remaining quarter of all maize production is meant for export, although this quantity is rapidly decreasing as the demand for bio-fuel in the US rises sharply.

Americans are not averse to consumption: almost 10 billion bushels of maize (a bushel is a measurement of quantity equal to about 36 litres) are used annually as food and for the production of (bio) ethanol. This demand has pushed the price of the yellow-gold cob way up. In 2006 that resulted in the 'Tortilla crisis'. Mexicans eat a huge amount of maize pancakes, called tortillas. For the poorest in the community, this food is the most important source of protein. The huge rise in the price of maize therefore hit the poorest Mexicans the worst. Unrest about the prohibitive prices of tortillas led to mass protests as Mexicans demonstrated to show their displeasure with the government's policy. In reality the Mexican government could do little, if anything, about the rise in the price of maize.

In Europe, Brussels bought up the European Union's surplus maize. When a few countries abused this aid scheme, it was decided to end it. Farmers no longer cultivated the crop for sale, but only in order to be eligible for the financial settlement.

Soybeans

Soybeans are bought as ready-to-use products, but they are also processed to derivative products like soy oil and soy meal, and there is a great deal of trade done in these separate products. Soy oil is used in for the production of bio-energy.

Many farmers cultivate as much soybean as maize. Each field is alternatively planted with soybeans and maize in order to avoid deterioration of the soil. This form of rotation was generally strictly adhered to; however, it was recently proven that the strict schemes were open to interpretation and rotation became a thing of the past when the difference in price between these two products became too great.

In the world of commodities, substitution is an actual phenomenon. The price of soy is influenced, among other things, by the amount of agricultural land available. As a result of the price rise in maize, increasingly more plots are being acquired for maize production, at the expense of the cultivation of soybeans. The surface area of maize-cultivated land, taken over the whole of 2007, was expected to rise 15% in comparison with the year before.

1.3.4 Tropical products

Prices are essentially determined by supply and demand. Prices of crops and their yields are chiefly determined by supply. The demand for crops is reasonably stable, or at least predictable, while supply has to contend with harvests that are not continuous but periodical. Supply can even be totally frustrated by political boycotts or harvest failure; for example, because of disease, deviant weather conditions or natural disasters. Because of this, the price risk of these sorts of products points chiefly upward, as opposed to the stock market, for example. The price of crops regularly fluctuates for quite some time around a certain level, and occasionally rockets up as a result of market disturbance. The price returns to a balance situation when the sting leaves the market.

Cacao
Cotton, rubber and orange juice are a few examples of tropical products. Cacao is another sort that falls into this category. The Ivory Coast is the largest cacao producer in the world; however, there has been civil war, and therefore chaos, in this country for years. Much of the work in the cacao, sugar and coffee sectors is forced labour. Slavery and child labour are the order of the day. Tony's Chocolonely jumped in the deep end and brought a 'slave-free' bar of chocolate to the market in 2007.

Coffee
Brazil is the world's largest producer of coffee beans, followed by Vietnam. More than sixty sorts of coffee exist worldwide, of which Robusta and Arabica are by far the most well-known. Robusta is particularly used for making instant coffee. The base product of Robusta is traded on various exchanges, where the traded coffee sort is dependent on the choice of the exchange. Robusta is chiefly traded in London, and in the US it is mainly Arabica.
Production is closely linked to weather conditions. A temperature of above 23 degrees or below 17 degrees is fatal. Continued drought or heavy rainfall are just as bad for the harvest and will result in higher prices. Price rises on financial markets are not always passed on to the consumer; when the price of coffee rises or falls on the financial market, the price of a pack of coffee in the supermarket hardly changes. Price elasticity

of coffee is not as large as the price elasticity of gasoline, for example. The price of gasoline is often passed on directly to the consumer when the market price of crude oil changes.

The cost of transport, marketing and production is often forgotten when looking at prices, but these have to be included in the price. Moreover, sellers of packs of coffee sitting on shop shelves are different parties than sellers of coffee beans. Each party is influenced by different market factors.

Palm oil

Palm oil is used in mayonnaise, margarine, shampoo, soap and edible chips, but recently demand for the product has risen because of the increasing need for bio-fuels. It is possible that in time palm oil will no longer be classed as a tropical product, but will fall under 'energy'. This will probably also influence the composition of various indices and many operating benchmarks.

Malaysia and Indonesia together account for 80% of global palm oil production. At the end of 2006, Synergy Drive, a merger company of three separate enterprises producing palm oil, was set up in Malaysia. As a result of this amalgamation, the largest palm oil producer in the world has come into existence. The annual turnover of this company amounts to 5.5 billion dollars, which is equal to a market share of 6%.

Sugar

Unrefined (or crude) sugar is a different product than refined (or white) sugar. Apart from as flavouring in foods, the sweet material is also used as a base material in the production of bio-fuels. Brazil is the world's largest producer of cane sugar: the country has vast areas planted with sugar cane.

1.3.5 Livestock

In addition to vegetable materials, live poultry, cattle and meat fall into the agricultural products category. This includes rummaging pigs and cows as well as beef and chicken fillet. Meat consumption is strongly dependent on prosperity. The average American consumes 125 kilos of meat per year; an inhabitant of Indonesia eats only 7 kilos in twelve months. South Korea has made a huge economic leap forward and this also applies to the eating habits of the Korean population: between 1980 and 2007, the average meat consumption per person rose from 12 to 50 kilos. Consumption requires production, and increasing prosperity therefore demands more animals. This goes hand in hand with more manure and inevitably more pollution. For every ounce of beef produced, 5.5 kilos of excrement is released. Moreover, animals need drinking water, and that pushes the price of water up. Unlike most other commodities, meat cannot be stored indefinitely; it is more like electricity, which also has a market without reserves. This results in extremely volatile pricing.

The price of meat is also influenced by political frictions, geographical developments and trade agreements. Once again, a comparison with energy markets is easily made. At the end of 2006, Russia and the European Union were in dispute over trade in meat. Russia threatened Europe with a boycott. Russian borders would be closed to all meat coming from the EU, even though the problem between the parties only related to Romanian and Bulgarian meat. As a result of the embargo, the EU missed out on 1.7 billion euros income per year. Only the Netherlands exported meat, livestock and meat products (to the tune of 28 million euros) to Russia in 2005. Meat from Poland was still being refused by the Russians at the beginning of 2007 because a number of Polish traders had once sold the Russians a consignment of second-hand meat for a considerable amount.

The price of meat is further influenced by the price of nutritious commodities. Because of the demand for bio-fuels, the prices of grains, maize and other crops have exploded. This has led to a rise in the price of animal feed. The consequence of this is that less livestock is being taken to slaughter, which in turn leads to a rise in the price of meat. Animal diseases can also put their oar in. In this sort of situation, meat is replaced by soy products; as soon as meat prices rise too much, the demand for soya also increases, and again, this at the expense of meat prices. Furthermore, meat production is far less efficient than grain production: the first process requires at least ten times more land than the second to produce the same quantity of calories.

1.4 Fundamental price drivers

It is essentially important to know something about pricing on the commodity market. This helps to create a clear image of the current energy problems and possible alternatives for scarce commodities, (fossil) fuels in particular.

Price is determined by supply (production) and demand (consumption). A rising price trend can level off because of two factors: decline in demand on the one hand, and increase in supply on the other. Supply and demand, in turn, are influenced by a broad scale of different factors. Demand is, among other things, related to demography and prosperity; supply is, among other things, determined by availability and production capacity. In this section, both issues are further highlighted and discussed, together with a number of other defining price factors.

1.4.1 Demography and economy

In order to obtain a clear idea about procedures on commodity markets, it is important to first acknowledge local demographic developments. Requirement (demand) is, in the first instance, dependent on the number of people: countries with many inhabitants are bulk consumers. As well as China and India, these include the US, Indonesia, Brazil, Pakistan, Russia, Bangladesh, Nigeria and Japan, among others.

	Population	GDP
World total	6600	
China	1303	1,709
India	1092	705
United States	297	42,000
Indonesia	219	1,283
Brazil	184	4,320
Pakistan	150	728
Russia	143	5,349
Bangladesh	136	400
Nigeria	128	678
Japan	127	35,757
Mexico	103	7,298
Philippines	85	1,168
Vietnam	83	723
Germany	82	33,854
Ethiopia	72	153
The Netherlands	16	38,618

Figure 6: Countries with the largest populations (in million inhabitants) (Geoatlas, Graphi Ogre, 2007) and their Gross Domestic Product (GDP) per capita (in dollars) (IMF, 2005).

Demographic developments must then be linked to the trend of the Gross Domestic Product (GDP) and economic growth. Demand for goods is not only determined by the number of people, but also by their financial situation. Countries like China and India together have about 2.5 billion inhabitants, equal to about 40% of the world's total population. Seeing as the economy in both countries is growing rapidly, inhabitants are improving their standard of living. This has significant results: the relationship between supply and demand is drastically disturbed. Demand for basic resources explodes. Partly because of this, macro-economic developments are of great importance for the pressing issues surrounding commodities.

	GDP
Luxemburg	80,288
Norway	64,193
Iceland	52,764
Switzerland	50,532
Ireland	48,604
Denmark	47,984
Qatar	43,110
United States	42,000
Sweden	39,694
Nederland	38,618
Finland	37,504
Austria	37,117
United Kingdom	37,023
Japan	35,757
Belgium	35,712
Canada	35,133
Australia	34,740
France	33,918
Germany	33,854
Italy	30,200
United Arab Emirates	27,700

Figure 7: Countries with the highest Gross Domestic Product (GDP) per capita (in dollars) (IMF, 2005).

The use of commodities is closely linked to economic well-being. The growth of prosperity in India and China is ensuring a clear shift in consumption patterns. Increasingly more high-protein foods are being consumed, which is increasing the demand for milk and meat.

1.4.2 Reserves, supplies and availability

Commodities are usually found in the ground. Countries that cover large surface areas have a lot of valuable raw materials, generally speaking. Russia is the front runner when it comes to the number of square kilometres of surface area. Canada is a good second, followed by the US, China, Brazil, Australia, India, Argentina, Kazakhstan and Sudan. Most of these countries are also high on the list of the world's largest commodity producers.

	Surface area
Russia	17,075,400
Canada	9,970,610
United Stated	9,809,386
China	9,560,900
Brazil	8,511,965
Australia	7,682,300
India	3,287,263
Argentina	2,766,889
Kazakhstan	2,717,300
Sudan	2,505,813
Algeria	2,381,741
Zaire	2,345,410
Saudi Arabia	2,200,000
Mexico	1,972,545
Indonesia	1,919,445
Libya	1,759,540
Iran	1,648,000
Netherlands	41,526

Figure 8: Countries with the largest surface area (in square kilometres).

The deepest mineshaft in the world is found 3,660 metres underground in South Africa. China began drilling in the Chuanke-1 oil and gas field in 2007: the intended depth of the drilling pipes is 8,875 metres. Russia drilled a hole that was 12,200 metres deep – which is nothing compared to the distance from the surface to the core of the earth, some 6,300 kilometres.

Untouched commodities are referred to as 'available reserves'. Often only a part of these is recoverable; firstly because technology won't allow more raw materials to be extracted from the earth (technical feasibility), and secondly because of the high costs that are coupled to it (economic feasibility).

Supplies are extracted commodities that have already been retrieved from the ground and are either stored or in transport. Commodities are generally put into storage and stored temporarily; often large consignments are purchased and transported. It is not usual for everything to be processed directly, and sometimes this is even a conscious decision. Safety supplies are kept back to be sure that company processes can continue even when the supply is diminished. Supply can be cut off by accident, like if a ship sinks, but it can also be cut off as a result of a broken electricity cable, burst pipeline or crisis situation (war or a terrorist attack). It is especially because of this last-mentioned reason that oil reserves are being kept back worldwide. All countries associated to the International Energy Agency (IEA) are obliged to keep a supply of energy for emergencies. This safety net can remove the biggest shockwaves on the market and pricing can run more steadily. When supplies are low they have to be replenished, which creates extra demand. Availability is therefore closely linked to geo-political tensions and developments, and these are therefore important forces behind the pricing process.

China's equivalent of the IEA, the State Reserve Bureau (SRB), is responsible for keeping stocks of commodities at a certain level. Exact figures about supplies in storage or reserves in the ground that this body provides are disputable. Sometimes countries or state-controlled organizations keep these figures secret or intentionally spread incorrect information, as a result of which it is impossible to make a proper prediction of existing reserves. A country like Saudi Arabia has been reproached many times for giving inflated figures in regard to oil reserves. Royal Dutch Shell was discredited in 2004 by a book-keeping scandal about reserves reported by the company. These proved to have been bumped up way too high. Unlike exchange-listed enterprises, countries are not obliged to divulge their supply figures. Reduced trustworthiness and suspicion are the direct results of this. It is then necessary to make estimates, which may have to be taken with a pinch of salt when it comes to the factual accuracy of the numbers.

1.4.3 Production and production capacity

There is still more than enough of most commodities in the ground, but that is not to say that these are directly available. Some elements or products can be found but the production capacity needed to extract them is lacking. Very few oil refineries were built in the 90s because the oil price was very low at the time. This supports the 'super-cycle theory'. This theory assumes that structural under-investing in the recent past later results in a mismatch between supply and demand. Increase in production capacity requires massive investment and a lot of patience, which creates long-term fluctuation (Kondratieff-cycle). According to experts, 20,000 billions dollars will have to be invested to ensure that global supplies of energy will still be able to meet demands in 2030. With an investment of an extra 5 to 10 percent, this could actually be done climate-neutrally.

As a rule, extracting commodities requires extensive operations, and complex installations are needed for this. Raw materials also have to be processed and transported, and all the operations within these various segments require capacity. There has to be sufficient capacity in all the links of the chain. If the supply falls short in one segment it directly leads to delay in the whole cycle.

Time and energy can be saved if products can be recovered from the surface (opencast mining), but products often lie deep underground (mining), underwater (on the ocean bed) or even under the permafrost or polar cap. Current technology still falls short on many levels and therefore (technically and/or economically) not all sources can be reached. Only 30 percent is recoverable from oil fields with the current expertise, the rest remains underground. In an attempt to keep the pressure in reservoirs up to a certain level so that more oil gushes up, water or gas is introduced.

In 2006, the Canadian company Petrobank claimed to have developed a technique of pumping up seventy percent of the existing oil from a source. It goes without saying that the price of the company's shares increased fivefold in the period 2005 to 2007. The price of Royal Dutch Shell remained the same during this period.

The increase in commodity extraction can therefore take place because of improved technology on the one hand, and by increased capacity on the other. Increase in production capacity is a long and expensive process; expansion has to take place throughout the whole production line. Copper smelters, for example, have to keep pace with enterprises engaged in copper extraction. In mining it takes on average between four and seven years before investment results in operational activity. The level of investment is a factor that has to be taken into account. Exploitation and extraction are both long processes. Accidents in mines can also be a cause of delay in the process, just like sabotage and terrorism. The capacity of various products is sometimes deliberately kept low in order to profit from high prices.

Production capacity is not only important for crude commodities, but also for the processing of them. Iran has vast oil fields and exports huge amounts of the black gold, but because of a lack of refining capacity it has been importing gasoline for many years.

1.4.4 Social factors and political policy

Social unrest is also a factor that has to be taken into account. Employees sometimes demand pay rises or better working conditions. Working conditions in the mining industry are usually wretched. Working in a shaft is extremely unhealthy and conditions are being increasingly less tolerated. Production volumes drop when miners go on strike, and in such situations governments have to intervene. Australia has adapted its legislation over the last few years, relaxed and refined it in order to fully profit from the developments in the commodity sector. Economically, the Australian government is trying to take full advantage of the oil hype. Flexibility and liberalization are the main things, but attention is also being paid to fringe benefits for miners. Political policy that influences pricing further includes all sorts of fiscal issues like subsidies and levies in the form of tax, excise duty and surcharges.

1.4.5 Transport

Commodities are physical products and, as opposed to shares, bonds and currency for example, they are therefore not transferable via a bank. Commodities are by definition, difficult to transfer. As a rule, the process requires a lot of time, mainly because of transportation. Moreover, sending commodities costs money. Depending on distance, the mode of transport employed and the shortage on the market, despatching commodities can cost a great deal of money. Which form of transport is recommended?

In the past, gas could only be sent through a pipeline; however, these tube systems often lie open and exposed on the ground and are therefore regularly subject to the whims and fancies of saboteurs. Fortunately it is now also possible to transport liquid gas (LNG) by ship.

In order to keep transport costs as low as possible, industrial processes often take place near the source, or near delivery and conveyance points (harbours). Foundries are near iron-ore mines, and preferably near a gas field. Refineries are often set up near oil sources, factories and power stations in harbour areas or close to other delivery points.

Despite all the effort, many goods still have to be transported and the costs that are coupled to this are an elementary factor in the pricing of commodities. The acute transport shortage, because of limited numbers of ships for example, does not make the situation any easier.

Transport capacity is also important in regard to energy. Networks for gas and electricity are linked together in order to integrate markets. Without sufficient transport capacity at such junctions, the market is imperfect. Price differences occur. By network and market linking, prices move simultaneously and price discrepancies are arbitraged away.

1.4.6 Geo-political interests and risks

The transportation of commodities is essential if production does not take place at the same place as consumption. Anyway, commodities are found scattered throughout the world, in one place more (sometimes significantly) than another. Certain raw materials are found concentrated in certain areas, while others are found widespread. Some countries are extremely rich in natural resources, while others get a really rough deal. It is remarkable that a few (former) under-developed countries have huge reserves. As a result of price rises over the last few years, these countries suddenly now count and have earned a place on the world stage. Because of this they acquire economic power and are able to continue their development.

Sometimes raw materials are found in several places but a number of large producing countries desperately need the products themselves. In such cases, export is out of the question. Think, for instance, about the position of the US with regard to oil, gas and maize. If only a few countries remain that supply these particular commodities, net-importers have to rely on them heavily. This increases the power of the suppliers, which is easy to see in political relations. If interests change, the position of countries can also change, which in turn can lead to a shift in the balance of power and in policy.

The suggestion that America invaded Iraq in order to secure the supply of oil has been made many times, but no-one would be surprised if this had indeed been the case. Russia exercised 'power-play' in Belarus and threatened to no longer supply the Ukraine with any oil or gas. This meant that the supply to Europe would also be uncovered. In addition, the Russians deprived Royal Dutch Shell of the majority interest in the prestigious Sakhalin 11 project. Russia and America are not the only countries that alter their positions to meet their interests. China is at the moment the most important buyer of a large number of commodities. The country is the largest consumer of copper (world market share 22%), iron ore (29%), coal (33%), palm oil (16%), rubber (24%), cotton (31%), rice (30%), and is a good second regarding oil (7%), tea (14%) and gold (8%). China has recently been offering financial support to many developing countries. Western countries criticize this policy; they think that the Chinese are merely acting in their own interest in order to secure the supply of fuels and other commodities, without taking account of human-rights and other sensitive issues taking place in development areas. The other side of the coin is that Western countries simply regard China as a competitor and happily use the issues mentioned as critical arguments without submitting them to objective analysis.

1.4.7 Quality

Commodities exist in varying qualities. Gold, for example, is available in various grades. The purity grade (the number of carats) is of defining importance. With diamonds it is the size of the stone that is important. The same thing applies to products in the energy sector; one product is not equal to another. Extracted coal, oil and gas each have a different calorific value. The amount of energy that a particular amount can generate always differs from that of the same amount extracted elsewhere. Oil extracted from the ground in Texas (US) is generally of a totally different quality than oil extracted in the Middle East. What's more, quality differs per source, even if the sources are right next to each other.

Different sorts of crude oil require different refining techniques and processing. This is why these products are not complete substitutes and why their pricing leads a life of its own. One sort of oil is more suitable for the production of certain products than another. That is also the reason that in standard contracts traded on exchanges, the quality requirements the underlying commodity has to meet is stated.

In this regard, electricity is an extreme example. Today's current is not equal to yesterday's. In contrast to (most) other commodities, it is virtually impossible to store electricity. Because of this, electricity today can have a totally different price than yesterday; it can even change minute by minute.

1.4.8 Exchange rates, inflation and negative correlation

Most commodities are priced in American dollars; the exchange rate of the dollar is therefore essentially important, especially for non-American companies. When the dollar falls, commodities become cheaper for those not living in the US. When the dollar rises, the opposite is true. In the period between 2000 and 2007, the oil price rose sharply when calculated in dollars, yet calculated in euros over the same period it was a bit cheaper. As a result, the price rise of oil clearly had less impact for Europeans than for Americans. Trade in commodities is sensitive to exchange rates; that applies as much for producers as for consumers. If desired, involved parties can cover themselves on the financial markets against any adverse consequences of swings in exchange rate.

When putting up their money, investors don't only look carefully at the exchange rates, they also look at inflation. If there is a question of devaluation, money will in time lose some of its value. Nevertheless, investors want to gain more return on their money than the financial loss inflation brings to their capital. In the past, commodities have often offered protection against inflation. The price rise of commodities has regularly compensated for devaluation, an advantage to investors in this sort of product.

It is often too quickly said that commodities are good against inflation and are therefore a stable investment. Usually, (rising) inflation paves the way for a rise in interest rates and this has an oppressive effect on share and bond prices. People forget that inflation is actually a gauge of the whole price climate of a country or region. The price of all sorts of commodities is already included in it, which supports the circular reasoning described above. In any case, inflation needs to be looked into. Prices of many commodities have risen drastically recently; however, when price development is looked at over a long period and prices are adjusted to inflation, the rise proves not to be too bad. It is even so that for some prices this is much lower than other investment instruments, like shares. Nominal amounts have to be adjusted to inflation. Mid 2007, the listing for oil used for warming homes (heating oil) was still under the inflation-adjusted top price of 1979. The aluminium price reached its peak in 1988 and mid 2007 (adjusted) was still only half that. The price of sugar was once, in 1974, 21 times higher than it is now.

The risk profile of commodities differs strongly from that of other asset classes like shares and bonds. The price development of commodities proves in the long term not to keep up with the price development of stocks and is generally of a contrary character. An investment portfolio that is optimally diverse therefore also includes investments in commodities. An adversative price relationship like this is also called negative correlation.

A compound investment portfolio which includes shares, bonds and property as well as commodities, has a lower risk profile, but it keeps the same performance prospect or a higher return with a similar risk. The reason for this can be traced to the economic cycle. The latest phase of this trend is, in general, a good time for producers of commodities because it is linked to relatively high growth. This is a stimulant for the price of commodities, while the prices of stocks actually drop then because the interest is high. Opposing developments apply to the other phases of the cycle. Investment results that can be achieved with different asset classes are not usually synchronic.

1.4.9 Seasonality and the weather

Supply and demand of commodities are both strongly seasonally driven (seasonality). On the one hand, supply and demand keep pace with economic developments, on the other they follow the standard patterns of a calendar year, or in some cases they even follow a day and night pattern. Less maize is produced and harvested in the winter than in the summer, and less electricity is used at night than during the day (peak and off-peak hours). Crops are harvested at specific times and the large supply resulting then generally creates price pressure. Weather conditions can also contribute. Farmers, especially, are sometimes plagued with bad weather and natural disasters: hurricanes, extreme drought, earthquakes, mud-slides and floods are not unusual phenomena. Some farmers cover themselves against the freakishness of the climate by using financial products. Derivatives can serve as a sort of insurance against unforeseen weather conditions.

Besides supply, demand is also influenced by the weather. The need for energy products greatly increases during severe winters. Warming homes during the coldest part of the year obviously takes more energy than in the summer. In the Netherlands during the three winter months, an average of 54% of all the natural gas used for heating on a yearly basis is used. During the summer, the Dutch only use 1% of the average 1,350 cubic metres that is used annually per household.

A similar pattern applies to the use of electricity for lighting. About 40% of the energy used annually for lighting is used during the winter. In the summer, 10% of the annual 560 kilowatt-hours is used.

1.4.10 Substitution

When product prices rise, people go looking for products with comparable application possibilities. If the price of natural gas rockets, for example, power stations will switch to stoking up coals or other sources of energy. From a certain level, substitutes can count on extra interest. The balance shifts, and the search for a new balance begins. But substitutes do not perform within certain margins: a coal-fired power plant cannot be stoked on gas, just as a gasoline-driven car cannot be driven on diesel. A refinery set up for the processing of heavy and sour oil cannot simply switch to light and sweet oil. Transformations like these require adjustments. Nowadays, substitution is not only price-driven; it also has to appeal to ethics. Environmental sustainability, the development of solar and wind energy for example, en ensures that alternatives are sought, at a higher cost, if necessary.

CHAPTER 2:
Fossil Fuels & Electricity

2.1 Introduction

Energy forms a separate category within the commodity spectrum. Because of the importance and indispensability of energy in today's world, attention to this specific group of commodities has risen hugely. Fossil fuels are hydrocarbon compounds that come from the residue of plant and animal life from the Earth's geological past. Examples of fossil fuels are: petroleum, natural gas and coals such as pit coal and lignite (brown coal). Even turf and peat can be included under the heading fossil fuel, but they have not yet been exposed to high pressure and high temperatures. Turf and peat are actually the forerunners of oil, gas and coal.

2.2 Oil

The world devours oil, especially the Americans, who are crazy about it. They use the most barrels of oil, both absolutely as relatively. In India, the average barrel use per person per year is less than one, but the results of local economy rising can easily be guessed. Until 1993, China exported any oil; now the country is the second largest user in the world and because of that is highly dependent on import. The total import of oil in China now amounts to about 12 million barrels a day.

United States	25
Europe	13
Thailand	5
China	2
India	1

Figure 9: The average oil use (number of barrels per annum) per capita in 2006.

Oil comes in all sorts and sizes. The oil price mentioned in the media usually relates to crude oil, but even with crude oil, a distinction can be made between types. There is, for example, Brent oil, which comes from the North Sea; West Texas Intermediate, extracted in the US; and oil from the Urals or the Middle East. The composition of the various types of oil differs significantly from one another. Because of the divergent compositions, the various types of oil have to go through different refining processes. A refinery is specifically geared to processing a particular quality of oil and cannot just start processing another sort. Relatively, heavy, sour oil is used a lot for the production of heating oil and asphalt. Sweet, light oil is more suitable for making gasoline. Most oil extracted in the Middle East contains relatively large amounts of sulphate (sour) and is, furthermore, very syrupy ('heavy' oil). Brent oil is light and sweet; it is very fluid and contains almost no sulphate. The so-called 'Maya' oil from Mexico is one of the heaviest types of oil in the world. 'Sweet Bonnie' from Nigeria is one of the purest oil sorts that could be directly used in an engine almost without refining.

Making a distinction between the existing oil sorts is extremely important. Apart from the different refining processes, the extent to which the type of oil can provide us with energy also differs greatly. The energy efficiency of light, sweet crude can sometimes rise to 60%. Forms of heavy, sour crude deliver on average only 35% energy value. This therefore greatly explains the price difference that exists between the two types of oil.

In refineries, crude oil is processed to a variety of semi-finished and finished products. Refining is the industrial purification of chemical material by means of distillation or extraction or by another process. Heating oil, gasoline, diesel and kerosene are generally-known end products of oil. Heating oil is used for heating, rail traffic and sea transport; lubricant is used for the production of grease, wax and paraffin. In petrochemistry, plastics and artificial fibres are produced from oil; bitumen forms the basis of asphalt and insulation materials. Fuels for modes of transport swallow up a great deal of the total oil produced. There were 600 million cars in the world at the end of 2005; together they accounted for about half the world's total oil consumption.

Today the world consumes about 1,000 barrels of oil (at 159 litres each) every second. This is equal to more than 86 million barrels a day, or 32 billion barrels a year. At a price of 60 dollars a barrel, this represents a total market value of 1,920 billion dollars a year. And with that, the economic interest of the oil sector is immediately proven.

When oil is mentioned, everyone immediately thinks of the Middle East, but the

Netherlands also contains oil. The largest oil field in Northwest Europe can be found in the Schoonebeek in the province of Drente. This source originally contained about 1 billion barrels of oil. Drilling stopped in 1996, but the field will be opened again in 2010. Up until now, 250 million barrels of oil have been extracted from Schoonebeek. It should be said that this black gold is exceptionally tough and syrupy.

	Reserves
Saudi Arabia	262
Iran	130
Iraq	115
United Arab Emirates	98
Kuwait	96
Qatar	15
Oman	6
Syria	2
Yemen	1

Figure 10: Proven official reserves of crude oil in the Middle East (in billion barrels). (BP Statistical Review of World Energy, 2003).

No-one knows exactly how much oil the Earth holds. Most oil resources today are state owned and details of the size of reserves are often scrupulously hidden from the outside world, yet there are some reserve figures in circulation that are considered reasonably reliable. It is essentially important to remember that particular areas of the world have not yet been (thoroughly) studied for the presence of oil. The frequency and extent of new oil source discoveries reduce with time, but here and there sources of some size are still being found. The Chinese government concern, Petrochina, made an important find in 2007: the Jidong Nanpu field in Bohai Bay, in the vicinity of Peking. This source contains oil and gas totalling 7.5 billion barrels of oil equivalent (BOE). And Brazil discovered a field worth 32 billion barrels off its shores in 2008, making it the largest find in recent years. At the beginning of the 1980s, a source worth 45 billion barrels of oil was found off the Russian peninsula of Sachalin. And in the Caspian Sea, in Kazakhstani waters, the Kashagan oilfield will be brought into production in 2008.

This field holds a total of 38 billion barrels of oil, of which 13 billion are extractable. Apart from these reports, it is often quiet for some time on the oil-discovery front. The hugest fields were actually discovered in the 1960s.

Large oilfields are called 'elephant fields'. Ghawar, in Saudi Arabia, is the largest oilfield ever brought into production. Fifty billion barrels of oil have already been pumped out of this well. The Saudi oil income amounted to more than 200 billion dollars in 2006. According to the latest figures, the remaining world supply amounts to 1,200 billion barrels. Of this amount, Saudi Arabia accounts for 250 billion barrels.

The largest field found to date lies partially under Canada and the American state of Alaska. This source has an estimated capacity of 150 billion tons, which is equal to about 1000 billion barrels. With this amount, the world could easily keep going for another 30 years, but unfortunately, this overfull field lies in a most inhospitable place. Exploitation of the field is impeded by the extreme cold of this region, which is why it has not (yet) been included in the figures. Apart from that, this unspoilt area is of great ecological importance. Until now, conservationists have managed to ensure that no wide-scale oil extraction can be carried out in this area. The volume of the oil supply found offshore has not been fully mapped out; further exploration must result in a thorough evaluation of the potential oil supply there.

	Reserves
Middle East	57%
North America	18
South & Central America	8
Russia	7
Africa	6
Asia	3
Europe (North Sea)	2
OPEC	75%

Figure 11: Proven petroleum reserves (CNUCED, 2003) as a percentage of world supply

The Middle East produces 35% of the total worldwide oil production. Its reserves are even more impressive; the region accounts for 57% of the world's total (see figure 11).

The Americans have already used up most of their reserves and therefore their import rate will increase rapidly (eventually reaching 100%). At the beginning of 2006 the US imported 27% of the world's production. In total, America now gets almost 70% of the oil it consumes from abroad. The percentage in Europe is 85, which means that the West is highly dependent on the oil production of other countries. The most oil-exporting countries have a reputation for being politically unstable. Seeing as energy consumption in upcoming countries is increasing, the pressure to ensure oil supply is becoming increasingly greater in other parts of the world. In that respect, the Chinese are becoming increasingly more prominent. They forage the market and try to conclude long-term delivery contracts. For this, among other things, the ties with Russia and oil-producing countries in Africa and in the Middle East are strengthened.

	Production
Saudi Arabia	9,050,000
Russia	9,750,000
United States	6,937,000
Iran	3,750,000
China	3,690,000
Mexico	3,640,000
Norway	2,640,000
United Arab Emirates	2,630,000
Canada	2,570,000
Kuwait	2,510,000
Venezuela	2,510,000
Former Soviet Union (excl. Russia)	2,380,000
Nigeria	2,240,000
Brazil	2,190,000
Iraq	1,920,000
Libya	1,750,000
United Kingdom	1,476,000
Algeria	1,350,000
Angola	1,320,000
Indonesia	860,000
Qatar	830,000
Netherlands	30,000

Figure 12: Production of crude oil (in barrels per day) (IEA, October 2006).

Before oil extraction can take place, enterprises have to obtain concessions, erect pumping installations, lay pipe-lines and build refineries. This requires not only a great deal of time, but also billions of euros. Such investments were not forthcoming in the 1990s because the oil price was very low at the time. The tide has since changed; oil can now be sold for very high prices. Unfortunately, oil cannot just be taken from the shelf. The 'Peak-Oil' theory (see Chapter 3, section 3.4) describes the ceiling in the production capacity of oil. The world has probably now used 25% to 50% of the available oil supplies – what remains is becoming increasingly more difficult to extract.

	Volume
Ghawar, Saudi Arabia	80
Burgan, Kuwait	70
Azadegan, Iran	26
Rumila, Iraq (and partly Kuwait)	20
Romashkino	17
Daqing, China	16
Kashagan, Kazakhstan	13
Prudhoe Bay, Alaska	13
Tengiz, Kazakhstan	8
Ekofisk, Norway	3

Figure 13: Largest known oilfields ever brought into production (in billon barrels of producible oil).

Economists have recently been paying a lot of attention to the oil price; that is because of the huge influence the value of oil has on the economy. The oil price has direct influence on production costs and, therefore, indirectly on the well-being of enterprises. The price level of oil also influences general price levels and, with that, inflation; which is why the general public complains when the oil price rises sharply. In 2006, the highpoint was around 80 dollars per barrel; that is equal to about fifty cents per litre, which is still quite a bit cheaper than a can of soft drink or a bottle of mineral water at the local shop.

Those who think gasoline is expensive can lodge a complaint with the government. Of the 1.35 euros per litre that the consumer paid at the Dutch pumps at the end of 2006, 0.92 went to the Dutch government in excise duties. It is not for no reason that a litre of 'super' is dirt cheap in the US compared to the price we are charged for the same amount. The comparison with Iran, Venezuela and Indonesia is even greater; in those countries, at the same time, gasoline cost less than a dime a litre.

Gasoline prices differ per country and that is not only because of the availability of the product; it is particularly the taxes, other duties and/or excise duties that push the price up. The gasoline price in the Netherlands is made up of production costs (29%), distribution costs (5%), VAT (16%), excise duty and taxes (46%), the gross profit margin for the oil company (1%) and the gross profit margin for the gasoline station (3%). Mentioned percentages are, of course, dependent on the moment of measurement and on the type of fuel and these relate to Euro95 at the end of 2006.

The production costs of gasoline include the cost of the basic product, crude oil. This has only a limited influence on the retail price in the Netherlands. Because of the addition of all sorts of taxes and duties, our gasoline price is less sensitive to changes in the price of crude oil than it is in America, for example. They apply less excise duty compared to the Netherlands, which means their car fuel price is more influenced by price changes in crude oil. The volatility of the gasoline price in the US is therefore markedly higher than in the Netherlands.

2.3 Gas

Like oil, natural gas is also a fossil fuel. It comes from the same sort of processes that lead to the generation of petroleum, but natural gas represents the lighter group of organic products from these processes. Natural gas is often found together with oil, but it regularly penetrates other layers of the earth than the much heavier oils. This results in the creation of specific gas fields.

Because of the frequent presence of gas in oilfields, it used to be regarded as a by-product of oil and was therefore often flared off. Only later did gas gain a greater (economic) value and people began to recognize the usefulness of this product. Gas-collection increased. Flaring off is now regarded as unethical because many greenhouse gasses are released during the process. But it is still happening in some places as it is sometimes dangerous or impractical to remove the released gas in any other way, on an oil rig, for example. In such cases, an exception rule applies.

	Percentage
Industrial processes	37 %
Power generation	35
Heating & cooking	25
Transport	3
Total	100 %

Figure 14: Application of gas (OECD, IEA, 2002)

Oil is chiefly used as a source of energy for transport, whereas gas is mainly used for heating homes and business and for firing power plants. In that last case, coal is seen as a substitute for gas. By contrast, a good replacement for oil for transport is not available. In a few areas, oil and gas are often considered substitutes for each other and the price development of both products is extremely closely linked. In gas contracts the price of the commodity is often coupled to the oil price. In Europe people regularly refer to Brent oil. The reason for this originated in the Netherlands, the first European country to switch largely from heating oil (among other things) to gas for heating homes in the 1960s. This was closely connected to the amount of gas available in the Netherlands after the discovery of the Groningen gas field (more information about that in Chapter 12: section 8.4).

Country	Reserve	%
Russia	47,800	27%
Iran	26,700	15
Qatar	25,800	14
Saudi Arabia	6,900	4
United Arab Emirates	6,000	3
United States	5,500	3
Nigeria	5,200	3
Algeria	4,600	2
Venezuela	4,300	2

Figure 15: Proven natural gas reserves (BP, 2005) in billion cubic metres and as percentage of the world supply.

Worldwide, Russia owns far and away the largest gas reserves (see figure 15) and is also the largest gas exporter. The Netherlands can in no way compete with this, yet the Netherlands is sitting on a huge gas deposit. The supply of the Groningen field, *the gas bubble of Slochteren*, still amounted to 1,510 billion cubic metres on 1 January 2006, whereas the original supply amounted to 2,700 billion cubic metres. To a large extent, Dutch production comes from Groningen, but gas is also being extracted in other places. The North Sea and, since 2007, the Wadden Sea are also locations where gas is being extracted. The Nederlandse Aardoliemaatschappij (NAM), a joint venture between Royal Dutch Shell and ExxonMobil, accounts for the largest part of Dutch oil and gas production.

In 2006, 71 billion cubic metres of gas were extracted in the Netherlands, of which 42.5 billion came from the Groningen field. In total, 45.6 billion cubic metres were extracted on land, while 25.2 billion were pumped up from the continental shelf (off shore). Seeing as new fields with a gas reserve of only 15 billion cubic metres were discovered in 2006, it is evident that new finds keep coming up short in respect of the growing need for gas. The Groningen field will have been so intensely exploited by around 2040 that it will be considered empty. The previously mentioned 42.5 billion cubic metres of gas from Groningen is an annual ceiling fixed by former Minister Brinkhorst in order to avoid the field being emptied too quickly. In this way, the Dutch government is trying to profit from the available gas supply for a few more decades. An important part of the, in total, 12 billion euros that the extracted gas brings in, according to the state budget of 2007, disappears into the General Fund pot, out of which a part of the government's expenditure is financed.

In comparison to production of 71 billion cubic metres, home consumption is only 43 billion cubic metres. The difference is destined for export. GasTerra, formerly owned by Gasunie but because of enforcement of the unbundling rule now a separate entity, has a 10-year contract with the English Centrica to supply an annual amount of 8 billion cubic metres. Seeing as Dutch production will decrease in time and the duration of existing export contracts still have years to go, the Netherlands will eventually have to import more in order to continue meeting its obligations.

Many European countries do not find themselves in the same luxury position as the Netherlands. Europe now imports 40% of all natural gas it uses from Russia; that percentage will rise to 70% over the next 20 years. Some Eastern European countries are already almost totally dependent on the supply from Russia. It is essential for the Russians to continue investing in the infrastructure of the gas sector otherwise, in time, the country may no longer be able to meet its export obligations. In 2007 the IEA wanted Russia to inject 17 billion dollars into the gas industry within twelve months in order for the activities to remain at the required level in the future.

In the winter of 2007, shortfalls in the area of extraction and transport were already so high that the Russian state enterprise Gazprom made it known that as soon as the temperature were to drop below minus 15 degrees Celsius it would supply no more gas to the Russian industry. Remarkable, seeing as the concern, with natural gas reserves of 29,000 billion cubic metres, is the largest gas company in the world.

The Dutch gas market is, to a large extent, in the hands of both Gasunie and GasTerra. Gas Transport Services (GTS), the transmission system operator, is a subsidiary of Gasunie, the government-owned enterprise that owns the infrastructure. GasTerra sells the gas. GasTerra shares are partly in the hands of Shell Nederland BV (25%) and Esso Nederland BV (25%); the balance (50%) is owned by the Dutch state. GTS is responsible for managing the whole Dutch gas network which, with a total length of 12,000 km, is enormously intricate. The extensive gas infrastructure is extremely valuable, certainly regarding the future position of the Netherlands on the Northwest European gas market. The Netherlands is in tenth place worldwide in regard to gas production and is seriously in the ball game in that respect. Because of gas extraction in its own country, the Netherlands has gained much standing in the field of gas technology over the years. The Dutch are also involved in all sorts of ways in gas extraction abroad, including various projects in the world's largest gas-producing countries, Russia and the US.

The importance of gas is becoming increasingly greater worldwide. Because of the ever-increasing need for energy, gas can be deployed as a conventional energy source; and burning gas gives off less CO_2 emission than stoking coal. In the US, increasingly more people are heating their homes by means of gas. From 2004 to 2009 America is investing 100 billion dollars in building new gas-fired power plants. The country has a considerable gas reserve at its disposal: in total it exploited 320,000 gas fields in 2003. At that time a little less than 300 million Americans were using just as much gas as 3 billion Europeans and Asian together.

The figure below shows that Russia and the US are the world's largest gas producers, but also that there are large differences between both countries. The production in Russia will increase over the coming years whereas production in the US will fall. Russian gas supplies are the biggest in the world; for the Americans, the end of gas is in sight. There are also large differences between the two countries in regard of gas consumption. While Russia uses a large part of its production for export, America's gas production falls short of meeting home requirements and it is therefore forced to import large amounts.

	Natural Gas Production
Russia	640
United States	515
Canada	185
Iran	101
Algeria	91
United Kingdom	88
Norway	87
Netherlands	73
Indonesia	73
Saudi Arabia	70
Malaysia	66
Turkmenistan	62
Qatar	45
Total	2,800

Figure 16: Production of Natural Gas (in billion cubic metres per year) (IEA, 2005).

Because gas is often used for generating electricity, it is also listed and traded in megawatt hours (MW*h) on the financial markets. The British operate in British Thermal Units (BTU), or therms for short. By listing gas in equivalents of electricity on exchanges, both forms of energy can be compared to each other to a certain level. Gas is also listed in equivalents of oil. In 2007, about 86 million barrels of oil were used on a daily basis worldwide; the daily consumption level of gas amounted to 52 million barrels of oil equivalent.

2.4 Coal

The amount of available coal on earth is enormous. Based on the amount of energy that can be generated from both, there is a hundred times more coal than oil reserve in the world at the moment. With this source of energy, the world can go on for another few hundred years. Partly because of this, it is claimed that there isn't an acute energy shortage, only an environmental problem. Coal may well be plentiful, but burning coal is coupled with serious environment pollution as a great deal of CO_2 gas is emitted during the process.

The geographical distribution of coal reserves is favourable to the largest economies. Oil is mainly extracted in politically unstable regions. The low risk component of extracting coal is partly expressed in the price of the commodity, which is relatively low, certainly compared to the price of gas and oil. The fact that coal is cheap makes it a very popular commodity sort. Coal can be regarded as a stabilizer of the world's energy supply; regretfully, the accompanying environmental problem that burning coal produces creates a nasty split.

United States	247
Russia	157
China	115
India	92
Australia	79
South Africa	49
Ukraine	34
Kazakhstan	31
Poland	14
Brazil	10

Figure 17: Proven coal reserves in billion tons (PM, 2005)

The Netherlands uses relatively little coal for producing electricity. Because of the sizeable gas reserves, many Dutch power plants are gas-fired, however, the Netherlands does transport a lot of coal; in total about 30 million tons per annum. Germany is a large customer for this 'Dutch' coal. It is true that the Germans also produce coal, but that has proven to be uneconomic there; the German government has to contribute about 3 billion euros every year. Coal is easily recoverable in South America, Australia and South Africa where it is often collected from the top layer of soil, which makes opencast mining possible. In Germany, however, coal has to be mined from deep underground, which results in high costs and, therefore, a high cost price. Because of this, German coal has a considerable competitive disadvantage compared to foreign variants of the dark commodity.

Besides the way in which coal is mined, quality is also an aspect that has repercussions on price. Half of all the coal available in the world is low quality, which is why the market for high-quality coal is tense. Japan and China, in particular, are importers of high-quality coal. German coal belongs in this category and produces 30% more energy than coal recovered from opencast mining. But the price that has to be paid for this extra quality coal is three times higher. In Germany, plans that must lead to the statutory subsidy on coal being lifted are being busily worked on. And all operational coal mines have to be closed. There were 8 in 2007, employing 40,000 people. Although all these jobs are hanging in the balance, the German government has promised that the plans are not coupled to compulsory redundancies. The possible approaching end of mining in Germany is really remarkable, certainly in light of the fact that the world's growing need for energy prompts more extraction, not less. France, England and the Netherlands are therefore considering reopening their old coal mines.

Lignite is also a particular form of coal (brown coal) and it is, therefore, also a fuel, but in that respect lignite, because of its chemical composition, is markedly less efficient than coal. Carbon is the most important element in fossil fuels and comes originally from plant materials. Dead plant residue is pressed together at high temperatures for years and eventually the matter changes into peat, lignite and coal, anthracite and finally graphite. The percentage of carbon rises during this process: 60% in peat, 75% in lignite, up to 95% in anthracite.

Nowadays, low-quality coal, like lignite, can be upgraded by means of complex techniques. This is advantageous for countries like Indonesia that have considerable lignite supplies. Upgrading coal is a costly process, which in turn increases the price of the product. Indonesian coal has yet another advantage; it contains little sulphate and ash which makes it more environmentally friendly than coal from other regions.

	Consumption	Production	Import/export
China	1,080	1,110	-
United States	570	580	-
India	205	200	-
Japan	120	0	Importer
Russia	105	140	Exporter
South Africa	95	140	Exporter
Germany	85	60	Importer
Poland	60	80	Exporter
South Korea	55	0	Importer
Australia	45	200	Exporter

Figure 18: Consumption and production of coal in million ton oil-equivalents (2005)

In Australia, the world's largest exporter of coal, Excel Coal is a producer of considerable size. In 2007, the price of coal rose sharply; firstly because of continuous demand, but also because of strikes in the Australian port of Newcastle. This refusal to work led to panic in the world's largest coal export harbours and tended towards exploding. Due to a shortage of ship capacity, specifically for transportation of coal, sea freight prices rose through the roof. In the middle of 2007, 60% of the price of imported coal in Amsterdam was determined by transport costs. And the problems kept mounting up. Later in 2007, 50 huge coalers were anchored in the port of Newcastle hoping to be loaded. China, in particular, suffered from these problems. Despite their large coal reserves, China has become a net-importer over the last few years; the country needs the fuel for its growing park of power plants.

2.5 Electricity

Fossil fuels, all of which are extracted from the earth, were dealt with in previous paragraphs of this chapter. On the other hand, electricity, popularly referred to as power, is not a commodity that is extracted from nature; it is a source of energy that is generated in power stations. Electricity can only be stored and transported in limited amounts; it is, furthermore, non-tangible. All of this makes it difficult for this product to be referred to as a commodity, but in the financial world, it is often included in this category. Most power is (still) generated by means of fossil fuels, which strengthens the (price) correlation between these products and electricity.

In central production locations, energy in the form of electricity is generated by heating water in a boiler. Various materials can be used as fuel. Coal is the mostly-used fuel worldwide but, of course, there are exceptions. Due to the large availability of gas in the Groningen field, the Netherlands has many gas-fired power plants. France creates 75% of its electricity in nuclear reactors. There are also a few power plants that work on oil, and lately there has been much attention given to power plants that burn biomass or waste. Some plants, especially new ones, can make use of several fuels; these so-called multi-fuel or combi plants can, for example, be fired on coal and/or biomass.

Each method of production has its own features. Scandinavia and the alpine countries produce a lot of electricity by the use of falling water; during periods of little rainfall, little water is available for generating electricity by means of hydro power. The price of electricity then rises. The Netherlands, on the other hand, has no mountains and therefore produces no hydro power. The price of Dutch electricity rises however when it is so hot that the temperature of the cooling-water in power plants rises above the permitted level. Power plants are generally located beside water, which is necessary for the production process. The water also functions as a coolant.

Nuclear power plants need the most cooling-water, followed by coal-fired power plants and then gas-fired power plants. During the very hot summer of 2006, water in the vicinity of Dutch power plants became so hot that cooling was no longer possible, which meant that no electricity could be produced. TenneT, the Dutch manager of the electricity grid, signalled 'code red', which actually put restraints on the production of electricity. The price per traded unity rocketed from 200 to 2,000 in two days and then immediately fell to 1,300 when it became evident that rain was on its way. The volatility of the electricity price is mainly due to the fact that electricity cannot be stored in an economically viable way; pricing is therefore regularly subject to extremes. The price of electricity is, moreover, very much linked to locality; this is because of the specific features of electricity and the local infrastructure. Electricity can hardly be stored and can only be transported through a grid, the availability of which is often limited. Unfortunately, transporting electricity by ship is impossible.

Electricity grids are often specifically for local or national use and transport. This sort of grid usually only has a regional coverage, which results in fragmentation of the market. The various grids are not, or are rarely well connected to adjacent networks. Existing connections often have limited capacity. This applies, for example, to the border between the Netherlands and Germany. Connection with other countries is indeed taking place more often now, and with larger capacity (see Chapter 12, section 12.7 about market coupling), but this phenomenon is still in its infancy. For now, the market remains very fragmented and that results in different regional pricing. Price differences between the Netherlands and Germany, for example, lead to a supply and demand existing for the transportation of electricity from the country in which it is produced most cheaply to the country where the price is highest. Apart from that, these price differences can alter quickly. For example, in one region there may be comparatively more windmills that only generate electricity when the wind blows, and when it does the price of electricity drops in that region because the supply has increased.

Germany has comparatively more coal-fired power plants than the Netherlands. This involves all sorts of peculiarities. The electricity production of coal-fired plants cannot just be increased or decreased and it takes a lot of time to get a plant that is not operational up to full power. A coal-fired plant needs significantly more time for that than a gas-fired plant; for a coal-fired plant such a process can take a few days. This is therefore the most important reason why such plants are not usually entirely switched off but left on a sort of stand-by. A plant kept at low speed is much less efficient, which, of course, doesn't help the price.

Because of it relatively large number of gas-fired plants, the Netherlands is reasonably flexible in the provision of its electricity requirement. If necessary, production can be quickly increased, which creates extra power supply.

In 2050, electricity requirement will have increased by a factor of four compared to its current level. Because of this, demand for fuels will increase dramatically. Most of the current plans are for coal-fired plants. Total annual Dutch coal consumption is now 2.4

gigatons, but by that time it will have reached a level of 6 gigatons. This development will push up the prices of fuel and electricity.

Because of the large number of planned power plants in the Netherlands, power production can increase by 35% over the next five years. This could make the Netherlands an electricity-exporting country instead of one with import status, which it is at the moment. The Netherlands imported about 20% of its total electricity consumption in 2006, mainly from Germany. Germany is going to close a number of its current lignite plants because they are exceptionally polluting.

Over the last few years, on average, China has started building a new coal-fired power plant every five days. In 2006, the country increased its electricity production capacity by 100 gigawatts. That is comparable to the total current capacity of England and the Netherlands together. For its future expansion, China will primarily rely on coal-fired and nuclear plants.

	Total	Conven-tional	Nuclear	Hydro	Wind	Geothermal
EU25	703,874	407,571	132,985	129,049	30,589	656
Percentage	100%	57.9%	18.9%	18.3%	4.8%	0.1%
Belgium	15,634	8,365	5,761	1,415	93	-
Czechia	17,418	11,498	3,760	2,160	-	-
Denmark	13,363	10,228	-	11	3,124	-
German	123,845	78,413	20,552	8,251	16,629	-
Estonia	2,375	2,375	-	-	-	-
Greece	12,435	8,866	-	3,099	470	-
Spain	69,392	35,477	7,577	18,118	8,220	-
France	116,342	27,387	63,363	25,235	357	-
Ireland	5,839	4,929	-	532	378	-
Italy	81,306	58,792	-	20,745	1,127	642
Cyprus	988	988	-	-	-	-
Latvia	2,132	590	-	1,517	25	-

Lithuania	5,710	2,473	2,367	870	-	-
Luxemburg	1,632	459	-	1,138	35	-
Hungary	8,628	6,711	1,866	51	-	-
Malta	387	387	-	-	-	-
Netherlands	21,712	20,153	449	37	1,073	-
Austria	18,564	6,254	-	11,750	560	-
Poland	31,724	29,402	-	2,282	40	-
Portugal	12,711	7,292	-	4,852	553	14
Slovenia	2,965	1,335	656	974	-	-
Slovakia	8,268	3,107	2,640	2,518	3	-
Finland	16,563	10,811	2,671	2,999	82	-
Sweden	33,649	7,424	9,471	16,302	452	-
United Kingdom	80,292	63,855	11,852	4,193	392	-

Figure 19: Power production capacity (in MW) of the EU25 (2004)

The elements that influence electricity pricing are enormously varied. Wind has already been mentioned, but the fact that markets and networks are shielded also has radical consequences. In the Netherlands, little electricity is generated by means of water, which is understandable as the country is as flat as a pancake. Countries like Sweden and Austria make full use of falling water as a source of generation. A reservoir can be used for the production of electricity; this form of production is very flexible because changing up or down takes hardly any time. A water reservoir is therefore a sort of forerunner of electricity storage and can, moreover, offer flexibility (as back-up facility) for wind energy.

Electricity pricing displays even more typical features. The current pattern in Europe shows that especially during the winter a lot of electricity is used for lighting; obviously, because it is then darker longer. In warm countries, in the Middle East for example, where much use is made of air-conditioning during the hot summers, the pattern is the other way around. In a country like Greece, a different phenomenon appears in the summer. In such countries, because of the huge influx of tourists, there are extra people during the summer months and this increase is so extensive that, in an absolute sense, energy consumption rises dramatically.

Energy source	Worldwide
Coal	39 %
Hydro power	16
Nuclear energy	16
Gas	15
Oil	10
Other	4
Total	100 %

Figure 20: Worldwide sources of electricity production (in percentages) (2006)

Electricity is produced worldwide by means of coal, hydro power, nuclear energy, gas and oil (see figure 20). It is true that a part of electricity generation is created by means of hydro power, nuclear fusion or by burning biomasses, but most electricity generation greatly contributes to the pollution of the planet.

The choice of the type of generation (read: fuel) is expressed in the price. The kilowatt-hour price of electricity generated with coal is considerably cheaper than electricity produced in gas-fired power plants. In the case of nuclear energy, the price of the commodity uranium only makes up a few percent of the kilowatt-hour price. Costs that weigh relatively much heavier are exploitation and the building and dismantling of nuclear power plants. In the case of oil or gas-fired electricity plants, the commodity makes up about 60% of the electricity price (2007). Of course, these percentages are highly dependent on the prices of the various commodities and developments in technology. Because of these factors, the amounts mentioned are subject to change.

CHAPTER 3:
Availability & Technique

3.1 Introduction

'Addiction' to energy involves a number of important issues. The following chapters expound on the most important of these individually. The availability of fuel is limited; not only because of limited reserves and supplies, but also because of inadequate production and transport capacity (Chapter 4). This sometimes leads to serious tension which can sometimes become so great that it results in new forms of political and military policies (Chapter 5). In addition, the environment becomes seriously polluted, which leads, among other things, to climate change (Chapter 6).

Just like fuels, the quantities of commodities are also limited. There is more supply of one sort than there is of another, and some products are more easily extracted than others of its kind or than equivalents. The wealth of reserves, in regard to volume, quality and extractability, varies per region. The availability of high-quality commodities will decrease, particularly because these, when and where possible, are the first to be extracted. This continually leads to rising extraction costs. The relationship between extraction costs and market prices is not linear but extremely complex. Among other things, this is traceable to monopolies, cartel formation, expectations, demand elasticity and the necessary costs for the introduction of additional production capacity.

Production is falling in 60% of all the countries where Royal Dutch Shell produce oil and gas. The total production capacity of Shell has been falling for years on end, and other large private oil companies are having the same problem. Because of the low oil price in the 1990s, (too) little was invested in production capacity; during that period, the focus lay on maximizing returns. The results of this are now only too noticeable.

Just like production capacity, the amount of available supplies and reserves are also limited. Pumping units on land and oil rigs at sea are both oil-extracting techniques. In recent years, the hurricanes Katrina and Rita caused massive damage in the US, and two years after the natural disasters some of the oil rigs had still not been repaired. As a result, production capacity during this period was less than it had been before. On the one hand, scarcity pushes the oil price up; on the other, lost income results in huge losses or even bankruptcy for the involved enterprises. The company Transocean, owner of the Deepwater Nautilus oil rig, lost 220,000 dollars a day in rent because of storm damage. Reparation of this construction weighing over 50,000 tons is not easy as it requires extremely specialized and time-consuming labour.

3.2 Definitions

Terms like supplies and reserves are used in the media all the time, which can easily cause confusion. This book does not argue in favour of standardization, it simply draws attention to the phenomenon. Forecasts about future extractable reserves of commodities are usually conservative, at least when these are based on current costs, prices, technique and knowledge of geology. However, the world is dynamic and influenced by change. One thing is indisputable: the numbers mentioned all over the place are often subject to debate. Even when determining such numbers has been done with the greatest possible insight, it is still impossible to say with certainty how much supply of a certain commodity there is in the ground. Many numbers mentioned in this book are also subject to debate. In general, the figures do give a reasonably reliable picture of the reality, mainly because when determining the figures appeal was made to both reliable and various sources, which makes cross-checking possible.

Estimations of the price of a certain amount of an extractable commodity can only properly be understood if a difference is made between reserves and supplies. The concept 'supply' relates to the total amount of a certain commodity that has been discovered or is presumed to exist. The term 'reserves' refers to that part of the supply that has been shown with certainty to be economically profitable to extract with current techniques. Supplies can, therefore, increase by exploration and new finds. Reserves will rise as a result of improvements in the field of technology and operational management, which will suddenly make previously mapped out supplies extractable. Many OPEC countries substantially upgraded their oil reserves in the 1970s and 80s as a result of new insights, although the outside world suspects that political interests played the major role in this.

	Abu Dh.	Dubai	Iran	Iraq	Kuwait	S. Arabia	Venezuela
1980	28.00	1.40	58.00	31.00	65.40	163.35	17.87
1981	29.00	1.40	57.50	30.00	65.90	165.00	17.95
1982	30.60	1.27	57.00	29.70	64.48	164.60	20.30
1983	30.51	1.44	55.31	**41.00**	64.23	162.40	21.50
1984	30.40	1.44	51.00	43.00	63.90	166.00	24.85
1985	30.50	1.44	48.50	44.50	**90.00**	169.00	25.85
1986	31.00	1.40	47.88	44.11	89.77	168.80	25.59
1987	31.00	1.35	48.80	47.10	91.92	166.57	25.00
1988	**92.20**	**4.00**	**92.85**	**100.00**	91.92	166.98	**56.30**
1989	92.20	4.00	92.85	100.00	91.92	169.97	58.08
1990	92.20	4.00	93.00	100.00	95.00	**258.00**	59.00
1991	92.20	4.00	93.00	100.00	94.00	258.00	59.00
1992	92.20	4.00	93.00	100.00	94.00	258.00	62.70
2004	92.20	4.00	132.00	115.00	99.00	258.00	78.00

Figure 21: Proven reserves with suspicious upgrading (in billion barrels) (Colin Campbell, SunWorld, 80-95)

Categorization of supplies can be further explored by differentiating between commercial, military, speculative, reasonably assured, and conventional supplies. The last-mentioned are geological supplies of which the concentration of the chemical element of the commodity is large enough to justify extraction at a certain price level.

Sometimes a particular material is also extracted as a by-product, which effects extraction as sometimes being profitable and sometimes not.

A number of countries, for various reasons, report no supplies, or at least, not all sorts of supplies. Because of this, estimation problems arise from time to time. Australia is an example of a country that, in respect of uranium, discloses supplies of reasonably assured supplies but no speculative supplies. The reason it gives for this is the already known supplies the country has; these are so extensive that, for Australia, further elaboration makes no sense. Information about extra supplies could negatively influence the psychology of the market, which could result in the price dropping, which would not be advantageous for Australia as owner of all this commodity.

Details about supplies under the North Pole are unknown. A few years ago, it was claimed that this area contained a quarter of the world's yet-to-be discovered supplies. This contention has now abated considerably. A 2000 report from the United States Geological Survey (USGS) estimated supplies in North East Greenland at 63 billion barrels of oil and oil-equivalents, whereas a 2007 prognosis from the same institute came out at barely 10 billion barrels. This considerable down-grading gives a totally different picture of existing supplies worldwide.

3.3 Exploration

Exploration is essential, but it is also an extremely expensive business, which is why only a few enterprises go looking for the extractable commodities that people are expected to need in the coming years. Exploration in the past was often so controlled that the volume of reserves remained at a reasonably constant level.

Generally speaking, the price of a commodity rises when consumption exceeds production. Because of price rises, non-economic supplies become reserves; a stimulating factor for exploration. A reverse situation is, of course, also possible. This mutual dependence is shown in the supply curve, a graphic representation of the volume of supply set against the cost price of extraction.

3.4 Peak Oil theory

Back in the 1950s, the American geologist King Hubbert predicted that oil production would peak in the future. He proved to be a good forecaster as the number of petroleum finds began to decrease in the 1960s. Since 1986 the world has been consuming more oil than it finds. On the basis of Hubbert's theory, others have predicted that oil production in the Middle East will reach its peak in 2010. On the basis of current estimations, it can be assumed that oil reserves still to be extracted lie somewhere between 1000 billion and 2000 billion barrels at the moment. It is highly likely that the production peak of gas will be reached between 2040 and 2050.

Hubbert's Peak arises from the so-called Peak Oil theory. This assumes that at a given time, more oil is consumed than is produced, for the simple reason that increasingly more need for oil exists while the available amount, and therefore production possibilities, are limited or even decreasing. Technological progress is crucial. When non-conventional oil (like oil shale and oil from tar sands, see Chapter 7, section 3) is included in the calculation, it will not be so much a question of a production peak, but rather of a production plateau. Technological progress can postpone the peak and, by so doing, shift the curve in the graphic representation forward in time.

3.5 Enhanced recovery techniques

The supposed energy crisis can be avoided, or at least postponed, through geological and economic causes. When prices rise structurally, more expensive techniques can be employed and economically-recoverable reserves increased. In the recent past, 30% of existing reserves in an average oil field were extracted. A similar story is applicable to gas fields, albeit with a higher percentage. More (and more expensive) drilling can increase this percentage for oil by a few percentage points. Extremely intensive production (speed) will, however, exhaust a field and thereby lower the recover rate.

Before crude oil can be produced it has, of course, to be located (exploration). Oil and gas fields are located and analysed by means of seismic and electromagnetic techniques. Often in the past, a spot on a computer screen turned out to be a salt-water layer or something of that nature, but because of improvements in various techniques over the last twenty years, the chance of discovering a valuable field has increased from 1 in 10 to 1 in 3, or less.

By making use of the most modern resources during extraction, continuous measurements can be carried out. The temperature, pressure and the flow of oil are immensely important for the adjustments of the pumps. By streamlining all this information, production is optimized. Often, a gas or water injection is administered to increase the pressure, which keeps the oil gushing upwards. Oil extraction increases by a few percent through application of these so-called 'enhanced-recovery' techniques.

The presence of water is essential for extracting oil, but it is far from easily available everywhere in the world. This is one of the reasons that oil fields in the Saudi Arabian interior are less developed than fields located on the coast. For an oil field to be operational, an enormous amount of infrastructure is needed, even if it is just to transport water through vast sandy deserts. In addition, oil extracted from the Saudi desert is predominantly heavy and sour in character, which more quickly rusts and rots metal pipes than light and sweet oil. And maintenance is more expensive.

A large portion of the oil found in the (vicinity of the) Persian Gulf is predominantly light and sweet. This sort of oil has a higher price, which makes extraction more attractive than heavy and sour oil (and therefore produced first). The latter variant is primarily found in the interior of the Gulf States and represents the largest part of current reserves.

Sometimes, instead of water, steam is injected into an oil well in order to make the syrupy material more fluid. This technique drastically contributes to increasing the total percentage of the fuel that can be extracted from a well, which is important to oil companies because the company that can extract the highest yield from a source has the best chance of obtaining a licence to exploit a source. This is also called a concession. Oil companies that wish to exploit the ground in a particular area must first, by means of bids and application procedures, obtain concessions to do so before they may actually begin drilling.

3.6 Production capacity

In order to produce energy, production capacity is needed. Exploration and production (E&P) are two of the first operations, but subsequent processes are generally just as necessary. Refining falls into the sector referred to as 'downstream'. 'Upstream', on the other hand, relates to the E&P. Both are relevant and they have to be geared to each other. If capacity on one or both fronts falls, all links in the chain are affected.

Every oil refinery is maintained once every three or four years; that means that the plant is inoperative for a while, and that causes a regression in production (capacity). Major maintenance generally requires about six weeks. When a lot of refineries close at the same time, because of maintenance or through damage caused by a hurricane or war, for example, this generally has an impact on prices. The price of refined products will develop relatively stronger than the price of (the underlying) crude oil.

In this sort of situation it is easier if parties have spare capacity at their disposal and are actually able to utilize it. OPEC occasionally uses a part of its spare capacity in order to produce extra oil. This enables OPEC to provide extra supply if the market requires it. In a reversed situation, the cartel would be inclined to use less productive capacity, by which the spare capacity would increase. Spare capacity is therefore actually nothing more than available capacity that is not being used.

CHAPTER 4:
Transport & Infrastructure

4.1 Introduction

Goods arrive at their destination by being transported from A to B. Transport of the source to its destination is generally carried out by road, water and air, so products reach their destination by being driven, shipped and flown. Transport of products via pipelines and other sorts of networks is also a possibility.

Power plants and industrial companies are set up, by preference, in the vicinity of ports; the reason for this is the availability of cooling water and the fact that delivery of fuels can then take place over the shortest possible distance. The closer to the place of supply, the lower the transport costs.

The extent of the costs is important, but transport of commodities involves more problems. With energy transport, the ceiling of available capacity is often reached. Logistics companies have to deal with councils, boroughs, ministries, port organizations, and many other bodies and authorities. Bureaucracy appears to be the transport sector's biggest problem. Schiphol Airport wants to continue expanding and the building of a second terminal seems unavoidable. The current terminal of the Netherlands's largest airport can handle 60 million passengers a year. The number of passengers expected to pass through Schiphol Airport over the next few years far exceeds this amount. However, airports play a much neglected role in the transport of energy.

Trucks can transport containers of goods and, as tankers, are also suitable for transporting gas and crude oil, or end-products like gasoline. There is a growth of about 400% expected in container transportation over the next few years. Transportation, which already assumes huge proportions, is expected to create even more problems because of this. In 2007, about 150,000 trucks were daily using Dutch roads. The A15, a crucial motorway for reaching Rotterdam, was so full during the week that many transport companies avoided the seaport during the day. A large number unloaded during the night in order to save time and money. Traffic jams in 2006 cost Dutch shippers a total of 740 million euros.

	Length of road networks
United States	6,395,705
Canada	1,408,800
Japan	1,182,593
France	994,354
Australia	810,263
Spain	665,636
Germany	626,891
United Kingdom	413,120
Poland	377,289
Sweden	212,000

Figure 22: Length of road networks per country (in kilometres) (Editions Atlas, 2003)

The eastern direction of the Betuwe railway line is particularly used for bulk transportation, like pit coal for German power plants. Until 2008 there will only be 7 trains a day on this route; a year later that number will rise to 50, and to 150 before 2012.

4.2 Shipping

4.2.1 Ports

Sea ports are central points for intercontinental connections. Inland shipping, together with pipelines, trains and trucks, take care of transport on the continent. Rotterdam, as the hub, is Europe's most important port, even (or maybe especially) in the field of energy. In the oil sector, Houston, Singapore, Fujairah and Rotterdam are the four most important bunkering ports. Each continent, or each time zone, has its own energy port. The oil price is roughly determined at these places.

		Tonnage
Shanghai	China	443
Singapore	Singapore	423
Rotterdam	Nederland	376
Ningbo	China	272
Tiajin	China	245
Guanhzou	China	241
Hong Kong	China	230
Busan	South Korea	217
South Louisiana	United States	192
Houston	United States	192

Figure 23: Largest ports in the world, top 10 goods transport (in million tons) (Wikipedia, 2005)

4.2.2 Vessels

Solid materials, like iron ore, grain and coal, are transported overseas in bulk carriers (*dry freight*). These gigantic ships are equipped for transporting very sizeable loads. Transportation overseas of liquid materials, like oil and LNG (see Chapter 7, section 4), is done by super tankers (*wet freight*). Pipelines are used for transportation over land. Of the total worldwide oil transport, about 2 billion tons a year, 62% goes overseas. The most important oil tanker routes begin in the Persian Gulf and go via the Malacca Straits to Asia, via the Suez Canal to Europe and along the Cape of Good Hope to America. Some super tankers, ultra-large crude carriers (ULCC), can carry more than 2 million barrels of oil at a time.

Handysize	10,000 - 35,000
Handymax	35,000 - 65,000
Seawaymax	10,000 - 60,000
Panamax	60,000 - 80,000
Aframax	80,000 - 120,000
Suezmax	120,000 - 200,000
Capesize	80,000 - 200,000
VLCC (Malaccamax)	200,000 - 320,000
ULCC	320,000 - 550,000

Figure 24: Vessels to maximum transport capacity measured by propulsion (deadweight metric tons, DWT)

Transport capacity with tankers and bulk carriers is determined by the number of vessels available. The restricted available volume of tonnage is positive for the results of tanker companies, but it results in high costs for consumers. Rates for chartering bulk carriers rose by 50% between the beginning of 2006 and the middle of 2007. The rate for transportation with a super tanker was 35,000 dollars a day in April 2006, and by August 2007 that had risen to 90,000 dollars. The cost price for tanker companies was, at that time, around 22,500 dollars a day. It should also be said that freight charges are generally highly season-related: heating oil requires a lot of transport capacity chiefly in the winter.

Moreover, there is a shortage of 'safe' ships at the moment. From 2010 oil tankers, in accordance with international agreements, will have to be fitted with double hulls. In the market sector of tankers for mineral and edible oil, there are about 5,000 tankers that desperately need to be replaced, yet at the beginning of 2007 a total of only 900 ships were laid up in shipyards for repair. Oil tankers are chiefly built in Japan, China and South Korea where, mid 2007, the time between order and delivery was about three years. Worldwide, due to the great shortage, many single-hulled ships are sailing with a temporary dispensation. Of course, insurance premiums for this sort of ship are considerably higher, which then affects the level of transport costs.

Building ships is, however, not the only solution to the biting transport problems. Ports must also be enlarged, as at the moment ships regularly have to wait a long time before they can actually be unloaded. As time costs money, this problem also requires the necessary attention. Not optimally utilizing available ship capacity is a factor that further increases transport costs.

4.2.3 Rotterdam

The Netherlands wants to be the junction for a number of important issues in the field of energy. This is because of its geographical location and its highly-developed infrastructure. The Netherlands as a 'gas roundabout' (see Chapter 12, section 12.7.3), the Netherlands as a spider in the web of the 'copper plate' creation (see Chapter 12, section 12.7.2) and Rotterdam as the energy port of Europe. This seaport fulfils an important role in the future plans of the Dutch economy; it is vitally important for Rotterdam that the port is transformed to an energy-hub. Clustering companies that complement each other is hugely important because interaction creates a reduction in costs. An area can become competitive with foreign countries because of this. Consumers and generators of electricity try to get together in order to keep transport costs as low as possible; which is why generators gladly set up in a port area like Rotterdam, close to supply and transport and sufficient quantities of available cooling water.

There have been a number of large refineries and a number of petrochemical industries in Rotterdam since way back. The seaport has the largest oil and coal terminals in Europe and natural gas would fit perfectly in that picture. Liquid natural gas is a new growth market. In 2007 there were already concrete plans for the building of at least two LNG terminals. Meanwhile, Rotterdam has already managed to gain a reasonably solid position in the area of bio-fuels. Bio-ethanol, bio-methanol and bio-diesel are already being traded, transferred and shipped in the Rotterdam docks. In addition, a number of new bio-fuel producing factories are being built.

Because of the great economic significance of transport, there is a lot of attention for the position of Rotterdam. The seaport is of vital importance for the future international position of the Netherlands. Rotterdam is unique on account of its deep sea port and favourable geographic position, both of which are of utmost importance for a good connection with the European hinterland.

Rotterdam is the third largest port in the world, after Shanghai and Singapore. In 2007, 10 million containers were transhipped in Rotterdam; it is expected that this number will rise to 38 million over the next 30 years. More than 1000 containers pass through the port of Rotterdam every hour. If a year's worth of these containers were placed side-by-side the length of the line would be equal to the circumference of the world. Some ships carry 12,000 at a time; this type of gigantic carrier cannot enter the ports of Antwerp or Hamburg, only Rotterdam. The *Berge Stahl*, a ship that carries iron-ore and is 342m long and 64m wide, only travels between Brazil and Rotterdam. The depth of the ship is 23m; the water level in the port of Rotterdam is 24m. Docking has to be done quickly as the 24m water level is only applicable at high tide. Entering the port is a huge job because slack water only lasts a few minutes, after which the water level drops quickly. Captains of the bulk carriers often have to hand over to special port-employed steersmen, who know the local conditions of the port like no-one else.

There are comparable capacity problems all over the world. The Panama Canal has trouble with the same sort of obstacle that Rotterdam has, which is why this waterway has to be dredged and widened. Building of the current canal started in 1880, but it only opened for shipping in 1914. Until recently, the locks were 32m wide, but nowadays the largest container ships are much wider. Thought is being given to digging a new canal further up, and Nicaragua is also considering starting a similar project at the moment.

	1990	2000	2004	2005	Share (2005)
Hard coal – Total	125,674	151,390	193,201	193,560	100%
Of which:					
South Africa	24,590	41,515	54,052	51,602	26.7%
Australia	18,515	28,374	30,175	26,861	13.9
Colombia	9,119	22,313	24,133	24,159	12.5
Russia	2,114	12,259	36,288	44,531	23.0
United States	46,752	19,395	14,631	14,367	7.4
Indonesia	241	8,664	13,425	14,246	7.4
Other countries	24,343	18,870	20,497	17,794	9.2
Coking coal – Total	44,688	43,423	40,644	41,079	100%
Of which:					
Australia	8,725	18,965	19,811	19,434	47.3%
United States	26,422	14,750	10,919	12,008	29.2
Canada	2,761	6,225	4,102	5,560	13.5
Venezuela	0	418	969	873	2.1
China	1	2	1,951	178	0.4
Other countries	6,779	3,063	2,892	3,026	7.4
Steam coal – Total	80,983	107,967	152,557	152,481	100%
Of which:					
South Africa	24,432	41,127	53,619	51,307	33.6%
Colombia	9,095	22,173	23,858	23,976	15.7
Russia	32	10,191	35,004	42,505	27.9
Indonesia	195	8,223	13,425	14,246	9.3
Australia	9,790	9,409	10,364	7,427	4.9
Other countries	37,439	16,844	16,287	13,020	8.5

- Hard coal: Coal, particularly suitable for the production of electricity
- Coking coal: Coal, particularly suitable for the production of coke
- Steam coal: Coal, particularly suitable for the production of steam and heating, in as far as not sorted under coking coal

Figure 25: Coal imports for the EU25 (in kiloton) (OECD, 2005)

As well as Rotterdam, the Dutch port of Eems Haven is also trying to win an important place in developments in the field of energy. This harbour can also serve as an arrival place for all sorts of energy products. The electricity connection with Norway (NorNed) is coming to this shore and, furthermore, Eems Haven is close to the Groningen gas field and it is the port connected to the intricate Dutch gas-pipe network. Especially because of this last aspect, Eems Haven is a very suitable place for the delivery of LNG, which can be stored in empty gas fields and then injected into the network.

4.3 Networks

East Siberia contains the majority of commodities present in Russia. About 85% of all Russia's natural gas comes from this region, as does 80% of all Russia's extracted oil and coal. In addition, gold, silver, platinum, diamond and nickel are found in this Russian region. East Siberia is also the primary wood-production area. Unfortunately, the area is neither people nor production-friendly. The intense cold can create severe conditions that make extracting commodities extremely difficult. The huge Vankor oil field is in the permafrost in the Arctic Circle; the temperature in these parts regularly drops to below minus 50 degrees Celsius. The consequences this has for activities being developed in the area are easy to imagine.

But even when production can be carried out in the Siberian Vankor, there is still the problem of the extracted material being transported over huge distances; via a pipeline, for example. Laying these pipeline networks costs a lot of money and is linked to a number of different questions. For example, where do the pipes need to go? Should they go over land or under sea? What sort of material is used for making the pipe sections, and under what pressure does the system have to function?

At the beginning of 2007, China had a pipeline network totalling 80,000 km, one of the longest networks in the world. Because of the fast growth of energy requirement in China, the country wants to expand its infrastructure. Between 2007 and 2010, China will lay another 50,000 km of oil and gas pipelines.

European energy networks require, according to the IEA, a total investment of 500 billion euros over the next 25 years. Each kilometre of new pipeline laid costs over 1 million euros.

4.3.1 Gas pipelines

Laying a gas pipeline with a diameter of 120 centimetres costs, on average, 2 to 3 million euros per kilometre. A pipe of this size can transport about 100 million cubic metres of gas every day.

Before the gas is pumped into the pipe, it is first brought to the correct pressure. A pressure level of 70 bar is very common for this. Whilst underway, the gas passes through all sorts of intermediate pressure stations that keep the pressure level up, which allows the gas to continue. Because intermediate stations are not used under water, the pressure in pipelines lying at the bottom of the sea is increased to 200 bar.

The Netherlands has two gas-transport networks: one for high-calorie gas, the other for low-calorie gas. All Dutch small-scale (household) consumers use low-calorie gas from the Groningen field. An alternative for this is converted high-calorie gas. To convert high-calorie gas to low-calorie gas (gas conversion), which is necessary for it to be used for the same purposes, nitrogen is added.

	2000	2002	2003	2004	2005	Share (2005)
Russia	107,213	101,762	108.515	108,655	106,839	36.7 %
Norway	48,715	64,342	67,280	68,523	71,285	24.5
Algeria	54,644	52,551	53,126	50,395	55,620	19.1
Not further specified	6,808	13,604	17,914	22,609	29,580	10.1
Nigeria	4,283	5,507	7,884	10,117	10,741	3.7
Qatar	293	2,070	1,893	3,770	4,606	1.6
Other countries	2,906	3,171	2,681	6,640	12,773	4.4
Total imports	224,862	243,007	259,293	270,709	291,444	100 %

Figure 26: Gas imports for the EU25 (in million cubic metres) (OECD, 2005)

Heated debate is taking place at the moment about gas and, to a lesser extent, about electricity. Buyers generally have to sign two contracts: one for their supply of gas and the other for the transport of that gas. Transport contracts are usually concluded for longer periods. The EU is against this as the phenomenon thwarts competition, especially because of the restrictive consequences it has for the availability of supply. Parties can purchase energy, but they are then not always certain of transport, and as has already been mentioned, availability of transport capacity is essential. Big players, like Gazprom, would do anything to gain control of cross-border capacity.

A few important projects are described below, but this is just a handful of the huge number of planned constructions.

Nabucco

The Nabucco pipeline goes from the Caspian region via Turkey to Austria. This pipeline network will become operational in 2011 and will award Turkey an important role in Europe.

The realisation of this pipeline was conclusively arranged beforehand. Turkey and Iran came to an agreement about the annual supply of 30 billion cubic metres of gas from Iran and Turkmenistan via this pipeline. The gas from Turkmenistan will be pumped from Iran to Turkey and from there to Central Europe (Austria) via the Nabucco pipeline. In this way, the Nabucco pipeline connects the Caspian Sea to European hinterland, which will make Europe less dependent on Russia. This has apparently offended Russia and is the reason Russia and the Italian ENI are now busy laying the so-called South Stream pipeline. This southerly route has to provide the EU with gas and offer competition to the Nabucco pipeline. The Russians have also reached agreements with Kazakhstan and Turkmenistan about the increase of gas supply from their counties, which has brought the viability of Nabucco seriously into play. The Americans have added to this because they do not appreciate the agreement between Turkey and Iran. They think that all transactions with Iran should be banned in order to isolate the country economically.

Blue Stream

The Blue Stream pipeline is an undersea connection between Russia and Turkey and is, therefore, a direct competitor of the Nabucco pipeline. Because of its strategic position, Turkey has access to about 70% of the worldwide oil and gas reserves, which are chiefly found in Russia and the Middle East. Turkey is, because of this, the energy corridor for the continents of Africa, Asia and Europe. Turkish oil and gas importance is known worldwide. The country itself uses its key position as a trump card during the process that leads to a membership of the European Union.

Nord Stream

The Dutch Gasunie and the Russian Gazprom work together on several fronts. Both gas companies signed an agreement at the end of 2006 which gave each an interest in the other's gas pipeline systems. Gasunie gained a 9% interest in Nord Stream, the Baltic gas pipeline project that will be transporting gas over a total distance of 1,200 km from Russia to Germany (under the Baltic Sea) from 2010. A branch of the pipeline system will also go to the Netherlands. The agreement also gives Gazprom an interest in the BBL pipeline from the Netherlands to England. This pipeline is only 235 km long, which made the laying considerably cheaper than that of the Baltic project. That is the reason that Gazprom received extra financial compensation from Gasunie in addition to the agreed exchange of shares.

In the middle of 2007, shareholders in the Nord Stream project, including Wintershall and E.ON, decided to change the route of the pipeline because of environmentally technical objections. The pipeline will now not be laid along the south side of the Danish island Bornholm, but along the north side.

BBL (Balgzand-Bacton line)

The BBL pipeline connects Balgzand in North Holland with Bacton in England. Gasunie (60%), E.ON (20%) and Fluxys (20%) are shareholders in this project. The difference between BBL and the Inter-connector, a pipeline that connects Zeebrugge in Belgium with England, is that the BBL line as yet only allows one-way traffic from the Netherlands to England.

4.3.2 Oil pipelines

A number of pipelines go across the bottom of the sea, but most go over land. One of the longest oil pipelines goes from Samara in Russia to Leuna in Germany and has a length of 3,640 km. Another Russian pipeline is the subject of heated debate at the moment. Transneft, a company that is controlled by the Russian State, has begun laying a pipeline from East Siberia to Asia. The pipe system will have a total length of

4,000 km and is coupled with enormous risk. It is a gamble whether or not the pipeline will be economically cost-effective because whether sufficient oil will be found in that part of East Siberia is not yet known. The total cost of laying the new pipeline has not been conclusively calculated, but the cost-price of the project is in the billions of euros. The project is, therefore, more a political and prestigious enterprise than an economically responsible one. Russia is, however, trying to show itself as a superpower in the field of energy; the nation wants to trade oil energy forms in all the furthest corners of the world.

A new oil pipeline to be laid between the Caspian Sea and the Mediterranean Sea has to become an alternative for the busy shipping route near Istanbul in Turkey. Russia has a 51% interest in the project; Bulgaria and Greece together have 49%. Kazakhstan has also expressed interest in becoming a potential partner.

	2000	2002	2003	2004	2005	Share (2005)
Former Soviet Union	118	156	174	196	199	36.4%
Norway	115	101	104	106	90	16.4%
Saudi Arabia	65	53	61	64	61	11.1%
Libya	45	39	45	50	50	9.2%
Iran	35	25	34	35	34	6.3%
Middle East (others)	13	20	12	9	9	1,6%
Other countries	127	111	94	86	103	18.9%
Total imports	519	507	528	548	548	100%
In million barrels	3,792	3,706	3,855	4,007	4,004	

Figure 27: Oil imports for the EU25 (in million tons) (OECD, 2005)

Druzba

Of the total Russian oil export, 28% goes through the Druzba, (or Friendship), pipeline. This pipeline system is 4,000 km long and connects Russia with Central Europe.

The Russian pipeline operator, Transneft, closed the Druzba pipeline at the beginning of 2007. Druzba means friendship, but there was absolutely no sign of that when the Russians suddenly turned off the tap. The system transports 28% (1 million barrels a day) of Russia's total oil export to refineries in Poland and the Danube countries. Russia itself refines about half of its total oil production; the rest takes place in other countries.

The trouble began when Belarus announced that it wanted to impose a tax on oil transit. It had reached this decision because Moscow was forcing it to pay extra for delivery of its natural gas from 1 January 2007. Russia forced its neighbour to pay double because the prices that Belarus was being charged were, according to Russia, no longer in conformity with the market. From 2011, Belarus will have to pay as much for gas as Western Europe does. Apart from that, the Russians stopped delivery of cheap oil to refineries in Belarus by imposing an export tax. As a reaction to that, Belarus threatened to block the transit of oil to Europe. Moreover, they tapped off oil, and that infuriated the Russians.

Primorsk

Political tensions around the Druzba pipeline are interwoven with all sorts of other issues. The problems actually began in 2006 when the Russians blocked the import of Polish meat, which led the Poles to frustrate the negotiations between Europe and Russia. Lithuania was also involved in this sparring match. In response to the take-over of the Lithuanian refinery Mazeikiu by the Polish Orlen, Russia threatened to stop the oil supply. A little bit before that, the Russians had forced the Americans to sell Mazeikiu to the Russian Yukos by threatening a similar action. After Yukos went bankrupt, Orlen bought up the Lithuanian oil industry; this to the great displeasure of the Russians who reacted to it in March 2007 by suggesting connecting the pipeline with one of their ports on the Botnic Gulf. In 2007, the Russians approved the building of an oil pipeline that would connect the Baltic port of Primorsk to the Russian hinterland. Oil can be transported via this line to Western Europe, for example, without it having to be dependent on former Eastern Bloc countries, which the Friendship pipeline is as it travels through other nations territories. The position of the Eastern European oil companies is seriously weakened by this initiative.

4.3.3 Power grids

For transportation of electricity for home use, high-tension, middle-tension and low-tension grids are used, but these days more and more electricity is being transported over borders. Cross-border electricity transport is desirable in order to better meet consumer requirements. On the one hand, by capitalizing on excessive supply and demand on one or the other sides of the connection; and on the other hand, because of the difference in price. As a result of historically-strong local or national government policy, this cross-border capacity is extremely limited in most places. The reason for this is can be traced back to 40-year old policy. The current electricity grids were built in the 1960s and are now seriously out-of-date. In the past, each country built its own electricity grid which connected to others in order for countries to help each other out in cases of calamity. This cross-border capacity is, however, extremely limited.
This limited supply of transport capacity becomes more harrowing as energy takes on a more important role. Since the liberalization of energy markets, more and more attention is being given to transport, increasing transport capacity and linking various existing networks. There are, of course, many initiatives, but the situation is not an easily-solvable one, which is why changes are essential.
The German energy producer RWE wants to build an electricity generating plant in the Dutch Eems Haven, but that has proved not to be possible as the high-tension lines there are already full. That means that all the available capacity has been booked by others. Long-term contracts have ensured that all available capacity has been taken until 2017 and that there is no capacity available for newcomers. The problem has been partly caused by NUON. This company obtained prior approval for building an electricity generating plant on the same spot. The consequence of this is that the plans that wind farms and bio-mass plants have for this region have to be shelved for the time being. Transport capacity is, as will have already become apparent, often a restrictive factor. Sometimes, because of this, energy cannot be transported; and for this reason, electricity traffic between the Netherlands and Germany is very limited. The desire for transport can be traced to the price difference that regularly occurs between the two countries. As soon as sufficient capacity is available, transport takes place until the existing price discrepancy is removed (price arbitrage). But because the limitation of transport capacity still exists, the price difference regularly reappears.
At the beginning of 2006, the electricity networks of Germany and the Netherlands were connected with a capacity of 3,650 megawatts. Recently, transmission system

operators TenneT and RWE decided to increase the cross-border capacity by 1,500 megawatts. This did not only benefit the electricity supply from Germany to the Netherlands, but also the electricity supply in the other direction. Apart from that, a lot of electricity is transported from Germany to France via the Netherlands and Belgium. The high-tension cable between Diele in Germany and Meeden in the Netherlands has also been increased and became fully utilized in October 2007. Investment, made by the German grid manager E.on Netz, ensured the increase of the available capacity from 850 megawatts to 1,400 megawatts, which to a great extent solved the congestion there had been until then. Of course, large changes in supply and demand will continue to cause problems. Over recent years, production of large volumes of electricity by means of wind parks has occasionally resulted in the Dutch grid becoming overloaded.

The application of information technology in the current situation is small. Overloading simply causes a part of the grid to be shut down. In order to reach an optimal situation, a lot of work still needs to be done in this area. In the future, 'intelligent systems' will be equipped with sensors so that management can be better carried out. Networks will be more economical, reliable and friendlier.

Another aspect is that some connections only allow one-way traffic, while two-way traffic is becoming increasingly desirable. This applies as much to electricity as to gas. Power is increasingly being generated locally and small-scale, which sometimes results in more being produced than is required. Market gardeners want to bring this extra electricity into the system so that it can then be sold to others. This so-called 'energy sell back' requires two-way traffic.

A great deal will (have to) change in the future. Once solar energy is adopted on a large scale, it will be mainly generated in countries around the Mediterranean Sea. This will lead to a lot of transport from Southern Europe to Northern Europe, which again will burden the network in a different way than was the case beforehand. It is also possible that an important part of power consumption will shift from day to night time, which will also influence the design of the electricity grid. For the time being, two overseas connections for expanding the link of several countries' systems are of vital importance to the Netherlands. The ultimate objective being strived for is the formation of one large copper plate in Europe (see Chapter 12, section 12.7.2).

NorNed

The NorNed cable between Norway and the Netherlands was completed at the end of 2007. The connection became operational in 2007 but the official opening will take place in the summer of 2008. On both sides of the cable are huge conversion stations where direct current is changed to alternating current. Direct current is used during transportation in order to restrict power loss. The capacity of the NorNed cable is 700 megawatts and laying the cable cost an estimated 600 million euros. The project came into being because of a joint venture between TSO TenneT and its Norwegian equivalent Statnett. The cable, which begins in Eems Haven, reaches 410 metres under sea level at its deepest point and is 580 km long, making it the longest undersea high-tension cable in the world. This record used to be held by the Basselink connection (290 km) that connects Tasmania with Australia.

BritNed

The BritNed cable will connect the Netherlands and England. If everything goes to plan, the Electricity connection between the Maasvlakte and the Isle of Grain will become operation at the end of 2010. The cable, which will be 260 km in length, will have a capacity of 1000 megawatts. The connection is especially interesting because England has a totally different composition of energy-production units than the Netherlands. The same is also true of Norway, but in the case of the BritNed cable, the hour time difference between the two countries will also be capitalized on. This will, after all, lead to a different purchase pattern. Additionally, heating in the Netherlands runs primarily on gas whereas the English mainly use electricity for heating.

All these differences create price differences. By linking both markets, energy companies in both countries can purchase electricity in the future and price differences will decrease or even completely disappear.

4.4 Costs of transport, storage and insurance

The costs of transport, storage and insurance are crucial in the commodities and energy world. Transport accounts for 20% of total energy consumption in the EU and the sector is actually 98% dependent on oil. Transport costs are ultimately calculated in the eventual price of goods, which is why the infrastructure of a country is so very important. Developing countries have to invest a lot in infrastructure, but there is much in western countries that needs replacing. Airports, roads, bridges, rivers and ports are essential for an economy to flourish. This also emphasises the importance of Schiphol, Eems Haven, Rotterdam, the Betuwe Line and non-congested motorways.

It furthermore proves how important supplying goods in large quantities is. Ultra large crude carriers (ULCC) can carry 2 million barrels at a time. These floating mega-constructions are more than 300 metres long and 60 metres wide and tall. The motors that propel such vessels have a capacity of 3 megawatts; enough to supply a small town with energy. Using such ships uses a lot of energy; some vessels even use up a part of their own cargo. The longer a journey is, the more the cargo is eaten into. The iron monster eats its own flesh, as it were.

This is why experiments are now being carried out with kites that hang at a height of a few hundred metres above a ship and pull it along. These *parasails* have a pulling power of 6,800 horsepower and can create fuel savings of 35%. There are, of course, costs attached, which is why the toy requires the efforts and undivided attention of a full-time crew member.

For a number of countries, the high cost of transport is one of the reasons to lay claim to parts of the North Pole region. Russia, Canada, Denmark, Norway and the US do not only bicker about the rights to the mineral commodity sources in the North Pole. Because of the melting polar cap, a northern navigation route may also become available. Sea transport between the US and Asia could be shortened by 6,500 km if vessels no longer had to use the Panama Canal. That this possibility would save a great deal of money, speaks for itself.

CHAPTER 5:
Geo-politics

5.1 Security of supply and safety aspects

This chapter is mainly about security of supply and the protection of own sources and resources. These are closely linked and are logical outcomes of transport (capacity), the subject of the previous chapter. When the subjects of safety or risk are reviewed they can include, apart from security of supply and protection of own sources, protection of the environment and working conditions. The Chinese factory inspectorate called for 10,000 small coalmines to be closed by the end of 2007. By the middle of 2008 half of all small mines must have closed. The Chinese actually have the most deadly mining industry in the world: 4,700 people were killed in mineshaft accidents in 2006. Corrupt local officials are actually the cause of many mines opening illegally. Unfortunately, little seems to help against personal enrichment in the form of bribes.

5.2 Focus on countries and regions

Countries with a lot of inhabitants, industry and/or energy sources play an important role in supply and demand in the energy world. Economic significance is more often and more sharply conveyed in the role that these countries play on the political stage. Countries of a large surface area generally also have a lot of commodities and are rich in energy sources. Large countries often have many inhabitants. Exceptions to this rule are Canada and Australia, both of which are large in size and have a lot of commodities, but both have relatively few inhabitants. Japan's total population is 130 million people, but it hardly has any energy sources of its own, which is why Japan strongly leans on the import of fuels. India is in a comparable situation, while this country is undergoing lightning-speed economic growth.

Every country produces and consumes energy, but despite that, countries are labelled as energy-consumers or energy-producers. It would be better, however, to designate countries as net-importers or net-exporters. Some countries have such huge reserves that they produce more than they consume; in such cases, a part of the total production is exported. These countries fall into the category of net-exporters. This group includes OPEC countries, Russia, Norway, Mexico, Oman, Australia and Canada. The US is indeed also a very large producer of oil, gas and coal, but it consumes so much oil and gas that on balance it still has to import fuels. Whether a country is a net-importer or net-exporter of energy is crucially important to the way in which (international) politics is practised. It is highly likely that the US invaded Iraq in order to secure oil supplies. And the invasion in Afghanistan seems to have been purely motivated by the securing of transport possibilities and increasing the grip on energy-rich regions. China is strengthening its connections with Africa in order to lay claim to the commodities there. In exchange for the oil and gas, the Chinese are laying railways in Nigeria. China is also offering economic aid to the civil-war-stricken Sudan via the United Nations. The western world reproaches China for not being concerned about human rights in the relevant countries, but the country itself is of a different opinion. China calls the West a hypocrite. Throughout the whole world, countries gear their policies to their own positions. Russia turned off the gas-tap to the Ukraine in 2006, interrupted the supply of oil by train to Estonia in the spring of 2007, cut Shell off from the Shachalin 2 project in 2006 and strangled BP in the exploitation of the East Siberian Kovykta gas project in 2007.

Life was also made difficult for Shell in Argentina, and Venezuela, Ecuador and Bolivia have expropriated diverse foreign parties in the telecom and energy sectors, although in this case there was talk of some financial compensation. At the end of 2007, Kazakhstan pulled a stunt on the Kashagan project. Kazakhstan tried to take control of the Kashagan field development away from the Italian ENI and its partners. In September 2007, Kazakh Prime Minister Masimov said about the pressure that was being exerted: *"Friendly talks are underway, but if our demands are not met we will implement plan B"*. In other words, the Kazakh state-owned energy company, KazMunaiGaz, had to acquire a majority in the project. These words probably sound barbaric to a western ear, but it has to be said that they were unequivocal. It seems that almost no-one on this planet is averse to intrigue and involvement. Alrosa, a company that has a state monopoly in Russian diamond mining, needed a loan in 2007 in order to take over the gold concern Polyus. Minister of Finance Kudrin granted the loan, which isn't surprising seeing the other positions he also held at the time. Kudrin was a Member of the Board of the VTB National Bank and Chairman of the Board of Alrosa.

5.2.1 Reciprocity clause

Placing commodities and enterprises under state control *and* expropriation are deplored by the West. In this sort of situation, Western countries usually come off second best and therefore lodge a complaint. Strange really, because in the past Westerners plundered their colonies. Yet the West is not without prospect as the European Commission has announced that adequate countermeasures will be taken if the legal rights of European companies are threatened. At the end of 2006, the EU and Kazakhstan signed an agreement in principle about collaboration in the field of energy. If Kazakhstan does not keep to the agreement it can expect harsh sanctions. Moreover, the EU has set up a defence against partiality in many areas within and outside the energy sector. Non-European companies with take-over plans in the Union can count on additional protection constructions. These measures will hamper future acquisitions. Europe's biggest fear is the participation of third parties in its infrastructure, like gas and electricity networks. Russia and countries in the Middle East will be faced with harsh conditions for potential investments. They will, hereby, be held to a so-called *reciprocity clause*, which means that non-EU countries receive exactly the same restrictions as European companies. In addition, the clause implies that countries like Russia and China may not participate in the EU if EU countries are not allowed to participate in Russia or China.

5.2.2 Regions

Every country has its own interests, which are expressed in its political set-up and policy. A number of countries and regions are focussed on below. Some regions are extremely important from a political point of view either because of the enormous mineral resources they contain, or because they are essential for the transit of these resources.

5.2.2.1 The Middle East

The Middle East contains the largest part of the world's oil and gas supplies. Countries in this region began nationalizing commodities years ago, and that is now happening in countries like Russia, Kazakhstan, Venezuela, Ecuador and Bolivia. State-owned companies in charge of large supplies of oil and gas are extremely wealthy. Over the last few years particularly, they have greatly profited from the huge price rises on the world market. Oil-rich countries used to be highly dependent on Western oil concerns, which were then the biggest enterprises in the world, for their investments. Nowadays, the Western concern ExxonMobil ranks only twelfth on the list of biggest companies. The company has less than 10% of the reserves that state-owned companies in Saudi Arabia, Iran or Iraq have. In comparison to what used to be done, several regimes in the Middle East are now trying to pump their income from the sale of oil and gas into the local economies. The populations of an increasing number of countries are benefiting from this because money is being released for improving infrastructure, education and health care. Government leaders are increasingly realizing that supplies with fossil fuels are limited and they are, therefore, trying to make their economies less dependent on this sector. Apart from that, increasingly more interests are being acquired in Western enterprises, as a result of which the risk in their portfolios is spread and their power increased. Because of the interests at stake here, the West has always taken much interest in the Middle East. The US, especially, tries to get, or keep, a foot in the door of several countries, which isn't easy because the region has, until now, been characterized by turmoil and violence.

5.2.2.2 Central Asia

After the Middle East and Russia, the Caspian region is the area with the largest oil reserves. Besides that, a lot of gas is found particularly in Kazakhstan and Turkmenistan. Few people realize that Russian home-land consumption and a part of the export is highly dependent on gas coming from Turkmenistan.

The status that the Caspian Sea has, has caused all sorts of legal clashes since the 19th century because the interests are great. If the Caspian Sea is regarded as a sea, the bordering countries gain exclusive rights to exploiting territorial waters, the volume being dependent on the length of each individual country's coastline. If the water is labelled a lake, the resources from the whole of the Caspian Sea are divided between the five countries and jointly exploited.

Kazakhstan	2,320
Russia	1,460
Turkmenistan	1,200
Iran	996
Azerbaijan	825

Figure 28: Coastline lengths of countries on the Caspian Sea (in kilometres) (Editions Atlas, 2007)

After the Middle East, it seems that Central Asia is now becoming the new region of tension. The area goes from the Caspian Sea, which is especially rich in oil and gas, to the Ferghana Valley, where Tajikistan, Uzbekistan and Kyrgyzstan merge. The area lies near Afghanistan and holds important potential transport routes, which is why all sorts of countries involve themselves in the politics of the involved countries. Everybody is trying to get a finger in the pie somewhere. As many of the region's leaders are getting on in years, the area will be characterized by much exchange of power over the coming years. The Americans have already spent years laying a connection between the Caspian region and the Pakistani coast to transport oil and gas. This route should then go from Turkmenistan via Afghanistan, or via the Ferghana Valley. Political efforts are translated into China and Russia taking a defensive position towards the US. Both countries want the American influence in the region diminished. They particularly want to see the American military leave. If this happens, China and Russia will become involved in a power struggle; both nations trying to come out on top. Iran, India and Pakistan are now also taking part in this increasingly-fierce struggle. Now the game is well underway, even they are trying to expand their sphere of influence. Iran has close ethnic and cultural ties with Tajikistan, while India has already set-up a military base there. This sort of initiative is not unimportant in an unstable region. The political situation in Kyrgyzstan, Tajikistan neighbour, is far from stable. Only time will tell how the relationship will actually develop.

5.2.2.3 Africa

The northern part of Africa (Algeria, Libya and Egypt) has for many years been known as a rich oil and gas area, but recently the struggle for fossil fuels has been increasingly directed towards other parts of the African continent. The Gulf of Guinea and the land that this stretch of sea encompasses is rich in oil and gas. Nigeria, particularly, contains significant amounts. The eastern part of Africa also has a number of interesting sources; Sudan and Uganda are, for example, rich in oil, but the situation in both countries is deplorable because of the furious civil wars that have been raging there for years. It is often suggested that the West doesn't want the African continent to develop economically. If this were to be the case, so much extra pressure on energy shortages would arise that the world would find itself in an even greater field of tension. This could be a reason why these countries do not receive extra support from wealthy countries.

5.2.3 Net-exporters

5.2.3.1 Russia

After the collapse of the Soviet Union, Russia tried for a long time to re-position itself in the world. This reorientation found new means in energy. Russia contains the largest gas supply in the world; it also has a lot of oil, coal and uranium at its disposal. In addition, Russia has an enormous land surface, on which of all sorts of vegetation can be cultivated for the production of bio-energy. The pressure the Russians put on the West clearly came to the fore when Russia turned off the gas tap to the Ukraine and Belarus. In the summer of 2007, the Russian flag was placed on the North Pole. With this action, Russia tried to lay claim to the commodities (oil and gas) present under the surface of the ice. If the temperature on earth does indeed rise, as experts say it will, access to the area will increase, and that is an advantage the Russians want to cash in on. Staking out the area by placing a flag did not sit well in international circles. It will undoubtedly give the Russians a stronger position at the negotiating table. It is logical that the Russians are looking for recognition. The situation in the country is still not radically different from what it was during the Soviet Union days; even then the country heavily relied on its natural resources. This partiality can still be found in the economic landscape. Growth figures of 1990, the last year that the Soviet Union existed, were only equalled again in 2006. The country didn't progress much in the intervening years; in fact, criminality and corruption even exploded. The potential of the country is indeed huge, but the result is, for the time being, of a dubious nature. Russia produces more oil than it consumes. A lot of oil is sold to third parties on the black market, something that chiefly lines the pockets of local rulers. The partiality of the Russian economy leads to dependence; a possible drop in energy prices will result in extra pressure on prosperity. Moreover, export pushes the price of a national currency unit up, which troubles other business sectors as it provides a competitive disadvantage. This phenomenon is also called the *Dutch Disease* because Dutch export suffered under its own power in the 1970s because of the increasing gas income. China and Russia were rivals for years, but they have been trying to get closer since the BorisYeltsin/Jiang Zemin era in the 1990s. Political and economic ties have been strengthened recently, as have those in the field of energy. In 2006, both countries even carried out a joint military exercise for the first time, and at the UN they regularly take shared standpoints flatly opposed to those of the Americans.

5.2.3.2 Saudi Arabia
Saudi Arabia contains the largest oil supplies in the world and it is, therefore, a particularly powerful country. The relationship between the US and Saudi Arabia has been particularly close for years. The Americans acquired the first interests in Saudi oil fields in 1933. First via Socal and later via Texaco, the US has built on an economic foundation that still exists today. The Sunnis Arabs who govern the country are not particularly charmed by the Shiite Arabs, like most Iranians. This leads to regular clashes and political power regularly grates against other sections within OPEC (see section 5.3.1). Because of its large supplies (and production capacity), Saudi Arabia occupies the most prominent position in the oil cartel. Saudi will is therefore regularly law. In the past, oil income has chiefly lined the pockets of members of the Royal Family, but over the last few years they have also come to realize that it is better to allow the population to share the benefits of all the wealth. That is why the country is also going to spend its highly increased oil income on the nation this time. The Saudi government has planned investments totally 300 billion dollars for the period 2007 to 2010. Four brand-new cities have to be thrown up, as do a number of new ports and airports, 3,800 km of railway line, 8,000 km of motorway, 77 new hospitals, 4 universities, 56 colleges and 2,000 training centres. These are rigorous plans, but at the end of 2006, the government already has 175 billion ready and waiting in its account.

5.2.3.3 Iran

After Russia, Iran has the largest gas reserves in the world, and it has the largest oil supplies in the world after Saudi Arabia. Iran's potential is enormous, but in practice, Iranian clout is limited. The country suffered from the war with Iraq in the 1980s, and from its own regime that has been led by radical Islamists since 1979. The economic and political boycott led by the US has also considerably contributed to the isolation of the country. By imposing all sorts of sanctions, the US is trying to force Iran to change its current regime. That isn't easy. The Iranian economy is bogged down and suffering from hyperinflation. Half of Iran's Gross Domestic Product (GDP) is dependent on oil income. In the US, the Iran Sanctions Act of 1996 forbids investment of 20 million dollars or more in Iran. This also thwarts possible initiatives that companies like Royal Dutch Shell and BP want to develop in Iran. The functioning of this law can be brought into doubt because many American companies maintain active relations with Iran. Until now, they have barely been punished for this, but in 2007, the American Democrats launched a motion for the Iran Counter-Proliferation Act. This act compels the American government to punish all companies, both American and non-American, if they trade with Iran.

Because of all these developments, Iran is lacking knowledge in the field of extraction, and there is a shortage of refining capacity for processing oil and gas and the infrastructure for transport is of a doubtful level. Iran is trying to counterbalance the imposed sanctions by conspiring with other world powers; Venezuela, for example. Furthermore, Iran is suspected of offering (financial) support to terrorist organisations like Hamas and Al-Qaeda. The struggle between the US and Iran reached a new peak with the debate about uranium enrichment and nuclear energy. The Iranians claim that they want to build a nuclear power station for scientific research and for producing nuclear energy, while the Americans accuse them of having nuclear-energy plans for military purposes; by producing a nuclear bomb, for example.

Within the scope of the impasse that has arisen between the two countries, the Iranians grab every opportunity they can to provoke the Americans. Iran has already proposed selling all its oil in a currency other than the dollar. In addition, the country has printed symbols of nuclear energy on its banknotes to draw out the Americans. Moreover, Iran is threatening to no longer observe the previously signed Non-Proliferation Treaty. The Head of the International Atomic Energy Agency (IAEA), Mohamed el-Baradei, warned about an escalation of the problems and tried to bring both parties to the table. Iran is increasingly benefiting from the position of Russia and China, which is increasingly deviating from American politics.

5.2.3.4 Venezuela

There was a reason that Venezuela was closely involved in the setting-up of OPEC. The country contains immensely large supplies of oil and gas, and it has at its disposal over one-third of the world's tar sand fields (see Chapter 7, section 7.3.1). President Hugo Chávez regularly conspires with his Iranian counterpart Mahmoud Ahmadinejad. Together they fight against western imperialism and try to block the path of their sworn enemy, the US. The offensive is mostly carried out in the media, in which both leaders regularly depict the American President George W. Bush as a 'donkey' or a 'devil'. Venezuela is following the trend prevalent in many countries that have 'mountains' of mineral commodities. At the beginning of 2007, Chávez announced the nationalization of companies in the telecom and utility sectors. Share prices and the national currency immediately went into free fall. Venezuela also stepped out of the IMF in 2007 and turned its back on the World Bank. Ecuador and Bolivia subsequently threatened to do the same. The IMF is increasingly losing power, certainly now that in Latin America and Asia more and more people are calling for their own regional financial emergency funds. The possibility of that happening is becoming simpler because the financial strength of individual countries continues to increase, especially in regions that are rich in mineral commodities. The shift of power that this phenomenon brings about will result in the creation of new consultative and aid bodies. This will be at the expense of classic institutions like the World Band and the IMF. As President of Venezuela, Chávez took more drastic measures and he has gained increasingly more power. He considerably curtailed the power of the central bank; he even called the body a *neo-liberal idea*. Westerners, however, accuse him of running a dictatorial regime. For instance, only people loyal to Chávez are allowed to work in the army or in the state-owned oil company PdVSA. Media that carry out smear campaigns against him loose their licences.

5.2.3.5 Brazil

As far as the general public is concerned, Brazil is not reputed to be an energy giant, but the country is becoming increasingly more important in this area. Brazil made gigantic oil finds at the end of 2007 and the beginning of 2008. Gigantic oil fields were discovered off shore and, partly because of that, Brazil is considering becoming a member of OPEC in time. In addition to the available oil and gas supplies, Brazil has a lot of potential and plans in the field of bio-energy. The country is pre-eminently suitable for cultivating sugar-cane and other commodities needed for the production of bio-fuels. Together with the US, the nation is even the largest producer of bio-ethanol in the world. Moreover, Brazil has a large process capacity for this specific category in the energy spectrum. In June 2007, the G8, the collaboration of the eight richest industrialized countries in the world, was in session; a session which, for the first time, the five strongly-developing countries of China, India, South Africa and Brazil were allowed to attend.

5.2.3.6 Australia

The number of Western countries that have large supplies of energy sources is extremely limited. Yet there are a number that have significant amounts in the ground and this enables them to export a part of the extracted commodities. Australia, Canada and Norway are shining examples, and it is striking that all three countries have a large land surface but only a limited number of inhabitants; respectively, 20, 32 and 5 million people. This is probably the most important explanation for the fact that these countries are able to supply other countries with energy. Besides all kinds of non-energy commodities, there is a lot of gas, coal and uranium in the ground in Australia, and the country is happy to export these.

5.2.3.7 Canada

In addition to large supplies of uranium, oil and gas, Canada also has gigantic tar sand fields; in total, one-third of the all the tar sand fields in the world. This unconventional energy source will become increasingly more important in the future. Production costs of a barrel of tar-sand oil are indeed many times higher than those of the same quantity from the Middle East, but it becomes profitable as soon as the price of a barrel of oil is listed at over 30 dollars.

Canadian wealth of mineral sources translates in economic prosperity and a more prominent position in the world. Over the coming years, the geographic line Saudi Arabia/Caspian region/Russia/Canada, better known as the SCRC Line, will become the most important vein in the field of energy.

5.2.3.8 Norway

Norway owns large oil and gas fields and is wealthy because of them. There has been no stopping the economy over the last few years and the country measures, after frontrunner Luxemburg, the highest GDP per head of population in the world. This is probably also the reason for Norway's decision not to participate in the European Union.

The Norwegians occupy a unique position in the world because of their knowledge of offshore drilling and extraction. In addition, the Norwegians have a great deal of technologic knowledge in the field of exploration and production under Arctic conditions. All this sets Norway apart from most other countries and it provides the country with an important position in the oil and gas industry.

5.2.4 Net-importers

5.2.4.1 The United States

The US is the biggest consumer of energy. Despite the impressive volume of its oil production, it is a net-importer of the black gold. Moreover, its dependence on import will only increase because the need for oil continues to increase, and because its domestic-production is declining because of the depletion of its own reserves. For the time being, natural gas production provides just enough for domestic consumption, but the turning point of also becoming a net-importer of gas has almost been reached. The US also still has large supplies of oil and gas in inhospitable areas like Alaska, but lack of technological knowledge and environmental-protection measures ensure that this area can not (as yet) fully serve as a source of extraction.

The country has more than enough coal, but that doesn't much help the transport sector as it runs almost exclusively on oil. The same also applies to the enormous American war machine. The US is often reproached for wanting to impose its will on the world. American international strategy could be explained as the striving towards a unipolar world with one superpower: the US as the centre of power, strength and decision-making. Now the Americans are threatened with losing their major role in the world, the question is how they will react. Former Russian President Putin called America's attitude a threat to peace because no-one is safe in a system with one dominant factor. No-one could appeal to international law.

5.2.4.2 China

In the coming years, China will overtake the US as the biggest energy consumer in the world. Both countries are also the biggest polluters on earth, mainly because of greenhouse-gas emissions. China will show the same signs that the US showed at an earlier stage. China is also becoming a net-importer, while the country actually has large supplies of oil, gas and coal, but it is guarding against fast depletion of its own supplies. The biggest problem the Chinese have is the lack of production capacity. Moreover, the country with a population of 1.3 billion is developing economically at breakneck speed, which, in itself, will exhaust the energy reserves very quickly. Dependence on other countries is also increasing. Asian countries like China, India, South Korea and Japan are increasingly taking more oil from the Middle East and are threatening the position of Western countries by so doing. Pressure on these countries keeps increasing, which increases the chance of confrontation. The Chinese keep emphatically positioning themselves in all sorts of areas, including East Africa and the countries around the Caspian Sea. China is doing what the West used to do: carry out trade, hand out loans and collect commodities. To the great displeasure of the West, China offers support to countries that form a threat to human rights. Loans handed out by China carry no conditions, like *good governance* (ethical trade), avoidance of corruption and political reformation. Everything is dominated by concluding long-term contracts for the supply of commodities like oil and gas. It is understandable that the West follows China's activities with suspicion, but the concerns may be exaggerated. Fear is a poor advisor. Reality teaches that the cultural differences between, for example, Africa and China, are huge and that those differences don't just disappear. The African continent still maintains close ties with Europe, as much culturally as historically.

5.2.4.3 India

India's economy is developing parallel to that of China, also at breakneck speed. The country has large supplies of coal, but is highly dependent on other countries for the rest of its energy supply, which is why its ties with old friends are being strengthened and working relationships with former enemies built up. India is trying to maintain good relations with all three of the superpowers, the US, China and Russia. Russia is an old friend from the Cold War and India has concluded energy and defence contracts with the Russians. The Russians are building new nuclear power plants in India, and India is investing in Russian oil and gas fields and purchasing fighter planes. India recently entered into a partnership with the US and agreed to supply nuclear energy.

The relationship between China and India has, to say the least, not been good, but both countries seem to realize that maintaining good relations brings in money. And that works wonders.

5.2.4.4 Japan

Japan can hardly fall back on it own energy sources; there is relatively little of this sort of mineral resource under the Japanese ground. The country imports 90 to 95 percent of its total energy requirement. The Japanese have set up their structure so that they can call on a broad spectrum of energy sources. Japan is currently by far the largest importer of LNG and it built nuclear power plants at a very early stage. The main thing is that the country's enormous industry continues to be supplied with energy in the future. One of the most important missions of Japan's politicians is for Japan to be an economic great, after the US and the European Union.

5.2.4.5 North Korea

North Korea is more known on account of the label *Axis of Evil* stuck on it by the Americans than it is for having influence in the field of energy. However, need for energy is increasing everywhere and supply is becoming more acute. This regularly entails new policy and a new attitude.

North Korea carried out its first nuclear test in October 2006. This shook the world to its foundations in all respects. After much lobbying by various countries, an agreement between North Korea and South Korea, Japan, China, Russia and the US was signed in 2007. In exchange for dismantling its nuclear programme, North Korea was promised, among other things, 1 million tons of crude oil. This it needs, as energy, also in North Korea, is essential for running the economy. The country needs more than 2 millions tons of oil a year in order to function as it should. Generating power in North Korea is extremely restricted at the moment; families only have a few hours of electricity a day at their disposal, and power failures occur regularly.

5.2.4.6 European Union

The European Union is on its last legs as far as energy self-sufficiency is concerned. At the moment, Europe is importing more than half its total energy requirement. If policy doesn't change, this will rise to 65% by 2030. Gas interest will rise from 57% to 84%, and oil requirement from 82% to 93%. Europe is becoming increasingly more dependent on Russia in as far as gas is concerned. Diversification of suppliers, like Algeria and Qatar, among others, and expansion of sustainable sources should decrease the pressure.

5.2.4.7 United Kingdom

In the 1980s and 90s, England sold off its gas potential at high speed. This sale started in the period that Margaret Thatcher held sway in the UK and it caused the country to use up almost its total gas reserve in less than two years. Recently, energy dependence has compelled England to conclude contracts with Norway, Russia (Gazprom) and the Netherlands (GasTerra). The import requires adequate infrastructure, including all sorts of new pipelines which are being laid at the moment. The early liberalization of the English energy markets has nevertheless ensured that the country has far and away the largest and most liquid gas market (power and gas exchange APX) in Europe.

5.2.4.8 The Netherlands

For years, this damp country has been able to rely on the gas supply chiefly formed by the Groningen field; however, the end of the gas bubble is in sight and that means that dependence on other countries will increase in the near future. The oil and coal reserves the Netherlands has are negligibly small, which is why these products have been imported for years. That is the reason that the Netherlands is included under the category 'net-importer'. Mainly because of its level of knowledge, advantageous geographical location and good infrastructure, the country has a key role within Europe. Rotterdam is the continent's most important seaport, the Netherlands can become the 'gas roundabout' of North-west Europe and was, furthermore, together with Belgium and France, one of the first countries to become involved in the formation of the European 'copper plate', a coupling of the electricity grids and markets of several North-west European countries.

5.3 Cartels

Defending own interests is not new. Association in organizations that promote joint interests will occur always, everywhere and at all levels.

5.3.1 OPEC

The Organization of the Petroleum Exporting Countries (OPEC) is an oil cartel that was set up in Baghdad (Iraq) in 1960 through the initiative of Venezuela. The Headquarters is in Vienna (Austria). Besides Venezuela and Iraq, Iran, Saudi Arabia and Kuwait were also co-founders of the organization. Qatar, Indonesia, Libya, the United Arab Emirates, Algeria, Nigeria, Ecuador and Gabon joined later. Ecuador and Gabon then left OPEC at the beginning of the 1990s and Angola joined OPEC in January 2007. The composition of the cartel does change from time to time.

The economies of member countries are highly dependent on oil income. The countries associated in OPEC together have over 75% of the world's total oil reserves and currently produce about 40% of the worldwide total. This gives them a considerable position of power, which they deploy from time to time. Most of the power lies with the world's largest producer, Saudi Arabia. OPEC therefore chiefly operates by the grace of this oil state. Saudi Arabia dominates because it is able to quickly increase or decrease its oil production (by varying the usage of its spare capacity). By influencing the supply of oil, OPEC attempts to control the market price. Every country has to conform to fixed quotas in order for the market to be able to move in the direction OPEC desires. Libya and Algeria don't take the rules too seriously, but control on policy is often difficult.

At the beginning of the millennium, member countries of OPEC had enough spare capacity to meet any unexpected shock in worldwide oil demand. Because of this, the power block was able to reasonably control the oil price and keep it within a certain price range, but since 2004, a lot of the buffer has been used up and the price is more susceptible to free market processes. OPEC doesn't at all regard itself as a body that helps give form to world economy, but it views the world from a micro-economic perspective. OPEC is only looking for the answer to the question of whether the market remains healthy if more or less oil becomes available.

OPEC members want to increase their production capacity by 25% over the coming years. They will have to take action in order to ensure that they can continue to meet growing demand in the future. The members have together reserved an amount of 100 billion dollars for this purpose.

5.3.2 Gas cartel

Russia, Iran and Qatar are at the moment discussing the possibility of forming a new gas cartel. If this initiative takes off, it will probably be called Gaspec. The countries mentioned, together with other interested parties, Venezuela and Algeria, have 60% of the proven gas supplies in the world, and together they control 50% of worldwide gas exports. Naturally, other gas exporting countries can also join this power block. The most prominent gas countries are, incidentally, already associated to the *Gas Exporting Countries Forum* (GECF), which was set up in 2001. The Netherlands is not a part of this forum and it is not expected that it will ever participate in this initiative as the country pursues a different policy.

The world is following the developments of a possible new gas cartel with suspicion because people are afraid of the gas market being manipulated. Particularly large concerns like ExxonMobil, Royal Dutch Shell, Total and BP will feel increasing pressure. State-owned companies will increasingly work together in the area of technology and capital. Until recently, that was a factor by which private concerns could differentiate themselves from the masses.

Apart from that, it is expected that the future gas cartel will operate differently than OPEC. Variation of product cannot be applied as easily as with oil because the gas market is dominated by long-term contracts. Moreover, it is usual now to link the gas price to the oil price when drawing up an agreement. So it is not only a question of whether or not a cartel is coming, but also whether it will be a price cartel or a collaboration in which investments are coordinated. In order to invest in large projects like the building of LNG terminals, people want to be sure that the price won't drop below a certain level, otherwise the results will hang in the balance. This seems to be a good reason to put heads together sometime and try to get everyone working in the same direction.

5.4 Independent energy policy

Each country has its own interests. Each country also has its own fleet and industrial parks, its own military set-up and its own economy; besides which, the amount of available energy sources differs per land. The energy mix per country can therefore differ from that of other nations, as shown in figure 29.

Energy source	US	France
Oil	40%	37%
Gas	25	15
Coal	24	5
Hydro	3	6
Nuclear	8	37
Total	100 %	100 %

Figure 29: Energy mix per country, divided per energy source in 2004 (BP, Statistical Review 2005)

It is clear to see from the figure that France generates a lot of energy by nuclear means. France has more nuclear power plants than all other countries, relatively speaking. Because of the difference in interests, difference will also arises in the policies that countries pursue. One thing is certain: all the large economic blocks in the world have to contend with serious oil and gas shortages, which makes them regard import as the spearhead. This has resulted in the *energy supply security* policy. Scarcity leads to politicization and militarization of energy supplies, production, extraction, process and distribution.

5.4.1 Strategic reserves

Seeing as Western countries import a lot of energy, they wish to be less dependent on unstable countries and regions like Russia and the Middle East. Energy transition of fossil fuels to sustainable solutions is not only happening because of the environmental problems, but also because diversification of energy portfolios makes importers less dependent on others. In view of decreasing availability, energy consumers are looking for security. In order to decrease risks, OECD countries, including the Netherlands, are obliged to keep supplies that cover the import requirement of oil (products) for 90 days. The International Energy Agency (IEA) controls these strategic supplies. The governing board of the IEA, which consists of representatives from all associated countries, decides when the supplies are deployed. At the beginning of 2007, more than 4 billion barrels of crude oil, gasoline and diesel were stored for this purpose.

The strategic oil reserve of the US was about 700 million barrels at the beginning of 2007, but President Bush wants to more than double this amount to 1.5 billion barrels. This would decrease the US's dependence on foreign countries and, moreover, large price fluctuations could be tempered. The US is the largest importer of oil; it imports almost 70% of its total annual usage.

In 2007, China also decided to increase its emergency oil reserves and made it compulsory for oil companies to keep larger supplies. In the *fifty year plan* for energy provision, it is ascertained that current reserves are not sufficient to cope with crisis situations. In 2009, the reserve will contain enough oil for Chinese society to continue unabated for two weeks. Totally different standards apply in Japan, where oil companies are obliged to keep a 70-day reserve of oil.

The US does keep reserves of crude oil, but no gasoline reserves, as opposed to some European and Asian countries that do do that. Apart from that, increasingly more countries want to have a strategic gas reserve. The disadvantage, however, is that storing gas is much more expensive than storing oil. It takes up a lot of space and requires new transport capacity.

5.4.2 State control

The energy politics of net-importers is directed towards *energy supply security*, whereas net-exporters are increasingly nationalizing companies in the commodities sector, which results in state-controlled energy concerns. Gazprom, the Russian state-controlled gas concern, has an export monopoly on gas from Russia; the only exception as yet being formed by ExxonMobil which exports gas from the Russian peninsula of Sachalin. Gazprom exerted pressure for this exception to be undone in the middle of 2007, and at an earlier stage had already taken over control from Shell in the Sachalin 2 project. Furthermore, Russia has for years refused to ratify the energy treaty, which also allows European companies access to the Russian market. It is now impossible for

European companies to trade or supply gas in Russia. Yet Gazprom wants to acquire interests in local infrastructures in all sorts of places in the world. As far as gas is concerned, the enterprise is very interested in vertical integration and would very much like to indirectly increase its range of influence. Russia is lying in wait for empty gas fields in the Netherlands that it wants to use for gas storage that can be deployed to manipulate the European market. In England and Italy, Gazprom is already directly supplying to end-users, which is more profitable than selling to retailers like utility companies. Incidentally, until 2011 Gazprom won't be earning much from selling to consumers in its own country because an agreement from the Russian government to sell gas at low rates rather than commercial prices is still applicable. At the moment, prices are being kept artificially low. Iran does something similar in its own country. The state lavishly subsidizes the sale of gasoline, among other things, which results in it being sold under cost price. The country recently did indeed slacken the reins, but a litre of gasoline in Iran still costs a little less than ten euro cents.

Gazprom	Russia	28,000
NIOC	Iran	26,600
Qatar Petroleum	Qatar	18,500
Saidi Aramco	Saudi Arabia	7,100
Sonatrach	Algeria	4,200
PDVSA	Venezuela	4,200
Rosneft	Russia	3,900
Adroc	United Arab Emirates	3,800
INOC	Iraq	3,100
NNPC	Nigeria	3,000
Petronas	Malaysia	2,800
Pertamina	Indonesia	2,500
KPC	Kuwait	1,600
ExxonMobil	United States	1,600
BP	UK	1,300
Shell	UK/Netherlands	1,300

Figure 30: The largest gas concerns (gas reserves in billion cubic metres (Energy Intelligence Group, 2005).

For some time now, private oil concerns like ExxonMobil, Shell and BP Amoco have not been the largest of their kind; they have been overtaken by a whole series of state-controlled oil companies. Many governments no longer intend to allow foreign companies to extract the riches that lie in their ground. By making oil companies property of the state, governments control the income and the capacity. These can be used for the country itself. Now that oil-rich countries are becoming even richer, they can even invest in production capacity. Private oil concerns are increasingly only being asked to do difficult jobs that demand a lot of technical knowledge. Because of that, oil multinationals are increasingly concentrating on deepwater drilling, liquid gas and exploitation of unconventional oil like tar sands. It is already possible with current techniques for some concerns to find oil at a depth of more than three kilometres below sea level.

Saudi Aramco	Saudi Arabia	260,000
NIOC	Iran	126,000
INOC	Iraq	115,000
KPC	Kuwait	99,000
PdVSA	Venezuela	78,000
Adroc	United Arab Emirates	55,000
LNOC	Libya	23,000
NNPC	Nigeria	21,000
Pemex	Mexico	16,000
Lukoil	Russia	16,000
Gazprom	Russia	13,500
ExxonMobil	United States	12,900
Yukos	Russia	11,900
Petrochina	China	11,000
Qatar Petroleum	Qatar	11,000
Shell	UK / Netherlands	7,000

Figure 31: The largest oil concerns (oil reserves in million barrels) (Energy Intelligence Group, 2005).

Governments take fiscal measures in order to protect their domestic reserves or to be able to profit from them. Oil extracting is generally heavily taxed by local tax authorities. In Venezuela taxes for oil companies are rising. Foreign oil companies have to hand over increasingly more royalties for the activities that they (are allowed to) carry out. In some countries, above a certain oil price ceiling, oil companies have to hand over near enough the full supplement to the state in which they extract oil. Nigeria, for instance, creams off 95% of the oil price. At least, it does for oil extracted on shore; less harsh division is applicable to offshore production. The distinction is understandable seeing as extra expertise is required for offshore production.

5.4.3 Vertical integration

Many enterprises in the commodities sector are sizeable conglomerates with activities in several sections within the same industry; from production via process and trade to transport, sales and supply. The Brazilian steel concern, Compania Siderurgica Nacional (CSN), owns its own port and is 30% owner of the railway that connects the mining district to this sea port. Such a coagulation of activities (vertical integration) is often a question of carrying out an independent policy. In this way, at least, dependence on others is limited as much as possible.

Saudi Arabia has its own state-owned company in Saudi Aramco. This oil concern is the largest of all the oil companies in the world and has far and away the most reserves. Saudi Arabia was one of the first countries to apply vertical integration, which is so very important to the oil branch. In addition to oil extraction, the country, via Saudi Aramco, has developed refining capacity to transform raw material into heating oil, diesel, gasoline or other refining products. The state-owned concern even owns, together with Royal Dutch Shell, three refineries in the US. Furthermore, this energy giant has its own fleet. In 1995, Saudi Arabia gained command of fifteen super tankers, with which the country navigates the world's seas.

5.4.4 Military issues

It is not a new body of thought that countries largely govern their foreign policy by energy requirement. In order to increase the security of energy source supply, countries use any means they deem legitimate. It is interesting to consider the background and private interests of various politicians. US President Bush comes from the oil sector and he still has large interests in it. The story goes that the war in Iraq was about serving politicians' own interests and those of people in their own circle. Vice-President Dick Cheney used to be Chairman of Halliburton, one of the world's largest service providers to the oil industry.

At the beginning of February 2007, the American government confirmed that it also recognizes the importance of Africa by setting up a special military command. The *African Command* will consist of entities that will concentrate on North America, South America, the Middle East and Central Asia, the Pacific and Europe. The American government explained that it had taken this decision because of the increasing strategic interests of the African continent. West Africa is today good for 15% of the American oil import, an amount comparable with the supply from Saudi Arabia. The US expects (or hopes) that countries on the Gulf of Guinea will provide 25% of America's import in a few years. The battle for favours from these countries is in full swing. China is also knocking on the same doors, and is also busy in East Africa. This last-mentioned region lies closer to China and is therefore of extra interest because of the lower transport costs.

The *Joint Development Zone* field lies in the Gulf of Guinea. The source contains about 14 billion barrels of oil, to which both Nigeria and Sao Tome may lay claim. It is therefore not surprising that the US has plans to establish a marine base on the island of Sao Tome. The military apparatus is being increasingly employed to defend the (increasing) interests of countries. The US has a military budget of 528 billion dollars, and that makes them far and away the world's front runners. Countries like Great Britain, France and Japan *and* China have budgets that vary from 45 to 60 billion dollars. Just like Western states, developing countries want to be independent in as many aspects as possible. The military apparatus in these countries is increasing in size. This is chiefly happening in order to add strength to the new standing with a show of force. In 2007 Saudi Arabia announced that it had already begun setting up a new security force. This force will consist of 35,000 men whose job it will be to protect oil fields from foreigners with malicious intent. In this way, the Saudi government wants to reinforce its reputation as a secure and reliable oil supplier. It won't come as a surprise that the American defence concern Lockheed Martin will be training the new army.

As a counterbalance to the influence of the US, Russia and China carried out a large-scale military exercise together with four Central Asian countries: Kazakhstan, Uzbekistan, Kyrgyzstan and Tajikistan. This exercise took place under the guise of a conspiracy against separatism, terrorism and extremism. The West suspects that the pact was forged to carry political weight. US influence in the Central Asian region is already waning and the problems in Iraq and Afghanistan are not helping.

CHAPTER 6:
Environment & Climate

6.1 Environmental pollution

Commodity extraction and the production processes connected to it regularly involve pollution. Burning fossil fuels damages the environment. Pollution can occur in all sorts of ways, and each variant has its own consequence. Certain forms lead to chemical contamination, soil pollution and unusable drinking water, whereas other types of pollution lead to radiation and are therefore carcinogenic. Yet in some areas, mankind is on the right path in preventing or limiting pollution. Emissions from installations are increasingly containing less particulate matter, and in increasingly larger quantities wastewater is being stripped of phosphate and nitrogen. Since the introduction of European regulations, sewage treatment plants are doing their utmost to protect surface water. Besides a rise in percentage of the polluting matter that is filtered out of the water, companies are increasingly using biological decomposition methods. Moreover, cars worldwide are emitting increasingly fewer polluting gasses, with the exception of carbon dioxide emissions. Emissions of lead and nitrogen fumes have greatly reduced since 1990.

Despite all the comforting words and good intentions, there are still many other issues that require our attention. Environmental damage caused by the oil industry, among other things, is enormous. In 2007, the Russian company Rosneft failed to report to supervisors that there was an oil leak in Siberia. The black syrupy liquid, amounting to about 2,000 barrels, flowed out of a defect pipeline and into the ground. On 24 March, 1989, the oil tanker Exxon Valdez caused one of the greatest man-made environmental disasters in history. By the ship steering into a reef, tens of millions of litres of oil leaked into Alaska's environment. Of course, governments severely tightened the belt after the accident. Companies must now suddenly conform to all sorts of new regulations. From 2010, all oil tankers and LNG ships will have to be double-hulled, but for now, new disasters are still happening on a regular basis. In 2007, the British oil giant BP halted production of the Prudhoe Bay oil field in Alaska for the umpteenth time because leaks had (again) appeared in the pipelines. In total, an amount of 6,000 barrels leaked into the environment. Cost-saving probably plays an important part in disasters being caused. Many measures are indeed being taken at the moment but, unfortunately, the situation is only being improved in dribs and drabs. So-called *blowout preventers* are installations that prevent oil under high pressure spouting out of a field that is being drilled. This technique is particularly used for underwater drilling. This contributes to the maintenance of the ecosystem.

For the moment, pollution remains an extremely complex problem, especially now that the economies of countries like China, India, Brazil, Mexico and South Africa are greatly improving. Earth is repeatedly having to cope with some very hard knocks. According to the World Bank, 16 of the 20 most-polluting cities are in China. Half of China's 600 largest cities do not have adequate water treatment systems. A large part of the country has to contend with acid rain and the biggest rivers are seriously polluted. 750,000 people die each year as a result of air pollution; poor quality water results in yet another 60,000 deaths. This makes the pollution even worse than the World Bank initially thought. The figures were kept secret for a long time out of fear for social unrest. The solution to the situation is another problem. In theory, China has set itself proper respectable guidelines, but executing them seems impossible because of resistance at local level.

In addition to all the situations mentioned, there are more causes of environmental pollution. Because of economic prosperity, the number of cars in the capital, Beijing, increased by more than 1,000 every day in 2007. There are now about 800 million cars on the world's roads.

Besides absolute numbers, energy-efficiency can also be referred to. It appears that Chinese households use twice as much energy as the average Dutch family. On the one hand, this could be explained by the huge temperature differences there are in China, but on the other, awareness, measures and the supervision of enforcement are totally different than in Europe. Chinese emission per unit of Gross Domestic Product is ten times higher than the average of more developed countries.

6.2 Climate change

Of all pollution, greenhouse-gas emission has been in the news most lately. These gasses lead to climate change and are therefore a much-discussed subject. If oil, coal and gas continue to be burnt as they are now, so much CO_2 will be pumped into the atmosphere that the temperature will rise by a few degrees Celsius. Estimates differ, but some experts expect a temperature rise of 6 degrees. This is, of course, a prediction, but it is based on extensive analysis. In reality, it may prove to be even worse. Some calculations show that there is already a significant difference compared with a few years ago.

For the Netherlands, 2006 was the hottest year of the last three centuries. The average temperature came out at 11.2 degrees Celsius. If this really is the result of the greenhouse effect, then there is much more to come. A change in climate has, for instance, a great impact on the cultivation of crops.

There are also some positive effects of climate change, but it has to be said that these in no way outweigh the negatives. Shifts can be expected in tourism; certain areas may become more pleasant as far as climate is concerned, whereas others may suffer. And as far as agriculture is concerned, the production of crops in certain areas could increase and more forests grow. CO2 is a necessary ingredient for that.

There has never been a warmer January day in the Netherlands than 9 January 2007. The average temperature was 12.9 degrees Celsius, which was a whole degree warmer than the previous record of 5 January 1957. That year is actually remarkable because the year before had produced the coldest February month with an average of minus 6.4 Celsius. But that's nothing compared to Oymyakon in Siberia, which is the coldest inhabited place in the world. In 1926 a temperature of minus 71 Celsius was registered there, but a temperature of minus 89 Celsius was once registered in Vostok, Antarctica, where it has actually never been warmer than minus 19. The lowest temperature ever measured in the Netherlands was minus 27 in Winterswijk on 27 January 1942.

Netherlands	Heat and drought records in April. January mildest month for 300 years
Belgium	More than 30 degrees Celsius (15 en 16 April)
Germany	May: the wettest month since 1901
England	May – July: the wettest period ever
Japan	Typhoon Man-Yi is the severest ever recorded in Japan in July
Oman	Cyclone Gonu is the first documented cyclone originating in the Arabian Sea
Australia	Heat record in February and cold record in June
Bangladesh	Cold record of 5 degrees in January causing 130 deaths
China	June to September: driest period for 20 years resulting in 7 million people being without water

Maldives	Abnormally high waves (3 to 4.5 metres high) washed over 68 islands
South Africa	May: cold record of minus 6 degrees confirmed
South Africa	June: unique snowfall of 25 centimetres
Sudan	Abnormally early and heavy rains resulting in worst flooding ever
Caribbean region	Hurricane Dean is third most-powerful hurricane to go ashore since 1850
Caribbean region	Hurricane Felix grew at record speed from a tropical depression to a 5th category hurricane in 51 hours
Uruguay	Worst flooding since 1959
Argentina	First significant snowfall since 1918
United States	Storms caused worst flooding for a hundred years
Canada	Never before was there so little ice in the Polar region, making the North-West Passage possible

Figure 32: Extreme weather conditions in 2007 (Dagblad De Pers, 6 September 2007)

In the film *The Inconvenient Truth,* former US vice-president Al Gore argues that global warming is caused by mankind intensifying the greenhouse effect. This opinion is however not endorsed by all climatologists and scientists. There is indeed a statistical relationship between CO2 concentration and the temperature, but that is not (yet) enough to confirm the cause and effect connection. It may well be that one is a result of the other, or it could be the other way around. It is also possible that both are the result of another, a third, factor. A rise in temperature will (more quickly) melt the polar caps and many cities will sink beneath water because of it. What about the man-made islands sprouting up off the coast of Dubai? The Netherlands will also suffer from the oceans' rising water levels - half of the country is below the present sea level. If all the ice on earth melts, the sea level will rise by a good few metres; but fortunately it won't come to that. About 90% of all the ice on earth is to be found in Antarctica. The biggest glaciers are in Antarctica and Greenland, and it is still freezing there, which is just as well as if it weren't, the problems would be incalculable. People would have trouble surviving and, apart from the ecological damage, the economy would suffer greatly. The real estate sector would be in real trouble. At the beginning of 2007, the total value of all Dutch houses situated below the present sea level amounted to more than 700 billion euros.

By 2020, according to research carried out by Wageningen University, the Netherlands will have to spend 62 billion euros on the effects of climate change: alterations in the landscape to create more possibilities for surplus water to be drained away, for example, or to steer the water of large rivers in the right direction. Together, these two projects cost about 26 billion euros. In order to take care of the problems surrounding salinity, droughts, drainage, flooding and copious rainfall, far more action is needed. Constructing climate-proof buildings will cost 23 billion euros and, according to the research, about 4 billion euros is involved in improving the sewage system.

6.3 Information asymmetry

When it comes to carbon dioxide emissions and climate change, scientists contradict themselves on several fronts. That excess CO2 emission contributes to climate change seems to have now been indisputably proven, but some climate sceptics believe and proclaim that the earth isn't warming at all. Or that it is, but not because of mankind. They claim that the measurements are not reliable. They think measurements in populated areas might have been influenced by the abundance of houses and offices. However, it now appears that the oceans are warming as well.

In general, scientists reach different and sometimes even contradictory conclusions. This often happens because of pressure exerted by the institutes that employ the experts. Consultancies are usually founded on a commercial basis, but a number of uncertainties also force scientists to work with assumptions and suppositions. Their calculation models are therefore not ideal and the assumptions used are often exactly the points on which the scientists are challenged. But critics also have to live with the same shortcomings, so their theories can't be blindly trusted either.

Over-simplified opinions are continuously being banded about. Some positions are worthy of debate because there is always a lack of sufficient research. Because of the excessive attention given to climate change, people tend to easily believe things dished up to them by others. It is however our own psyche that incorrectly assesses relativity.

This enables us to unjustly pay more attention to certain issues than to others. This phenomenon is called information asymmetry.

We live in an age of information; that means that the media pays a great deal of attention to each exceptional situation. There is so much information being collected and analysed at the moment that new conclusions can be drawn again and again, and it is quite easy to hunt for records in certain classes. The wettest January of the century gives a more relevant picture than the wettest 29 February or the wettest Wednesday night of the century. The conclusions that can be drawn from both of the last two are none too valid.

It has to be said that a too-high carbon dioxide percentage indeed has negative consequences for the climate, but the gas is basically essential for the growth of trees and plants. Vegetation takes CO_2 from the air and with water (by means of photosynthesis) converts it to oxygen (O_2). Oxygen is released into the air and offers us the chance of life. In addition, CO_2 is an ingredient of glucose: a hydrocarbon converted to cellulose. This last-mentioned material gives plants strength.

6.4 The long-term perspective

That the climate is constantly changing is beyond dispute. It has always done so and will always do so. The temperature on earth in the distant past was also not always constant, and in the future it will continue to rise and fall. Somewhere between the years 12000 and 40000 another ice age will occur. Climate changes manifest themselves in fits and starts and they are irreversible. The sea level rises without a change in CO_2 emissions. In the period between the last two ice ages, the Eemian interglacial period, the sea level was six metres higher than it is now. During that period, there was actually no ice at all in Greenland.

There is not a linear connection between the factors temperature and CO_2 emissions, chiefly because of the unknown number of factors that play a part. The key questions are whether, and to what extent, global warming is being accelerated by mankind (excess emission of CO_2 gasses). The starting point has to be one of objective data because research must not suffer under excessive exposure to only one side of the story. That would do an injustice to the complexity of the climate system. It is also worth noting that the average temperature on earth dropped between 1940 and 1975.

We could therefore ask ourselves whether or not we can actually have any influence on the developments of the temperature, and whether or not we should interfere with it anyway.

According to the current consensus, increased concentrations of CO_2 essentially result in a rise in temperature. From that point we can go in two directions: 1) the temperature rises and the consequences are not very reassuring, or 2) the increased temperature has a levelling or neutralizing effect. In the case of the latter, a rise in temperature will cause more vaporization of the oceans' water, which will create clouds. These in turn will obstruct solar rays and that will (indirectly) have a measurably restraining effect on the temperature. These are long-term effects and are therefore only measurable after a passage of time. Volcano eruptions also have to be included in climate analysis; ocean waters cool significantly after each severe eruption. Sunspots also influence the temperature on earth.

But global warm may not be the biggest problem the world faces. Changes occurring in the atmosphere play, according to some people, a much more important role. Over the last few years, air circulation in the world has mostly been from West to East; the flow from North to South is also important. The frequency of air displacement in both directions has greatly increased; that is important because a large majority of the earth's surface is in the Northern hemisphere. Northerly flow causes higher temperatures there and southerly flow results in the area being colder. The warm airflow from the South brings more rain with it in the winter. These *Meridional flows* bring a type of weather that differs from the climate we are used to. Strange temperature changes, heavy downpours and periods of drought, can be the direct result of that. For the Netherlands, the alleged global warming could turn out completely differently. The warm Gulf Stream, that for the most part determines the relatively moderate climate, could be impeded by the changes that occur. If the warm Gulf Stream no longer reaches the Netherlands, the country will become colder than it is now. The melting polar ice could result in lower salinity in the North Sea. Salt water is heavier than fresh water which could stop the warm Gulf Stream reaching the North Sea.

6.5 The greenhouse effect

The greenhouse effect has come about as a result of the presence of certain gasses in the atmosphere. An increased concentration of these gasses causes the average temperature on earth to rise more than could be expected on the basis of the combination of the sun's heat radiation and the internal heat of the earth. The temperature of the earth's surface is determined by the balance of a range of factors. On the one hand, heat is added by the radiation from the sun that is not directly reflected, and on the other hand, by the earth's internal heat. In addition, heat is also taken from the earth's surface; the cause of that being infrared rays. Infrared rays radiate from the earth towards space. The heat added by the sun and the extraction from radiation are, in a very complex way, dependent on a number of factors. Clouds bounce back sunlight but they also impede radiation; and ice and snow decrease the amount of radiation, as do absorbed solar rays. Moreover, greenhouse gasses do not only absorb radiation directed towards earth, but also that directed towards space. Soot also causes clouds to reflect less, while sulphur oxide has exactly the opposite effect. Finally, particles in the air form a shield which reflects light, so the earth is warmed less by the sun and clouds are more readily formed.

Incoming radiation is visible to the human eye, while outgoing (infrared) radiation is not. Greenhouse gasses absorb infrared rays and even bounce them back to earth. This happens to a greater extent than absorption of incoming solar rays. The result is a rise in the temperature on earth. All this falls under the greenhouse effect.

Greenhouse gasses exist in several forms: vapour, carbon dioxide, methane and ozone are the most important. The last two, methane and ozone, contribute about 4% to 9% to the total. Carbon dioxide is responsible for 10 to 25% of all greenhouse gas, and (without taking the clouds into account) vapour causes 35 to 70% of the greenhouse effect. Nitrous oxides and sulphur oxide are the worst culprits of acid rain. Emission of harmful gasses happens everywhere. Large-scale industry, power production and transport greatly contribute to the amount of polluting gasses. Gasoline consists of 85% carbon and 15% hydrogen. To burn just one litre of gasoline, about 2.7 kilos of oxygen is needed. During the burning the oxygen combines with hydrogen and makes water (1.1 kilos) and with carbon to make carbon dioxide (2.4 kilos).

	SO2	NOx	CO2
Natural gas	0	35	56,000
Gas oil	95	50	73,000
HFO 1%	500	50	78,000
Coal	640	50	91,000

Figure 33: Greenhouse gas emission in grams per gigajoule fuel (Distrigas, 2007)

Power plants in the Netherlands account for 11% of the total Dutch energy consumption, but they are responsible for a disproportionately large share of Dutch CO_2 production: 30%. This huge portion is indeed substantial, but in comparison with the rest of the world, the situation in the Netherlands is still reasonable. Worldwide, power plants actually cause 47% of all CO_2 emissions. The reason for this lies in the fact that most countries have coal-fired plants, while the Netherlands chiefly fires on less-polluting natural gas.

Electricity and heat generation (A)	39.1%
Industry (B)	15.5
Households (C)	12.2
Services & other things (D)	6.8
Transport (E)	26.4
Total	100 %

Figure 34: CO2 emissions per sector for the EU25 (Eurostat, 2004)

Emissions development follows different paths in different sectors. Time has shown the following:

Year	Total A	B	C	D	E	of which: E1	E2	E3
1990	3790 1493	728	489	289	790	672	85	12
1991	3810 1504	680	534	291	801	683	86	11
1992	3706 1460	648	493	281	824	703	88	11
1993	3646 1400	627	503	276	840	715	92	11
1994	3608 1406	621	471	265	845	717	96	10
1995	3647 1408	638	474	270	857	726	100	10
1996	3752 1431	634	514	287	885	749	105	10
1997	3684 1391	635	489	266	904	763	110	10
1998	3710 1418	610	478	265	939	789	120	10
1999	3671 1400	578	467	257	968	812	128	9
2000	3692 1425	596	452	247	972	812	134	9
2001	3754 1444	593	481	257	979	825	130	9
2002	3770 1481	598	457	246	988	836	129	8
2003	3845 1517	591	472	263	1002	844	133	8
2004	3863 1512	599	470	262	1021	859	139	8

Figure 35: CO2 emissions per sector for the EU25 in million tons (Eurostat, 2004) (E1 = Road transport, E2 = Air transport and E3 = Train. For A to E see figure 34)

As of now, these figures state the truth. The 25 largest cities in the world, including Mexico City, Cairo, Bangkok and Tokyo, produce 15% of the total CO2 emission. Incidentally, that pollution can be created somewhere other than where the consequences take place. 25% of the air pollution in California (US) originates in Asia. Stale vapours can travel over huge distances.

It is rumoured that about 50% of all CO2 emissions until now has been absorbed by seas and oceans, which is why pollution has been less visible until now than the damage that has actually been done. Seas and oceans are becoming more acidic and this is affecting the ecosystem. Mussels and other shellfish are suffering badly under their changed living conditions. Acidification causes problems for calcification, which is important for the housing of shellfish, conclude researches in *Geophysical Research Letters*.

6.6 Emission compensation

Fortunately, ethics shows its head from time to time and calls people to account for their standards and values. Not only individuals but also enterprises have to do their bit. Some companies go in for CO_2 compensation; as soon as they book a plane flight, they immediately purchase certificates from an organization that takes care of planting new trees. Vegetation is actually a possible source for solving the problems: large trees breathe in about 20 kilos of CO_2 every year and convert it to clean matter. Every person needs about ten trees to compensate for the pollution they cause during their lifetime.

	Energy intensity (= DC/GDP) toe/Meuro	Carbon intensity (= emission/DC) ton CO2/toe	DC per capita kgoe/inhabitants	CO2 emission per capita kg/inhabitants
1990	220	2.43	3535	8600
1991	218	2.41	3567	8607
1992	212	2.39	3493	8343
1993	208	2.35	3478	8179
1994	201	2.34	3458	8075
1995	200	2.31	3527	8143
1996	203	2.29	3647	8361
1997	197	2.27	3618	8195
1998	194	2.25	3659	8238
1999	187	2.23	3641	8136
2000	181	2.23	3658	8163
2001	182	2.22	3732	8272
2002	179	2.23	3701	8272
2003	182	2.23	3772	8398
2004	179	2.21	3798	8396

Figure 36: Energy indicators (European Union / Eurostat, 2006). DC = Domestic Consumption

According to involved parties, purchasing certificates guarantees that the amount of emitted CO_2 is compensated for by planting new trees or to a saving on emissions through sustainable projects. Climate credits, or CO_2 compensation certificates, can be purchased to offset 'debt' or contribution to the greenhouse effect.

By way of compensation for fleets, flight travel and other issues, operational management, up to and including heating and lighting, is made climate-neutral. Credits can be purchased via the normal channels (Kyoto Protocol, see 6.7) as voluntary trade (all individual initiatives). The absence of transparency and measurability of activities makes the CO_2 market vulnerable, which makes fraudulent practices relatively easy. Some companies claim to plant trees in exotic regions, but latch onto projects that were already in the planning. This undoubtedly benefits entrepreneurs and local politicians. We need to be alert otherwise a noble cause will only profit corrupt parties.

6.7 The Kyoto Protocol en emission rights

There are initiatives worldwide to limit the emission of greenhouse gasses. It goes without saying that a price has to be put on the emission of harmful gasses, otherwise every plan is doomed to failure. Worldwide governmental intervention is essential and political decisions must be internationally carried out. Big polluters like the US and China must participate otherwise the tide will not turn. Participation of all countries is essential, otherwise countries that do participate will price themselves out of the market. Energy transition and development of technology require a lot of investment before new techniques and applications become profitable.

The Kyoto Protocol was drawn up in 1997 in the Japanese city of Kyoto. It is the most important initiative to combat the emission of harmful gasses. The treaty regulates the decrease of greenhouse gas emissions and is a supplement to the United Nations Framework Convention on Climate Change (UNFCCC), for which the United Nations is responsible.

In the Kyoto Protocol, industrial countries have agreed to reduce the emission of greenhouse gasses (carbon dioxide, methane, nitrous oxide and a number of fluoride compounds) by an average of 5% compared to the level of 1990 between 2008 and 2012. The reduction percentages do indeed differ per country as economic power and current emissions are taken into account. The European Union as a whole must commit to a reduction of 8%. Seen in that light, it is remarkable that a country like Luxemburg

has to reduce its emission by 28%, while Portugal is allowed to increase its emission by 27%. A reduction of 6% applies to the Netherlands, and that is under the EU average.
The Kyoto Protocol provides a trading system for greenhouse gas emission. These CO_2 emission rights or credits are aimed at stimulating companies into taking steps. Energy must be saved and used more efficiently because by 2050 total energy consumption will be double what it is now. By then, it is expected that 70% of energy will be extracted from fossil fuels (26% oil, 26% coal and 18% gas) and 30% from sustainable energy and nuclear power plants.
According to the Kyoto Protocol, companies are obliged to have certificates for the emissions they make. If companies emit more than was agreed they have to purchase additional credits on the market. Organisations that do save energy or that operate more efficiently have credits left over. These credits can be sold on the same market where this sort of contract is traded.

	Emissions
United States	21
Germany	10
Sweden	6
France	6
China	3
India	1

Figure 37: CO_2 emissions per capita (in tons per year) (Het Financieele Dagblad, 16 January 2007)

6.7.1 Emission Trading System

The Emission Trading System (ETS) started in the EU on 1 January 2005. Six months later, only in the Netherlands, emission trading in nitrous oxide (NO2) was also introduced. CO_2 emission trading initially took place between companies in the heavy industry and the power sector because it is chiefly this type of business that is responsible for a great deal of all emissions. From 2008 other business sectors will also have to get involved. Trade in CO2 emission credits is a part of the climate policy. With this policy, governments are trying to encourage all target groups to achieve domestic objectives; from households, traffic and industry to agriculture, trade, customer-related services and even the government itself.

With CO2 emission trading, companies are allocated a fixed number of emission credits: the absolute emission ceiling (cap). The ETS arose from European regulations, in which is laid down that every member state must conform to these regulations. This makes mutual trade in these credits possible between European companies. The European *cap and trade* system is complex and difficult to manage, chiefly because the market consists of a wide range of parties who are not easy to categorize. By introducing CO2 tax, for example, the problem is tackled more at its roots.

Also included in the Kyoto Protocol is that industrial countries may realize a part of their reduction obligation via regulations abroad. Countries can take over emission credits from each other in order to realize their own reduction objectives. Emission trading leads to gas emission being forced to the place where it is cheapest. At the beginning of 2007, the price of emission credits outside the EU was about one fifth of that of European credits. In 2007, the Netherlands bought up emission credits from other countries; this was done via the *Clean Development Mechanism* (CDM) and *Joint Implementation projects* (JI), both covered in the Kyoto Protocol.

The American merchant bank, Morgan Stanley, is also buying emission credits for 2007 to 2012 by financing projects in developing countries that lead to reduction of carbon dioxide emission. The merchant bank then sells these credits on to European companies. Credits are cheaper in developing countries because it is easier to drive back pollution there. The disadvantage, however, is that there are risks involved, and procedures are often lengthy.

The European Commission has determined that countries may only realize a limited amount of their emission obligation outside their own borders. Spain said it wanted to realize 39% of its total abroad, but heard from Brussels that trading with others may, at the very most, be a supplement to domestic policy.

ETS	Emission Trading System	A mechanism under the Kyoto Protocol whereby EU countries organize their greenhouse gas emission reduction.
CDM	Clean Development Mechanism	A mechanism under the Kyoto Protocol whereby developing countries can finance their greenhouse gas reduction emission or environmental projects. The countries receive credits in exchange that count towards their own reduction.
JI	Joint Implementation	A mechanism under the Kyoto Protocol whereby developing countries can receive emission reduction units when they help to finance projects that contribute to emission reduction in other developing countries. Generally, the receiving country is an economy in development.
EUAs	European Union Allowances	Emission permit defined conform ETS
CERs	Certified Emission Reductions	Emission reduction unit given in accordance with CDM
ERUs	Emission Reduction Units	Emission reduction unit given in accordance with JI
VERs	Verified Emission Reduction	Emission reduction unit that has been verified by an independent auditor but which has not undergone the procedures and requirements for verification, certification and CER issue (in the case of CDM). Purchases or VERs accept the specific policy and all carbon-specific regulatory risks (the risk that the VER won't ultimately be registered as CER or ERU). Purchasers therefore tend to opt for a discount for the VER in compensation for the regulatory risk.

Figure 38: Types of mechanisms and emission rights

In the middle of 2007, Russia gave notice that that the country expected to dump a lot of credits on the European market. It is relatively easy to improve the old Russian electricity park, and by so doing, Russia expects to bring 300 million tons worth of CO_2 rights (10% of the total surplus) onto the market within a few years, earning itself 6 billion euros. Russia also wants to be able to sell still more credits and has, therefore, lodged a complaint about the calculation process. 1990, a benchmark year, was not a good year for the Russians because the Russian economy was then at a low level. Now the country is experiencing better times, it is being dealt with by standards that are too severe, at least according to the Russians. There are many other disadvantages to the current trading system, but that is understandable considering there has never before been a trading system like it.

The Russian strategy concerning the selling of emission credits is also called the *Kyoto rip-off* because the Russians earn twice from Europe. Firstly by selling bulk gas to Europe, and secondly by selling emission credits to European countries that desperately need them because of gas burning. This is an unintended result of the Kyoto Protocol. The protocol intended, among other things, that Western countries could purchase a part of their reduction commitments abroad, which would create the money needed for developing countries to improve their energy efficiency.

There are more irregularities in the ETS and it is still far from balanced. If German energy giants have to transport their coal to the East via Rotterdam, this will result in extra CO_2 emission. Building a new plant in the port of Rotterdam would be a more obvious solution. The system of emission credits therefore needs to be looked at with regard to Europe, and not merely to nations.

Emission trading in its present form contributes too little to cost-effective climate and energy policies. The reason for this lies in the free allocation of emission credits to newcomers and not including certain sectors. Lengthy discussions have taken place about whether or not the aviation sector should have to participate. By not including other sectors, less is being invested in sustainable energy than is desirable.

A company wanting to build new production capacity in the form of a coal-fired power plant is allocated more credits per kilowatt hour than a gas-fired plant or a windmill. These credits represent a particular value, and energy companies are certainly not averse to that. It explains the application by various parties for five coal-fired power plants. In this construct the effect is therefore counterproductive as electricity producers are not stimulated in this way. Energy generated from fossil energy sources doesn't become more expensive and consumers of this energy are therefore not stimulated into economizing.

A similar problem arises when considering the closure of a particular plant. If it involves inefficient capacity and the emission rights are withdrawn as soon as the capacity is disposed of, this does not stimulate investment in clean generation. The result is that old, polluting coal-fired plants are kept open longer than is desirable. The objective of emission trading is therefore totally missed. The system will only work when the scarcity factor comes into play, or when a tough standard is laid down. In addition, governments must contribute to the whole by creating good infrastructure for transport and storage of CO_2, and sensible choices must be made regarding locations. Utilizing the residual heat of power plants, in the port of Rotterdam for example, could lower the price of carbon dioxide. This would provide Rotterdam with a cost advantage.

6.7.2 Classification in periods

The progress of the Emission Trading System is divided into three different periods. The first covers the period between the beginning of 2005 and the end of 2007 (phase 1); the second covers 2008 to 2012 (2nd phase). The Kyoto Protocol ends at the end of 2012 and a new agreement will be launched (post-Kyoto phase).
In the Netherlands, only heavy industry and power producers were subject to the trading system in the 2005-2007 period. In the 2008-2012 period that will be expanded by 155 businesses, resulting in a total number of 362. During this period a few small businesses, like hospitals, greenhouse market gardeners and various manufacturers, will also be obliged to participate in the system.
The total amount of emission credits in the first period was so big that no scarcity appeared. The price of emission credits dropped severely because of that, almost to nothing. Because more business sectors fall under the regime during the second period, more efficient operational management will be implemented if the number of credits remains constant. It will, after all, be more difficult to stay under the approved CO_2 emission ceiling. In the Netherlands during the first period, a lot of emission credits were given away for free. This led to the appearance of so-called *windfall profits*: energy companies passed on the price of the free emission credits in their rates. Stavros Dimas, Member of the European Commission for the Environment, reacted to this by intervening in nine out of the ten submitted national allocation plans for CO_2

emission credits for the 2008-2012 period. From 2013 it is the intention to auction off 100% of all credits and no longer give any away for free.

From 2008, the focus is on still more sectors. The European Commission is wrestling with the questions of which sectors should be included in the ETS, under what conditions this should take place and when. Transport forms and important part in this.

Road transport	84.1%
Air transport	13.6
Train	0.8
Other means	1.5
Total	100 %

Figure 39: CO2 emissions in de transport sector for the EU25 (excluding shipping) (Eurostat, 2004)

From 2012, the categories of road transport and aviation will be fully included. Emission caused by international shipping also requires attention. This business sector emits more than the aviation sector, and it is growing faster. Both sectors are putting up a fight but it looks at the moment that the European Commission (EC) will impose its demands. Emission credits will be established for the aviation sector from 2011. These will be given free of charge, not via auction. Transatlantic air traffic will be exempt from participation until 2012, by which the EC is somewhat meeting the criticism from America and others. It is also important to know that whether emission credits for aviation will only apply to departing passengers or also to transfer passengers and cargo flights is still to be determined.

Tension is also running high in the motor industry. In the middle of 2007, the EC took the standpoint that from 2012 a new car in Europe may emit no more than 120 grams of CO2 per kilometre, whereas at that time the average emission per car was 163 grams. The motor industry has implemented several environmental measures over the last few years, including more economic engines, aerodynamics, less clutch friction, more economic tyres and more efficient electricity consumption and use of materials. Unfortunately, the profits from these measures were partly negated by extra security provisions, including a particular design of wing mirror. It is partly because of this that the motor branch is now so disappointed about the new, strict guidelines.

Ferrari 612 Scaglietti	474
Porsche Cayenne Turbo S	378
Audi Q7, 4.2 FSI	326
Jaguar Daimler Super Eight	299
Volvo (average of total production line)	195
Golf 1.6 Trendline	176
Renault (averaged)	149
Fiat (averaged)	139

Figure 40: Grams of CO2 emission per driven kilometre

Chiefly German car manufactures are having difficulty meeting the objectives, whereas French car companies and the Italian Fiat are well on the way. The Germans want the environmental requirements to be divided over various classes, and not that they apply per make but, for example, per weight class. Moreover, the motor sector believes that the solution should not only be sought by car manufacturers. According to them, combating traffic jams and driving more slowly should also be included in the package. Germany is already considering implementing a lower maximum speed on motorways.

Recently, many questions have been reviewed that have now been partly answered and solved, but the majority still needs to be answered. This vagueness creates uncertainty, therefore more regulation is essential. Is free issue of emission rights a disguised form of illegal support given by the government? May European parties outside the Union purchase emission credits in order not to have to deal with the emission in their own countries? If so, how many? Does a party that stores CO_2 get emission credits? Jacqueline Cramer, the Dutch Minister for Housing, Regional Development and the Environment, said in the middle of 2007 that energy companies would receive emission credits as soon as they captured and stored CO_2 during power production.

Both the environmental policies that countries follow and their emission plans must quickly be made concrete. Energy companies must, after all, know what they are up against. During the first five to ten years after 2007, the world is going to replace about 40% of its generation capacity. This capital-intense investment will then last between 30 and 50 years. Investors run the risk of making the wrong decisions and losing a large amount of capital. Policy must therefore quickly indicate which way it's going. That also means that a new climate agreement has to be concluded with a wide range of countries, with China and the US up front. Until recently, the Americans had harsh criticism for the climate pact and opposed the treaty because of it. Fortunately, the country has since decided to endorse international agreements regarding climate control from 2012.

	Total	Coal	Oil	Gas	Nuclear	New	Others *)
EU25	1,747.2	311.9	650.6	417.6	254.4	109.5	3.2
	100%	17.9%	37.2%	23.9%	14.6%	6.3%	0.2%
Belgium	54	6.1	20.1	14.6	12.2	1.2	0.7
Czechia	43	19.5	9.4	7.8	6.8	1.4	-1.3
Denmark	20	4.4	8.3	4.6	-	2.9	-0.2
Germany	347	85.8	125.4	78.7	43.1	13.8	1.0
Estonia	6	3.3	1.1	0.8	-	0.6	-0.2
Greece	30	9.1	17.5	2.2	-	1.6	0.2
Spain	140	21.1	68.9	25.2	16.4	9.0	-0.3
France	273	14.1	92.8	39.2	115.6	17.3	-5.3
Ireland	15	2.3	9.3	3.6	-	0.3	0.1

Italy	184	16.6	85.0	66.0	-	12.5	4.7
Cyprus	3	-	2.4	-	-	0.1	-
Latvia	5	0.1	1.4	1.3	-	1.6	0.2
Lithuania	9	0.2	2.6	2.4	3.9	0.7	-0.6
Luxemburg	5	0.1	3.0	1.2	-	0.1	0.3
Hungary	26	3.4	6.3	11.7	3.1	1.0	0.7
Malta	1	-	0.9	-	-	-	-
Netherlands	82	9.2	31.6	36.7	1.0	2.4	1.4
Austria	32	4.0	13.8	7.6	-	6.8	0.6
Poland	92	54.6	22.0	11.9	-	4.3	-0.3
Portugal	26	3.4	15.0	3.3	-	3.9	0.6
Slovenia	7	1.5	2.5	0.9	1.4	0.8	-0.1
Slovakia	18	4.5	3.6	5.5	4.4	0.7	-0.1
Finland	37	7.5	10.9	4.0	5.9	8.8	0.6
Sweden	53	2.9	15.4	0.9	20.0	14.1	-0.2
United Kingdom	232	38.3	81.5	87.4	20.6	3.7	0.6

*) electric energy and industrial waste

Figure 41: Domestic Consumption in Mtoe (Eurostat, 2004)

6.8 The Stern Report

On 30 October 2006, the British economist, Sir Nicholas Stern, presented the *Stern Review on the Economics of Climate Change*. He caused a worldwide sensation with this 700-page report by specifying which economic consequences climate change would bring with it. The calculations of this former World Bank economist teach us that global warming will cost the world 5% of its GDP. The material damage will cost about 5,500 billion euros in total, if policy remains unchanged.

In 2006, total CO_2 emission amounted to 8 gigatons, so if the principle of the polluter having to pay is observed, the CO_2 price should actually be 42 euros per ton. The

Intergovernmental Panel on Climate Change (IPCC) also calculated the economic burden to the world of steering the environmental problem in the right direction.

6.9 Intergovernmental Panel on Climate Change

At the beginning of 2007, the United Nation's climate commission, IPCC, issued the *Climate Change 2007: Impacts, Adaptation and Vulnerability* report, wherein is stated in no uncertain terms that climate change is a fact. According to this summary for policy-makers, it is 90% certain that human activities have led to global warming; the most significant cause being CO_2 emissions as a result of fossil fuels. At its present rate, the concentration of the mentioned gas in 2100 will be double what it was in the pre-industrial age. Based on calculations, a rise in temperature of 2 to 4.5 degrees is the most likely. According to the report, the temperature on earth now is already five degrees higher than it was during the last ice age.

It is almost certain that there will be fewer extreme cold days, while the number of heat-waves and heavy down-pours will greatly increase. The sea level is expected to rise between 20 and 60 cm over the next hundred years. It is also expected that the sea-level will continue to rise for another thousand years, even if greenhouse gas emission stabilized now.

By 2100, according to the report, the ice of both poles will totally disappear in the summer. Personally I have my doubts regarding the South Pole because this is about the only place on earth where the temperature has not yet risen. Moreover, some places in the world will actually cool down because of all the changes. And even if it does become warmer at the South Pole, the temperature will still remain well under zero. A possible rise in temperature of a few degrees will have little influence on Antarctica's ice cap, chiefly because the average temperature there is 40 degrees below zero - the majority of the ice would still not melt.

In its first report of February 2007, the IPCC laid down that the greenhouse effect and global warming are based on human activities. In its second report of April 2007, the climate panel showed the negative consequences of the warming. In its third report of May 2007, the IPCC calculated that global warming could be steered in the right direction for 300 dollars per world citizen per year. By spending this amount, a series of measures could be taken which would restrict the temperature rise to only 2 degrees in

2050. It can be concluded from this that control is not only technically possible, but also economically. Without taking drastic measures, CO_2 emission will be 90% higher in 2050 and lead to a temperature increase of 6 degrees. Countries agreed in an international treaty not to allow the temperature to rise by more than 2 degrees because then no irreversible damage would be caused. This limit of 2 degrees is very restricted because if a limit of 3 degrees had been fixed, the costs would drop considerably. Instead of 3 percent of worldwide gross product, this would then only amount to 0.6%.

Criticism of the IPCC's policy is that the panel is formed by scientists who have made climate change their work. Astrophysicists and geologists look at climate change differently than the climatologists of the panel. All sorts of people with various skills are involved in the problem in question. Geologists point chiefly to ice ages, astronomers focus on the changing force of the sun and meteorologists only analyse temperatures. Insurers, however, feel hugely supported by the conclusions the IPCC has drawn as they can now finally adjust their premiums on the grounds of the above-mentioned argument. Over the last few years, insurers have been victims of a number of catastrophes for which gigantic payments have had to be made. Hurricanes were a significant cause. The IPCC does not, incidentally, expect that hurricanes will increase in number, but it does expect that the force of these destructive storms will increase.

CHAPTER 7:
Energy transition

7.1 Introduction

The previous chapters covered a number of bottlenecks that arise in the energy markets, such as problems in the field of production capacity, transport, geopolitics, the environment and climate. Only when these problems have been solved will security of supply be raised to a more acceptable level. This could be realized by bringing (more) flexibility into the market. This means new products and product forms, alternative transport, environmental measures and other issues. This chapter deals with a number of alternatives in the field of fossil fuels. Chapter 8 deals with sustainable energy sources.

7.2 Changing the energy mix

The availability of fossil or conventional fuels is becoming increasingly scarce and, moreover, the burning of them has harmful consequences for the environment, which is why mankind is searching for alternatives. This means that the energy mix will change; a process that is also called energy transition. This business is time-consuming and the transition cycle takes decades. History shows us that it has never been any different. When need is high, the composition of the energy mix changes drastically. This dynamic can also be found in the fact that until the 19th century, wood provided almost 100% of the energy supply. Apart from that, spermaceti was used for lighting lamps. When the availability of spermaceti decreased due to excessive whaling, people had to look for alternatives. Coal and oil were found and the usefulness of both was soon recognized.

The oil crises of 1973 and 1979 also greatly influenced the energy mix. Nuclear energy was given a huge boost, and the world is again now on the verge of building a massive number of nuclear power plants. At that time it was chiefly in order to become less dependent on oil, whereas nowadays the argument is for decreasing CO_2 emissions. Environmentally-friendly solutions, including sustainable energy, will in time drastically change the energy portfolio.

In the framework of converting its energy portfolio, China wants to double the share of natural gas in its energy consumption to more than 5% in the period 2005 and 2010 (see figure 42).

144

	2005	2010*
Consumption		
Coal	69.1 %	66.1 %
Oil	21.0	20.5
Gas	2.8	5.3
Hydro power	6.2	6.8
Nuclear energy	0.8	0.9
Sustainable	0.1	0.4
Total	100 %	100 %
Production		
Coal	76.5 %	74.7 %
Oil	12.6	11.3
Gas	3.2	5.0
Hydro power	6.7	7.5
Nuclear energy	0.9	1.0
Sustainable	0.1	0.5
Total	100 %	100 %

*Figure 42: Energy mix China, in percentages (Reuters, 2007) (*2010 figures are based on estimates)*

Energy transition can be stimulated in three ways: by making good developments compulsory, by subsidizing, or by taxing businesses that have a negative effect on energy transition. But the most important thing is a clear policy. Because of that, Britain has long translated long-term objectives to short-term commitments. In England, the Prime Minister is responsible for the climate policy, whereas in the Netherlands about four departments or ministries apply themselves to it, which results in nobody having final responsibility and that is not beneficial to all the important work that needs to be done. Smooth energy transition requires a long-term policy for developing alternative energy. That includes sustainable solutions, like solar panels, wind-turbines and hydropower plants (see Chapter 8), as well as solutions that go further than the well-known forms of application. The following section deals with this last category.

7.3 Non-conventional oil

In addition to the most well-known form of oil (petroleum) and oil production (by means of drilling), the black gold can also be extracted in other ways. Extracting fuel by non-conventional means requires sophisticated techniques and a lot of energy; this results in high costs, but with the recent oil price developments and with a view to the future, these are interesting alternatives. Tar sands and oil shale are two popular forms of non-conventional oil sources.

7.3.1 Tar sands

When oil is talked about, conventional oil or petroleum is generally meant. This crude black liquid is found in sources under the earth's surface. Tar sands can be used for production of a relatively new form of oil and drilling is not needed because tar sands can be dug up. This form of opencast mining is comparable to the extraction of iron-ore, which is found on the surface of the ground.

Tar sands are deposits of sand, clay, water and bitumen. Bitumen can be converted to oil, which is fortunate as there is a lot of this material available. Oil reserves concealed in tar sands are much greater than conventional oil reserves. The potential of tar sand in Canada that can be exploited just by opencast mining is greater than the petroleum reserves of Saudi Arabia (250 billion barrels). Total worldwide oil reserves from tar sands are, according to some sources, even equal to 6,000 billion barrels of petroleum. Canada and Venezuela each own a third of that. In Canada, the majority of the tar sand is found in the Athabasca region (Alberta), and in Venezuela the precious material is chiefly found in the Orinoco Delta.

Oil from tar sands is the heaviest variant of the black gold, yet barrels of oil produced from tar sands can be sold for a lot of money, as long as the price of crude remains high.

The reason for this is that the crude oil is firstly intensely upgraded. The oil is made lighter by adding hydrogen and removing the sulphur. The residue is called synthetic crude oil, but such a process requires a huge amount of energy. The Canadian fields are usually frozen and first have to be heated with hot water. All this makes the production process expensive and that is why extracting this oil is only profitable at a high oil price of more than 30 dollars a barrel. In 2006, the average production cost for Shell of one barrel of oil was 7.73 dollars, whereas the company's costs were 13.55 dollars for oil from tar sand (almost double). In that year, the Canadian government received 9.92 dollars for every barrel Shell produced from tar sands and, furthermore, decided not to bother with the Kyoto Protocol. CO_2 gas emission from producing oil from tar sands is indeed sizeable and far from good for the environment. It's a continual compromise between the environment and access to energy.

In addition, other pros and cons can be weighed. For Western countries, Canada is a more reliable partner than Venezuela, but the conditions in the South American country offer a number of important advantages: tar is lighter, outside temperature is higher and there is more water available in the region.

7.3.2 Oil shale

Oil shale, or clay stone, is rich in organic material. Under high pressure and temperature, oil can be extracted from this rock. If the hydrocarbons remain in the rock and don't seep through to other underground reservoirs, oil shale is created. The IEA estimates world supplies of oil shale to be 2,600 billion barrels of oil, of which the majority can be found in the US. This means that just as many hydrocarbons are trapped in oil shale as in all known conventional oil supplies. Oil shale production is, however, still in its infancy, so much experimentation is still taking place. It is a technically sophisticated process that is only profitable when the oil price is high. That shows in particular that the expensive oil in the world is chiefly found in Western countries, whereas cheaply-produced oil is mainly found in the Middle East.

Just as extracting oil from tar sands, production of oil shale also requires the necessary heating, which makes this method of production an energy-intensive process. Furthermore, the oil is very heavy and therefore requires intensive refining. Oil shale has a lower tar level than tar sands and is therefore, in an ecological respect, friendlier.

7.4 Liquefied Natural Gas (LNG)

Transport is one of the most prominent problems in the energy sector. Energy has to be transported from A to B, so infrastructure is crucial. All possible transport variants are conceivable: from road transport to transport by train or ship. Oil, gas and electricity can also be transported through a network of pipes and cables.

Networks are occasionally expanded, but the structure remains more or less the same, which means that transport flexibility is very limited. However, oil has also been transported by ship for centuries and that has a few significant advantages. Natural gas can, fortunately, also be transported by ship these days, but for that gas has to be made liquid (liquefaction). Liquefied gas takes up 600 times less space than it does in gas form. Liquefaction of gas occurs under high pressure (in liquefaction facilities), at a Celsius temperature of 162 degrees below zero. The liquid product, Liquefied Natural Gas (LNG), is then loaded onto a tanker ship. Incidentally, LNG must not be confused with *gas to liquids* (GTL). GTL projects entail processes in which natural gas is converted to naphtha, diesel and other fuels.

Seeing as LNG tankers can travel to any place on earth, this form of gas transport is more flexible than transport via pipelines. By using this method of transporting LNG, countries worldwide can purchase gas, just as they do coal and oil. But the receivers do have to have special terminals as after delivery the liquid has to be returned to gas form (regasification) in special factories (regasification plants).

Gas transport via pipelines in not very much faster than by boat because the average speed of natural gas through a pipe is (on average) only 20 km per hour.

South Pars, Iran / North Field, Qatar	15,000
Oerengoj, (Polar region) Russia	10,000
Shtokman, (Barents Sea) Russia	3,200
Karachaganak, Kazakhstan	1,800
Slochteren, Netherlands	1,500
Greater Gorgon, Australia	1,100
Shah Deniz, Azerbaijan	800
Tangguh, Indonesia	500
Sachalin 1, Russia	485
Ormen Lange, Norway	400

Figure 43: Large gas fields (size measured in billion cubic metres).

Qatar has a population of only 150,000 and the island lies somewhere in the middle of the Persian Gulf. The country isn't large but it is located above the largest gas field in the world. A part of this field lies in Iranian waters and is called South Pars; the part within Qatar territory is called North Field.

80 billion dollars has already been invested in the Qatar production park of Ras Laffan, as a result of which gas production could be tripled from 2005 to 2015. It is already doubtful whether this is realistic. The relative size of the park is indeed overwhelming, but it also forms a direct threat. The terrain is an extremely concentrated workplace, whereby stability takes on erratic forms. LNG ships, production parks and storage places could be targets of terrorist attacks. One bomb attack on Ras Laffan would close down production for years, and that, considering its importance, is worrying to say the least. Together with Indonesia, Malaysia and Algeria, Qatar is one of the largest exporters of LNG in the world. Indonesia and Malaysia chiefly supply the Asian market, whereas Algeria's market is chiefly Europe.

Indonesia	28.8
Malaysia	22.1
Algeria	20.6
Qatar	19.3
Trinidad & Tobago	11.2
Nigeria	10.1
Australia	9.7
Brunei	7.6
Oman	7.2
United Arab Emirates	5.9
United States	1.3
Libya	0.5

Figure 44: LNG export per country (size in billion tons per year) (BP, June 2005).

China wanted to build a large number of import terminals, but these projects were postponed at the beginning of 2007 because they proved not to be cost-effective at the low prices of the time. Remarkably, these prices had been fixed by the state. Seeing as the manufacture of one average import terminal costs about half a billion euros, this puts enormous pressure on the initiators. The return on their investment would be open to huge risks. But many countries are building import capacity; the most important reason for this is the growing dependence on various energy sources.

In the Netherlands, both Vopak and 4Gas want to build an LNG terminal in Rotterdam. ConocoPhillips and Essent have similar plans for Eems Haven. Taqa, a company from Abu Dhabi, one of the United Arab Emirates, wants to build a large installation off the coast of Rotterdam that has to be operational by the end of 2008. Taqa wants to allow ships from all corners of the world to deliver LNG which will then be returned to gas form on a special ship off shore. Because of the considerable distance from civilization, that is a bit safer than loading and unloading at the wharf. Taqa will store the gas in two empty gas fields that the company owns; these fields (P15 and P18) can store a total of almost 20 billion cubic metres of gas. The fields are about 30 km from shore and are already connected to land by pipelines. This project is of great significance for strengthening the Netherlands' position on the European gas market.

	Number	Percentage
Japan	25	54 %
United States	5	11
Spain	4	9
Korea	3	6
France	2	4
Belgium	1	2
Taiwan	1	2
India	1	2
Italy	1	2
Greece	1	2
Turkey	1	2
Portugal	1	2
Dominica	1	2
Total	47	100 %

Figure 45: LNG receiving terminals per country (and in world percentage) (IGU PGC D, LNG Journal, 2004).

Delay in the building of capacity is, however, chiefly expected on the export side. Potential customers are building more terminals than exporters, which will result in supply and demand not remaining in balance and this will bring problems for the terminals that are to be built. The profitability of these terminals will come under enormous pressure.

Shortages exist not only in the area of import and export capacity, but also in the area of ships and qualified personnel. Due to a great shortage of LNG-tanker captains, their salaries rose from 6,000 dollars in 2004 to 20,000 dollars in 2006. The need for vessels is just as great, but the capacity to build these is extremely limited. In 2005, about

20 ships were being delivered per year, but that number will be about 35 in 2008. There were only 200 LNG tankers operational worldwide in 2006, whereas this number will probably have risen to 350 by 2010. Most ships are being built in South Korea. The country does not only have the reputation of being an important builder of LNG tankers, but it is also one of the most significant importers of LNG in the world.

Insight into costs structure is essential for weighing up interests and for making choices. The costs turning point for choosing LNG instead of pipelines is at a distance of approximately 2,500 to 4,000 km. That is why particularly Japan and Korea are very active in this area; the countries are situated at large distances from gas sources. The importance of LNG as a commodity will also increase for other countries in the future. In 2004, LNG took up only 6% of the total gas market and 26% of the total international gas trade; the rest was transported by pipe. But this will rapidly change, not least because it is expected that in the period 2002 to 2030, the US will import a factor 40 more gas.

Average costs for producing LNG varies per field, but in Algeria the average price in 2006 was 1.5 dollar cents per cubic metre. In addition, it costs between 4 and 5 dollar cents to make the gas liquid. Transport costs about 3 or 4 dollar cents per 10,000 km. And finally, the process to convert the liquid back to gas costs approximately 2 dollar cents.

7.5 Gas storage

It isn't only LNG that offers the gas market flexibility; gas storage also helps. Gas storage contributes to supply security because energy concerns or other companies are more easily able to meet peak demands. Apart from this social flexibility, there is also commercial flexibility: a peak in demand affords parties the opportunity to offer stored gas at high prices. This situation also occurs when the cause is not only the usual day/night or summer/winter pattern, but also when the market is subject to incidental extremes like strikes, damaged production installations or political tension. With a supply of natural gas, a market party can take up more trading positions than without any form of storage.

Gas is generally stored in empty salt caves or former oil and gas sources. Most locations do not, however, lend themselves to that, which results in there also being a shortage in this sector. Both Nuon and Essent have storage space of a few hundred million cubic metres in Epe, in Germany. These spaces are connected to the Dutch network by pipes. In Norg and Grijpskerk in Groningen, GasTerra has storage with a capacity of 17 billion cubic metres. That is quite a bit more than the few hundred million the other large Dutch energy companies have and can, therefore, be more easily regarded as guarantee for supply security. The storage energy concerns have is chiefly intended to contribute towards profit. Because of the mentioned shortage in the market, gas storage has indeed become a lucrative occupation, which is probably the most important reason gas storage owners try to keep other people out of their facilities. And that is also one of the reasons why the European gas market as a whole does not function optimally.

7.6 Clean Coal

'Clean fossil' relates to the production of electricity by means of burning fossil fuels. The carbon dioxide emitted from this process is captured and stored. This method is particularly suitable for coal-fired power plants because these are the biggest polluters. Such production processes are therefore also labelled with the term 'clean coal'. The totally environmentally-friendly process is called Carbon Capture and Storage (CCS).

Seeing as a lot of CO_2 is released during the burning of fossil fuels, it is essentially important that electricity power plants produce more cleanly from now onwards, and that governments impose stricter emission standards and emission rights. That also applies to the Netherlands, because even though the country chiefly has gas-fired plants, there are also coal-fired plants. And what's more, there are chiefly plans for building coal-fired plants. Coal is, after all, the most important source for electricity production worldwide.

The German energy company, EON, began building a new coal-fired plant with a capacity of 1,100 megawatts at the beginning of 2008. Due to improved technology, the stricter environmental standards can be met; CO_2 emission will be 20% lower than existing coal-fired plants. EON expects the new coal-fired plant to become operational in 2012, by which time the company will have invested 1.2 billion euros in the project. Besides EON, there are many others who want to build new coal-fired plants: Nuon and Essent want to build five together with their Belgium and German partners Electrabel, RWE and EON. This needs to be looked into because the Dutch coalition agreement states that the Netherlands must have the cleanest energy supply in Europe. The government wants to have about 30% less CO_2 emission in 2020 than there was in

1990. However, since the liberalization of the energy markets, the government may not lay down what type of electricity plant an energy company is allowed build. And environmental services may not lay down that companies have to capture CO_2 because with the implementation of the emission trading system, it was determined that no demands in respect of carbon dioxide may be included in the environment permit. The European Emission Guidelines only regulate how much CO_2 companies in Europe are allowed to emit. As long as a country stays within the agreed limits, it may determine for itself what sort of power stations it builds.

In order to be able to build new coal-fired plants, they have to produce 'cleaner' than was formerly the case. Capture of CO_2 gasses could be a solution. The captured gasses could be stored, possibly underground, in empty gas fields. The technology needed for that is being developed now. That also means that cost calculations have to be amended because, for the time being, capture and storage costs could mount up considerably. According to research by the German government, it will only be possible to capture a few percent of CO_2 in the next few years. That will increase slowly, but on the basis of the current data, the Germans expect that a maximum of 65% will be able to be captured in 2020.

Apart from that, there are also many other catches. A so-called pulverized coal-fired power plant neutralizes the CO_2 it produces by storing it in the ground. This process costs a lot of (extra) energy, which in turn costs a lot of money and, moreover, results in the emission of more CO_2. In addition, the yield from such a plant drops to 35% instead of the usual 45%.

There are, of course, other techniques to store CO_2, but these are still in the development phase. There are experiments, for example, whereby carbon dioxide is captured in magnesium carbonate. Furthermore, there are new coal-fired plants that do substantially provide a higher efficiency than existing coal-fired plants. Certain variants can also stoke biomass.

Underground gasification of coal is also an alternative for the production of energy. A coal gasification installation and a turbine work together; the former having the function of a chemical factory, the latter represents the power plant. Synthetic gas is extracted from coal in chemical installations and during this process, carbon dioxide is removed. During the burning of the gas, no harmful matter, like carbon dioxide, mercury or sulphur oxide is released.

Removing carbon dioxide from the smoke gasses that escape from the chimneys of normal coal-fired plants is a complicated chemical process that is also extremely energy-intensive. This results in the plant's profits dropping a few percent. With coal gasification, the capture of carbon dioxide is quite a bit easier.

The mentioned technically-sophisticated alternatives are good initiatives that contribute towards taking a new path, but technological development alone is not enough. There is urgent need for a mental shift. Moreover, specific infrastructure must be created in order to make the desired developments possible.

Bulk consignments of CO_2 have the same characteristics as other bulk goods. Adequate supply offers economically-interesting possibilities. An added advantage of storing carbon dioxide in gas fields is that the pressure increases, whereby more natural gas can be extracted from a source. The Dutch energy company Eneco and the company Seq are together building an electricity installation that emits absolutely no CO_2 but captures and stores it all. This is called a Zero Emission Power Plant (ZEPP). The plant extracts natural gas from the earth and squeezes CO_2 back in its place. The plant will be built on a gas field in the Dutch province of Friesland and will, according to plan, become operational in 2009. In this way, carbon dioxide even gains (positive) economic value, whereas this has been negative until now. The market will even be prepared to pay for CO_2. That also applies to greenhouse market gardeners, to whom CO_2 is sold because it stimulates plant growth.

Rotterdam is uniquely positioned and can accept the function of CO_2 hub. Firstly because the harbour area is close to where the aforementioned market gardeners are situated; secondly because there are a few oil and gas fields off the North Sea coast of Rotterdam that could be used for CO_2 storage; and finally because Rotterdam has a lot of heavy industry that produces residual heat. Because CO_2 capture requires a great deal of heat, this appears to be a perfect combination.

But before that happens, other things will have to be done. It is highly likely that CO_2 storage will be easy to implement. Technically it shouldn't be too difficult because the gas is quite a bit 'thicker' than natural gas and becomes liquid under reasonably low pressure. But legally and economically it won't be so easy. The Mining Act has all sorts of provisions for bringing up gas, but no regulations for putting it back again. Before companies can begin storing, all sorts of permits have to be obtained. There is even more uncertainty with regard to capture. At the moment, technology is severely under-developed, but that will undoubtedly change because of all sorts of projects that are currently underway. Incidentally, there is a risk that the stored CO_2 could still leak out and penetrate the air, which is why capture in another way is being considered. By allowing CO_2 to react with minerals, it is actually chemically captured: a reaction with silicon oxide results in sand. And, as a crowning touch, energy is even released during the process. There are, of course, costs involved in purchasing the required minerals, so the economic feasibility requires a lot of money. The actual investment and the yield to be achieved are dependent on various prices. Time will tell how these techniques develop, but if something concrete comes out of them then it can be expected that the price of the most suitable mineral will rocket and probably create a new *hype*.

CHAPTER 8:
Sustainable energy

8.1 Sustainability

Sustainability considers future generations and is about ethics. Within the energy sector, sustainability means dealing with nature, the environment and commodities in a way that will help them last. For companies and organizations it also means that they have to treat personnel and other interested parties in an ethically-responsible way. Sustainability also has a social character. Some companies commit themselves to international standards, like *Principles for Responsible Investment* (PRI) and *Equator Principles* (EP). With PRI, companies promise to consider environmental and social aspects when making decisions. EP is directed towards environmental and social sustainability awareness of project financing.

Sustainable energy is energy that is available to people for an unlimited period of time; the use of which damages neither the environment nor the future perspective of following generations. Sustainable energy includes, for example, bio-fuels and energy generated by the sun, wind, hydropower, hydrogen and compost installations. The ingredients and possibilities of producing energy are quite diverse. By using different production processes, risk is spread and dependence on other countries is reduced.
The aim is that in 2020, at least 20% of all energy consumed will come from sustainable sources and greenhouse gas emission will be 20% less than it was in 1990. In addition, 2% will have to be saved on energy consumption annually. The European Union is prepared to reduce CO_2 emission by 30% in the period leading up to 2020 but only if the most important industrialized countries commit to strict agreements. In Europe at the moment, 7% of all energy comes from durable sources, like wind and biomass. There is therefore still a lot of work to be done in order to reach the desired level. This requires mental, technological and organizational transformations. Industrial policy will have to undergo a third industrial revolution; this time an ecological one. These sorts of developments are taking place all over the world. Europe, for instance, is very much involved in generating sustainable energy, waste management and recycling. Japan has a leading role in the area of hybrid cars and fuel cells, while America is leading the way in bio-plastics and bio-fuels.

	2005	2010 (target)
Austria	60% *)	78 %
Sweden	52	60
Finland	24	30
Denmark	22	28
Spain	18	28
Portugal	14	38
Italy	11	25
France	9	21
Germany	9	13
Greece	7	20
Ireland	6	14
Netherlands	5	10
United Kingdom	3	10
Luxemburg	2	5
Belgium	2	5

*) nuclear energy is not seen as sustainable here

Figure 46: Sustainable generation of electricity (in percentages of the total)

8.2 Sun

In essence, solar energy is the basis of all forms of energy. Petroleum, coal and natural gas are all derived forms of solar energy. Fossil fuel is actually nothing more or less than the transformed residue of living things from the geological past. All this living matter was supported by photosynthesis. Wind energy is derived from differences in temperature and hydropower also indirectly comes from the sun. Vaporized water falls to earth as rain, is collected in huge reservoirs and id then converted into electricity by use of energy falling water.

The sun, the star closest to earth, is one huge ball of energy. The sun gets its energy from the so-called *proton-proton cycle*. The enormous pressure that the sun's own gravity has on the material in the sun's core combined with and the high temperature, changes hydrogen to helium. 600 million tons of hydrogen is converted to 596 million tons of helium every second. The 4-million ton difference is radiated in the form of electromagnetic energy. This fusion reaction forms the basis of the hydrogen bomb.

The sun radiates an amount of energy in the form of light and heat equal to 3.8×10^{26} joules per second. This is more energy than mankind has used in the last hundred-thousand years. Of all this energy, the earth receives only a two-billionth part.

The temperature on the surface of the sun is 5,500 degrees Celsius, but the temperature at the core is 15 million degrees. Mankind, however, has to be satisfied with the heat of the sun that reaches earth. The sun's yield is at its highest at the equator; namely a maximum of 1000 watts per square metre at ground level. It would be a sin not to make use of this, which is why we are increasingly focussing on the use of solar energy.

The Netherlands is unfortunately not the most suitable country for the production of solar energy as it has far too few hours of sun. The sun shines 85% less (brightly) on the shortest winter day than it does on the longest summer day. It lights the country for less than eight hours on that shortest day, and for 17 hours on the longest day. The sun doesn't make an appearance for an average of 37 days in the winter, but only 5 days in the summer.

	Renewables	Biomass	Hydro	Wind	Sun	Geothermal
EU25	109,539	72,274	26,128	5,033	743	5,360
	100%	66.0%	23.9%	4.6%	0.7%	4.9%
Belgium	1,161	1,119	27	11	3	1
Czechia	1,363	1,188	174	1	-	-
Denmark	2,926	2,346	2	566	9	2
Germany	13,755	9,367	1,812	2,173	269	134
Estonia	607	604	2	1	-	-
Greece	1,560	953	402	96	108	1
Spain	8,977	4,853	2,713	1,341	62	8
France	17,304	11,927	5,179	49	19	130
Ireland	325	214	54	56	-	-
Italy	12,528	3,791	3,671	159	19	4,888
Cyprus	97	5	-	-	92	-
Latvia	1,649	1,377	267	4	-	-
Lithuania	734	698	36	-	-	-
Luxemburg	73	59	9	3	1	-
Hungary	965	860	18	-	2	86
Malta	-	-	-	-	-	-
Netherlands	2,364	2,175	8	161	20	-
Austria	6,766	3,450	3,132	79	86	19
Poland	4,325	4,126	179	12	-	8
Portugal	3,894	2,877	849	70	21	78
Slovenia	822	470	352	-	-	-
Slovakia	737	379	353	-	-	5
Finland	8,805	7,498	1,296	10	1	-
Sweden	14,131	8,883	5,170	73	5	-
United Kingdom	3,671	3,055	424	166	25	1

Figure 47: Gross Domestic consumption in ktoe (Eurostat, 2004)

Since its creation, the sun has become about 25% hotter, which is perfectly normal as the older stars get, the harder they burn. And that directly announces the end of the world. A few scientists believe that life on earth will be over in 500 million years. If the temperature continues to rise, the earth will boil dry, as has already happened to Venus. But mankind will die out long before it is burnt alive. The sun will continue to exist for another 4 to 5 billion years (at the moment it is only halfway through its life), and then it will definitely be all over. The sun will swell and consume Mercury, Venus and (probably) Earth before imploding to a fraction of its original size. In the end, only a cold dark and lifeless 'solar system' will remain. In that respect, even solar energy is not completely sustainable.

That doesn't sound good, but at the moment the sun is our most prominent source of life, and we can profit from it in many ways. Solar energy exists in many forms: water can be warmed in solar boilers or solar collectors; with the so-called Concentrating Solar Power (CSP) technique, mirror farms produce large amounts of solar power; solar towers capture hot air power; and photovoltaic cells convert radiation to electricity.

If 1% of the earth's surface was covered with solar panels, the whole world's energy needs could be provided for. That would mean that the number of solar panels we have now would have to be increased by factor 3000. Solar energy is a hot item. In Europe in 2006, more than 2,000 megawatts of solar capacity had been set up; a year later that amount had been increased to 3,000 megawatts. For the last five years, worldwide capacity has grown by 50% per year. BP is the world leader in photovoltaic energy. In the field of solar cells, it is building a factory in Madrid, the largest in Europe, and is doing the same in India. Annual production capacity in Madrid will amount to 300 megawatts. Much of the future production is now already being sold on a large scale by means of future contracts. Shell, together with the French Saint Gobain, started an enterprise for building solar panels under the name of Avancis KG. Shell, incidentally, does not focus on standard solar cells but chooses the development of thin-film solar cells. Thin-film technology brings a layer of complex metallic compound onto glass, through which light is converted to energy.

	Target 2010	Total 2004	Hydro	Wind	Bio-mass	Sun	Geo-thermal
EU25							
EU25-Percentage	21.0%	13.7%	9.6%	1.8%	2.1%	0.0%	0.2%
Belgium	6.0	2.3	0.4	0.2	1.8	0.0	-
Czechia	8.0	3.3	2.4	-	0.9	-	-
Denmark	29.0	25.1	0.1	16.3	8.8	-	-
Germany	12.5	9.6	3.5	4.2	1.9	0.1	-
Estonia	5.1	0.5	0.2	-	0.3	-	-
Greece	20.1	10.0	7.9	1.9	0.2	0.0	-
Spain	29.4	18.0	11.3	5.6	1.1	0.0	-
France	21.0	11.5	10.5	0.1	0.9	0.0	-
Ireland	13,2	5,4	2,5	2,6	0,4	-	-
Italy	25.0	18.2	14.1	0.6	1.8	0.0	1.8
Cyprus	6.0	-	-	-	-	-	-
Latvia	49.3	68.2	66.3	1.0	0.8	-	-
Lithuania	7.0	2.2	2.2	-	0.0	-	-
Luxemburg	5.7	5.8	2.6	0.9	2.1	0.2	-
Hungary	3.6	2.8	0.6	-	2.2	-	-
Malta	5.0	-	-	-	-	-	-
Nederland	9.0	6.6	0.1	1.9	4.6	0.0	-
Austria	78.1	61.6	56.8	1.4	3.3	0.0	-
Poland	7.5	2.0	1.4	0.1	0.6	-	-
Portugal	39.0	27.9	21.9	1.8	4.0	0.0	0.2
Slovenia	33.6	27.6	26.8	-	0.8	-	-
Slovakia	31.0	13.4	13.4	-	-	-	-
Finland	31.5	29.9	17.6	0.1	12.2	0.0	-
Sweden	60.0	45.4	39.6	0.6	5.2	-	-
United Kingdom	10.0	3.7	1.2	0.5	2.0	0.0	-

Figure 48: Electricity production on the basis of sustainable sources (in percentage of the electricity mix) in the EU25 (Eurostat/Directive, 2004)

Solar panels consist of a large amount of solar cells; the basis of each solar cell is silicon. This commodity is becoming increasingly more scarce and expensive, despite the fact that it is extracted from sand. The earth's crust is made up of 25% silicon, but unfortunately it is not to be found in a pure form in nature. Compounds with oxygen can be found in sand and clay and refining both materials can result in 99.9% pure silicon, which is also called polysilicon. This material is not only the basic material of solar panels, but it is also suitable for the manufacture of computer chips. Of the total 30,000 tons of polysilicon that was produced in 2006, about half was used for making computer chips, while the other half was used for making solar panels.

Sand is indeed sufficiently available worldwide, but the refining capacity is lacking. That is why the price of a kilo of pure silicon rose from 30 to 150 dollars from 2005 to 2007. A well-developed spot market for silicon does not exist, resulting in double having to be paid from time to time. It is expected that supply and demand will be more balanced in 2010, but until then, manufacturers of solar panels in particular will be troubled by the price rises. Most manufacturers of computer chips have concluded long-term futures contracts with silicon suppliers and, moreover, silicon makes up only a limited part of the cost-price of a chip.

The process of making silicon from quartz sand devours energy as a temperature of 1,700 degrees Celsius has to be reached. This energy is generally gained from burning fossil fuels, which again emits CO_2. Therefore, solar energy generation also indirectly pollutes the environment.

8.3 Wind

Electricity can be generated by use of the sun, but wind also offers that possibility. This process occurs in windmills or turbines. The Netherlands is still known abroad for its windmills, but that's for the historical variety. Nowadays, the Netherlands is a net-importer of modern wind machines. In the Netherlands in 2006, a record number of 336 wind turbines were built, whereas the total number in 2007 was 1,848. Together, these wind turbines have a capacity of 1,615 megawatts, and because of that, wind energy occupies the most prominent position in the area of sustainable energy.

Present-day windmills are generally steel constructions fitted with two or three rotor blades. These days, windmills, or turbines, are even developed with a vertical rotation axis; this type only provides a capacity of 10,000 kilowatts at the moment. They are particularly suitable for inhabited areas because wind is also captured when they are placed close to buildings or put in places where the wind often changes direction. The turbines are aesthetically responsible and noiseless. Production of wind energy is developing fast; turbines are getting bigger and they generate more power (see figure 49).

Year	Capacity	Diameter
1980	50	15
1985	100	20
1990	500	40
1995	600	50
2000	2,000	80
2006	5,000	125

Figure 49: Size of windmills (in kilowatt capacity and turning circle diameter)

In total there was 75 gigawatts of wind-induced production capacity on earth in 2007, two-thirds of which was in Europe. On this continent, wind energy covers 3.3% of the total electricity requirement. The eventual capacity is greater, but because the wind doesn't always blow optimally, windmills turn, on average, at only a quarter of their peak capacity. The electricity grid, for that matter, can only handle 25% of the maximum utilization. Electricity production by means of wind is characterized my many peaks and lows. Intermittency of wind power is a problem for electricity supply. Sometimes it hardly blows at all, and sometimes it blows too hard. In the first case, the rotor blades hardly move, and in the second, windmills are temporarily taken out of service and no electricity becomes available. That is why a back-up facility must be created for every installed megawatt of wind energy capacity. Gas-fired power plants are preferable to coal-fired plants hereby because gas-fired plants can be quickly regulated. The energy concerns Essent, Nuon and EON have together put forward an alternative: the building of an underground installation for storing wind energy. During periods that there is wind, water would be pumped upwards; on windless days this mass would fall down again and could be used to generate energy. An extra power plant would then be unnecessary.

An additional 15 gigawatts of wind capacity was built worldwide in 2006, at a cost of 18 billion euros. The Americans expanded their capacity most, accounting for 2.5 of the total gigawatts. Germany is the largest producer of wind energy; windmills there generate power for 8 million households. At the beginning of 2007, the country had more than 20 gigawatts of installed capacity; twice as much as the US.
The Germans began building the first German off-shore wind farm off the coast of the West Frisian island of Borkum in 2008. Twelve wind turbines will stand in the North Sea. With the current state of technology, that's a difference of factor two. The subsidies granted in the Netherlands for the development of wind energy on land and at sea vary considerably. Over the next few years, a maximum of 57 million euros subsidy will be granted for wind energy on land, whereas wind energy at sea can count on 200 million euros' worth of government support.
The capacity count in China at the moment is 2.3 gigawatts. This has to be increased to 20 gigawatts by 2020. Until that time, the Chinese government is allocating about 190 billion dollars for sustainable energy projects. 75% of the country's energy portfolio at the moment is still made up with highly polluting coal.

Despite all the good initiatives, comments can be made on the production of wind energy. The hype in sustainable energy is as yet no guarantee of financial success. The Danish company, Vestas Wind Systems, is the world's largest windmill producer. In 2006, the company made a profit for the first time in three years. The incomes of many new wind farms hardly covered the interest on their loans, but the problems are more sizeable than just this. At the moment, electricity generated by means of fossil fuels is still far cheaper than wind energy.
That parts or production capacity are not, or not sufficiently, available for building the necessary apparatus, is just as true for wind energy as it is for solar energy. Criticism is also coming from environmental movements; they refer to the high mortality rate

of birds as being a result of wind farms. It is true that no carbon dioxide is emitted with wind energy production, but Dutch windmills kill 30,000 birds every year. It is, therefore, premature to say that wind energy is, by definition, good for nature.

8.4 Water

8.4.1 Water as an asset class

Water is possibly not directly a commodity thought of as belonging in the energy sector, but it is used for generating energy by means of falling water or the tide. In addition, water is used to pump oil out of the ground and to irrigate crops, like grains suitable for bio-energy. Water can contribute in various ways to energy production and consumption. As drinking water, it belongs to the primary necessities of life and, partly because of that, it is an asset class.

10% of the world's surface is covered with ice, and 75% of all fresh water on our planet can be found in ice masses like glaciers, icebergs and the Polar Regions. The ice layers in Artic regions are sometimes almost 5 km thick.

Water is an indispensable link in the world; it is needed for everything. 400,000 litres of water are needed to produce just one car; one kilogram of American grain requires 3,000 litres of water, and a huge amount is needed for pumping up oil. And what about the consumption of pure drinking water? More water is being used per head of population than ever before. At the turn of the millennium, an inhabitant of Cambodia used less than 5 litres of water a day, while in the Netherlands a person needed 140 litres of water for quenching thirst and for sanitary use. The Americans are the biggest consumers of water, with a daily consumption of 260 litres per person. This is remarkable, seeing as about 2 million children die every year from diseases caused by lack of clean drinking water and sanitary facilities. More than 1 billion people have no access to clean drinking water and almost 3 billion people live without toilets.

According to the United Nations' development programme, every investment in good sanitary facilities and drinking water is automatically recouped in savings on health care and productivity stimulus. In Egypt, infant mortality figures have dropped 60% as a result of improvements in the field of sanitation. Clean, fresh water is, nevertheless, increasingly scarce, and that brings problems. Upward price pressure can therefore also be expected. Water can then also be regarded as an asset class in which it is possible to make lucrative investments.

Water is increasingly extracted from crucial regions. Irrigation demands much of rivers, lakes and other sources. In combination with pollution and climate change, deltas, ground water, seas and rivers are being threatened by irrigation. According to the World Nature Fund, even the existence of ten large rivers is threatened. These include the Danube, the Nile, the Yangtze, the Mekong and the Ganges. Stress situations are occurring everywhere. The Dead Sea has been shrinking for years, and the Aral Sea in Central Asia and Lake Chad in Africa have almost totally disappeared. In the 1970s, the Soviet Union diverted two rivers that until then had flowed into the Aral Sea. The Russians changed the course of the flow for the irrigation of cotton fields in Uzbekistan and Kazakhstan. Agriculture is a large-scale consumer of water: the sector accounts for 70% of worldwide water consumption. Efficient use is therefore a must.

The United Nations' climate commission, the IPCC, has already stated that in 2010, between 1 and 3 billion people will be confronted with water shortage. Climate change is causing less rainfall in the regions around the equator. It is expected that 20% less rain will fall in the Middle East and North Africa. There will be more desertification (see Chapter 10, section 10.5) with all the catastrophic consequences that entails. This will lead to, among other things, a water shortage for agriculture. Furthermore, the water supply of millions of people will be threatened, as will fish stocks, and with them the food chain of the local population. In view of the importance of clean and fresh water, water problems can also lead to political tensions.

Wastage worsens the problem. Many pipes are old and sometimes even made of wood, like in New York. The World Water Council expects that just in developing countries 140 billion dollars needs to be invested annually in order to renew the infrastructure. Saudi Arabia expects to have to invest more than 80 billion dollars by 2025 to fix desalination plants and sewer systems.

8.4.2 Water as an energy source

Hydropower plants at dams and reservoirs generate electricity from water. The Three Gorges Dam in the Yangtze River (China) is the largest dam in the world. The dam will become operational in 2009 and a lake with a length of more than 600 km will be created. The energy yield will be 19.8 gigawatts, comparable to that of 18 nuclear power plants. In order to get this project off the ground, 1.9 million Chinese were forced to leave their homes as the lake floods their residential area.

Generation of electricity in Europe by means of falling water generally takes place in mountainous regions, like the Alps and Scandinavia. In the Netherlands, water can be profited from in another way. The difference in sea level as a result of the tides can also serve to produce electricity. In addition, combining salt and fresh water is another application that releases electrical energy, but the water must flow along special membranes. The migration of salt ions produces electrical power in a plant.

Water has many more applications forms. Thermal springs (geothermal energy) can be used for heating buildings. The temperature a hundred metres below the earth's surface is about 15 degrees Celsius; for every additional hundred metres deeper, the temperature increases by 3 degrees. It was sometimes 40 degrees in the deepest shafts of the marl mines in Limburg. In countries where volcanoes are active, like Italy, Iceland and Japan, significant use is made of geothermic processes.

Using aquifers is another way of profiting from the specific characteristics of water. With heat pumps, hot water can be stored in the ground in summer that can then be used in the winter. The process can be reversed in the summer whereby cold water from the ground can be used for cooling buildings situated close to the underground reservoir. Former mine galleries are sometimes used for storage space.

8.4.3 Combined heat and power systems

Cogeneration systems work on the basis of a Micro Hydropower Plant (MHP). An MHP is a sort of mini power plant that can be placed in the home: it is comparable to a central-heating boiler that provides electricity as well as heat. By this combination, losses resulting from transport of heat and energy are greatly limited. Moreover, using a MHP is a great way to capitalize on peaks in the electricity market. MHPs are frequently used by glasshouse market gardeners; they sell (back) the generated electricity to the grid and in so doing recoup a portion of their costs. An added advantage for market gardeners is that vapour engines produce CO2 in addition to power and heat. This CO2 gas is essential for the daytime growth of plants and is most desirable in these proportions, which is why the engine is on all day. The price of electricity is at its highest during the day, so this action is also economically justified. According to the Central Bureau for Statistics, market gardeners in the Netherlands generated 4.3 million megawatt hours of electricity in 2006.

About 400 glasshouse market gardeners have united in order to produce energy via micro hydropower plants. Together they represent a production capacity comparable to a thousand-megawatt power plant. Eneco cooperates with the purchasing body of this collaboration. In this way, the energy company can have extra capacity at its disposal during peak hours without having to apply for a licence.

8.5 Hydrogen

Vehicles that run on hydrogen emit nothing other than water. No other (pollutant) material is released. Cars that run on hydrogen no longer need exhaust pipes, nor gaskets nor gearboxes. Hydrogen reacting with oxygen forms water; this process releases a lot of energy and this is exactly what the user wishes to utilize. Fuel cells, or *stacks*, are boxes the size of a really large shoebox. The process is comparable to that of a battery, but with hydrogen. The stacks contain the precious metal platinum, and that is what pushes the price up. However, by means of recycling, a part of the precious metal can be extracted and re-used.

Fuel generators (or cracking catalysts) convert fuel such as natural gas to hydrogen. At room temperature and normal pressure, this material is a gas. The use of hydrogen results in a worldwide universal product because it involves a pure chemical element; hydrogen in Germany is identical to hydrogen in China or Australia, and that shows its similarity to electricity. This similarity does not apply to commodities as quality and purity differ each time.

Hydrogen is not the actual source of energy but a carrier of it, which is why hydrogen is not primarily the solution to the energy problem. Hydrogen has to be extracted, from gas, oil or coal, for example. Production of hydrogen is not only possibly by burning natural gas, for example, but also by electrolysis of water. Electrolysis is a clean method of production, but it does require energy. This energy can be supplied in the form of fossil fuel, but sustainable energy is also suitable. Production of hydrogen through fossil fuels is, however, not a solution for the energy problem. Hydrogen is indeed an alternative for fossil fuels as longs as sustainable energy provides the energy required.

Hydrogen can also be produced in nuclear power plants cooled by helium or sodium. Because of the high temperatures, water is immediately broken down into oxygen and hydrogen via thermo-chemical processes. This form of hydrogen production is much more efficient than electrolysis of water.

Reality dictates that it will be at least 15 years before economically-responsible hydrogen cars are on the road. Hydrogen cells are unfortunately not as reliable as combustion engines. Apart from which, costs are as yet still a problem, although these have recently decreased dramatically. One added advantage is that fuel cells are twice as efficient as diesel engines. The present gasoline stations will have to become hydrogen stations, but this will only happen when sufficient hydrogen cars are available.

8.6 Bio-energy

Biological fuel, shortened to bio-fuel, is fuel extracted from plant or animal material. To discover fossil fuel, man only used bio-fuel, which includes wood, charcoal, dried excrement, vegetable oils and animal fats. Nowadays, the emphasis is on bio-ethanol, bio-diesel and bio-gasses (extracted from biomass).

8.6.1 Wood

Wood can be regarded as a sustainable energy product. Electricity plants sometimes generate power by burning compressed wood chippings or pallets. Wood can, as biomass, also serve as an ingredient for the production of bio-energy (see section 8.7.3).

Wood can be burnt in the hearth and also in special wood-burning stoves to provide us with heat. Burning wood in average hearths yields 20%, which means that 20% of the amount of energy contained in wood is released in the form of heat. Sophisticated wood-burning stoves have a yield of 75%. The difference in temperature can even rise to a factor of five and therefore there is little ash formation with good stoves. In addition, burning wood is CO_2 neutral (providing new trees are planted).

The price of wood is largely influenced by the housing market. The building sector is partly responsible for demand having exceeded supply for years. Worldwide consumption of wood was 1.6 billion cubic metres in 2006, which is comparable with the total consumed quantities of cement, steel, plastic and aluminium put together. Fortunately, 2000 hectares of trees are gained every day thanks to sustainable forestry, but that is unfortunately nowhere near enough to meet the rising demand. Afforestation in Australia and New Zeeland would be the most effective because it appears that wood grows faster there than in other places in the world.

The price of wood can be determined in a number of ways; one way is by taking a look at the *stumpage* price. This relates to the price an owner of a forest receives for his wood. Corrected for inflation, this price has risen for a hundred years (with a factor of 200 in total) and is therefore one of the most stable investments. Moreover, the price has a low correlation with other financial products and only grows when the market is subject to a correction.

Another way to determine the price of wood is to take the thickness into account. The similarity between diamonds and wood is that the price increases more relatively depending on size. For diamonds, the price per carat exponentially increases if the diamond is bigger. Similarly, the price per measure of a thick piece of wood is also relatively high.

8.6.2 Bio-ethanol and bio-diesel

Ethanol and methanol are alcoholic materials. Bio-methanol is used for the production of bio-diesel. Bio-diesel is a sustainable fuel manufactured from vegetable oils or animal fats. The name indicates how much of the end-product that consumers use is a mixture of bio-diesel and diesel gained from petroleum. The designation B-20 means that 20% of the mixture comes from sustainable sources. Straight Vegetable Oil (SVO) is a bio-fuel that has been completely extracted from oil-yielding seeds or pips, like coleseed and sunflower seeds. SVO is actually biologically stored solar energy. The first diesel engine actually ran on oil manufactured from peanuts. Present-day diesel engines are no longer suitable to run on SVO without adjustments; they emit too much carbon black (soot) and are much too viscous. Current bio-diesel is chemically processed SVO and is extracted from coleseed oil or palm oil.

(Cane) sugar and grains, like wheat and maize, are used for the production of bio-ethanol. Bio-ethanol can be regarded as a synthetic form of gasoline, and the success of it can be measured in the large number of ethanol factories that are being built at the moment. 55 million tons of maize was processed in 2006; in 2007 that was 86 million tons, and the expectation for 2008 is 139 million tons. In order to meet 2008 quantity requirements, farmers have to greatly increase their acreages of maize. This would appear to be impossible. Here again, just as with fossil fuels, there is limited production capacity. Furthermore, little land would be left over for the production of crops for food.

At the end of 2006, the equivalent of 770,000 barrels of oil was produced of bio-ethanol and 65,000 barrels of bio-diesel daily. Between 2005 and 2010, the market for bio-diesel will grow by an average of 30% per year. In Europe, the production will increase by a factor of three, and in China it will increase fivefold. From 1 January 2007, 2% of gasoline and fuel brought onto the Dutch market by oil companies must be bio-fuel. In 2012, the EU will oblige its member states to match 5.75% of car fuels with bio-ethanol or bio-diesel. Bio-fuel is mixed with fossil fuel. Much of this sort of fuel is sold locally to councils, transport companies or public-transport companies. At the beginning of 2007, the Dutch government still imposed excise duty of 38 cents per litre on bio-fuel. This is not a good stimulant for the consumption of sustainable energy.

There are all sorts of initiatives in the area of bio-fuels elsewhere in the world. Bush wants the US to use a fifth less gasoline by 2017 by offering alternative sources a chance. This, of course, stimulates the price of maize and wheat, among other things. The US produced 19 billion litres of ethanol in 2006, of which the majority came from maize. 37 billion litres is expected in 2008, for which 3.8 billion bushels (at 27.2 kilos) is needed. The production of one litre of ethanol therefore requires approximately three kilos of maize.

In 2006, Brazil and America together produced 70% of the world's total ethanol production. The Americans, however, used most of it themselves and still imported large quantities. The Brazilians, with 3.5 billion litres, were the largest exporters of the product in 2006. Brazil produces bio-ethanol from sugar cane; at 22 dollar cents per litre, that is quite a bit cheaper than the American method of using maize, which costs 30 dollar cents per litre. European production is still more expensive because grain and sugar beet are used. This means that the various producers of bio-ethanol can be competitive at different levels of the oil price.

The EU applies an import tax on bio-ethanol, but not on bio-diesel. In order to protect its own market, America imposes import tax on ethanol from Brazil; it also gives its own domestic producers a subsidy of 13 dollar cents per litre on their production. The country is criticized for this by other governments, who want to see an end to these regulations.

Argentina (bio-ethanol from soybeans), Malaysia and Brazil regularly transported their bio-diesels via the US because they could pocket the subsidy. Because of this, the competition between bio-diesel from Europe and bio-diesel from the US was not fair.

8.6.3 Biomass: second-generation bio-fuel

Second-generation bio-fuel is produced from biomass and not at the cost of crops for food, as is the case with the production of bio-ethanol and bio-diesel (first-generation bio-fuel). Biomass relates to non-edible commodities and waste products like wood, straw, foliage and plant stems. The production of second-generation bio-fuel requires a totally different approach than the production of bio-ethanol or bio-diesel. Certain processes are started by means of catalysts. Petroleum consists of long chains of carbon and hydrogen atoms. Biomass also consists of oxygen atoms. These oxygen atoms have to be removed with the help of catalysts because otherwise the fuel would provide too little energy. The most effective and efficient catalysts are vehemently being sought in various laboratories. It is possible that in the future even plastics will be able to be made out of biomass. It is already possible on the basis of petroleum, but it will be a long time before it succeeds with biomass. In Stockholm busses and taxis are already running on bio-gas extracted from sewage sludge.

The production process of second-generation bio-fuel is therefore more complex, and partly because of that, more expensive. The commodities are cheaper because, in this case, they are actual waste which means that the product does not compete with food. At the end of 2006, the European Commission claimed that first-generation bio-fuel is about one and a half times more expensive than fossil fuel (at an oil price of 50 dollars a barrel), while second-generation bio-fuels are two and a half times more expensive. It has to be said here that the CO_2 emission from first-generation bio-fuels is roughly half that of ordinary gasoline or diesel. With second-generation bio-fuels, CO_2 emission is only a tenth.

Fossil fuels, like oil, gas, coal, peat and turf, are carbon compounds that are created as residue of plant and animal live from earth's geological past. Actually, fossil fuels are therefore a form of solar energy that was stored in plant and animal carbon compounds millions of years ago. In total, 200 tons of plant material that has been rotting and degenerating for millions of years and then exposed to high pressure and temperature is needed to produce one litre of oil. However, one litre of synthetic fuel can be directly produced from just 15 kilos of plant material. We can ask ourselves whether the price of the existence of the product should be calculated in the price of the energy product. At the moment, the price of oil is determined by extraction, refining and distribution, but calculation of the required millions of years is omitted. Plants can be quickly cultivated and harvested and, moreover, this process can be repeatedly endlessly.

The earth offers massive possibilities. Forests, fields and other overgrowth can offer an annual yield of about 10%; this means that 10% can be used for the production of crops destined for bio-energy production without exhausting earth. Planting, afforestation and natural growth can reduce possible net decline. However, excessive harvesting through cutting down forests and the production of crops leads to over-cropping. 60 billion tons can be produced annually in a responsible way; at the moment only 2 billion tons are being used for food and 10 billion for the production of energy.

By using crops that also serve as food (grains, maize, sugar), energy and food are in competition. This caused the Tortilla crisis in Mexico, and it is also the reason why China determined no longer to make bio-ethanol from products that can also serve as food. Second-generation bio-fuels will be substantially used. Maize, wheat and sugar are therefore banned as commodities for the production of bio-fuels. Plant-waste left over after picking corncobs or the stalks left after spikes have been picked are used. Though it is not only these stalks that are used; what about the household refuse and other materials that we generally regard as rubbish? Bio-gas is a gas compound that is created as a result of biological processes (read: rotting). The main components of bio-gas are methane and carbon dioxide. The gas is created as a result of anaerobic fermentation of organic matter like manure, sewage sludge, activated sludge or household refuse. This can occur in large quantities, whereby organic matter becomes full of bacteria in a few weeks. Methane is an example of naturally created bio-gas; fermentation of sewage water sludge is another form that leads to energy extraction. The term *aquatic biomass* refers to algae that are suitable for (third generation) bio-energy production. These micro-organisms seem to be an extremely efficient ingredient for the production of bio-diesel; even better than cole-seed or sugarcane. Algae oil can already be bought, and an added advantage to this form of energy product is that algae absorb a relatively large amount of CO2 during cultivation.

8.6.4 Future expectations

Not all sustainable alternatives are equally useful, but it is beyond doubt that energy producers will increasingly build more combi-plants that are able to stoke a certain percentage of clean biomass. The required biomass can be produced on a large scale by southerly-situated countries. These are generally the poorer countries. Developing countries may now be able to catch up. Biomass is therefore also referred to as *the energy of the poor*. Nigeria produces 6 million tons of waste a year and could totally meet its own energy requirements.

Sustainable energy is praised for its advantages, but the disadvantages are often forgotten. Firstly, first-generation bio-energy is won at the cost of food; secondly, the production of products like bio-ethanol also costs energy, by which environmental profit is partly lost as soon as this energy flows from fossil fuels. Thirdly, transportation of fuel costs a great deal of energy, even when its biomass; and fourthly, bio-diesel is biodegradable, contains no sulphur or aromatics and is not toxic, but the aromatics that are used during the production process are poisonous. When bio-fuel is burnt, less CO2 and sulphur oxide are released than by burning fossil fuels, but nitrogen oxide is emitted.

During the Dutch Balkenende-Zalm cabinet, bio-fuel was still more expensive than a litre of ordinary gasoline, while a car with bio-fuel didn't get as far. Nowadays, bio-diesel in Europe costs less than ordinary diesel. Subsidy, of course, plays its part in this.

CHAPTER 9:
Nuclear Energy

9.1 Sustainable or risky?

Nuclear energy is energy generated by nuclear reactions, like fusion or fission. These are reactions whereby the nuclei of atoms are involved. Nuclear energy is made available in the form of heat, which can be converted to electricity in a nuclear power plant in conventional ways via steam, turbines and generators.

Some people regard nuclear energy from fission as a form of sustainable energy. There is something to be said for this as nuclear power plants do indeed emit negligible amounts of CO_2, so in that respect, nuclear energy could be regarded as an antidote to global warming. But if an accident occurs, radioactive material can cause huge damage.

Those who regard nuclear energy as non-sustainable, refer, among other things, to the depleting supply of uranium. At the current tempo and considering all predicted new construction, this will certainly last for another one or two hundred years. Nuclear energy is then also seen as an interesting interim solution. If depletion is the only criteria, then even solar energy can no longer be regarded as sustainable: at some point, the sun as an energy source will be depleted and it will no longer shine. This implies that the concept of sustainability is elastic.

As has been said, nuclear power plants expose people to all sorts of specific dangers. Apart from the fact that these plants are ideal targets for terrorists, there is always the risk of serious radiation escaping as a result of leakage. Who doesn't remember the Chernobyl disaster in Russia in 1986? This catastrophe is public knowledge, but behind the scenes things are happening that don't reach the media. Japan produces nuclear energy because the country itself has no significant sources of energy. Japan is regularly exposed to danger. Fire, leakage and earthquakes threaten the power plants with some regularity, but many accidents are kept quiet out of fear of unrest. These sorts of disasters, and the lobby of green movements in various countries, contributed to nuclear power plants being closed and nuclear energy no longer being applied. The emphasis was put on coal-fired power plants, which is now a problem worrying the world.

In order to limit possible damage to their own nature, population and economy, countries often built nuclear power plants close to borders. Should, heaven forbid, an accident happen whereby radiation is released, the damage in one's own country remains limited; half of the misery and misfortune is shared with the neighbouring country.

Storage of poor or used material is also a tricky business. It takes thousands of years before radiation drops to an acceptable level. In order to justify the stamp of sustainability, attention must be paid to keeping nuclear waste as low as possible. Nuclear fuel rods are exhausted after a few years and must then lie in cooling water for more than a year, after which time they are transported to a place of storage or a reprocessing plant for recycling.

Apart from that, other (usually fossil) fuels are used somewhere in the nuclear energy cycle, so even with nuclear energy there is often indirect CO_2 emission. This emission will be about equal to 30% of the emission from the most common gas-fired plants. With a modern plant based on cogeneration, the emission difference between nuclear power plants and common gas-fired plants can even be ignored. This again shows that it is difficult to make comparisons because plants are of different sorts and types. Technology is making continuous progress, with the result that universal conclusions cannot be drawn. As yet, it can be said that in general nuclear energy is quite a bit cleaner than burning fossil fuels (coal, gas and oil), providing production goes without a hitch. At the current price level, nuclear energy is even cheaper than electricity generated by means of coal.

France, which of all countries relies most on nuclear energy, indeed claims that nuclear energy is sustainable. Many other countries totally disagree. This causes friction within the European Union when determining alternatives that member states may choose to reduce CO_2 emission. France was prepared to drop its objections to stringent standards for renewable energy in exchange for recognition that nuclear energy also contributes in the battle against climate change.

9.2 Nuclear power plants

France is the absolute front-runner when it comes to the production of nuclear energy. The French get about three-quarters of their total energy requirement from nuclear energy; their level of knowledge is therefore extremely high, and this head-start gives them an economic advantage. Very large French suppliers and nuclear power plant builders are Alstrom and the state-owned concern Areva. Together with the Russian company Atomenergomasj, Alstrom builds nuclear power plants in Russia. Between

2007 and 2027, forty new plants will spring up there. The country is investing 26 billion dollars in nuclear energy until 2017.

In addition, Areva is helping India, among other countries, build nuclear power plants. Countries with strong economic growth and enormous populations, like India and China, are pulling out all the stops to ensure continued provision in their energy requirements.

Nuclear power plants in use	440
Being built	30
Planned until 2020	100
On the drawing board	158

Figure 50: Number of nuclear power plants in the world (2007)

There are now about 440 nuclear power plants worldwide and 30 are being built at the moment; another hundred will be built by 2020. The Americans have plans for another 30 new plants, and the discussion recently flared up again even in the Netherlands. Because of the many disadvantages of nuclear energy, the Netherlands only has one nuclear power plant, and that is in Borssele. In the Balkenende-Bos-Rouvoet coalition agreement, it states that the Netherlands will build no new plants for the time being. Minister Cramer (Ministry of Housing, Regional Development and the Environment) emphatically confirmed this resolution on 1 October 2007.

The 'Borssele Nuclear Power Plant Covenant' includes agreements about keeping production going at Borssele providing sustainable energy is promoted. The shareholders of this plant, Delta and Essent, agreed to jointly invest 250 million euros in innovative projects between 2006 and 2012.

First generation plants:	up to 1965
Second generation plants:	1965-1995
Third generation plants:	1995-2010
3+ generation plants:	2010-2030
Fourth generation plants:	from 2030

Figure 51: Generations of nuclear power plants

Uranium is the most important commodity for nuclear energy. Important exporters of uranium are Canada, the US, South Africa and Kazakhstan, but the front-runner is Australia. This country owns over 40% of the world's uranium reserves. Even the Australians only had one nuclear power plant at the beginning of 2007, but the country will certainly build another 25 by 2050. Then Australia will be able to get a third of the total energy requirement from nuclear fusion.

9.3 Uranium enrichment

Uranium appears in nature in compounds with oxygen. Uranium oxide contains uranium that comprises 0.7% U235 and 99.3% U238. In order to keep a chain reaction in a reactor going, about 4% U235 is needed as only U235 is fissionable. The percentage that comes directly from nature is therefore 3.3% too low. Enrichment has to change that. In advance of the enrichment process, the uranium is first chemically treated so that it can be made into a gas. Fluorine is added to create uranium hexafluoride (UF6) which becomes a gas after heating. It is then transmitted to ultracentrifuge and turns in a vacuum at more than a thousand times per second. Because of the centrifugal force, the relatively heavy U238 is forced to the outside. The U235 remains in the middle and after being drained, 4% is left. To get from 0.7% to 4%, about 7 times as much basic material is needed. 7 kilos of commodity provides 1 kilo of enriched uranium and 6 kilos of depleted uranium. However, for 1 kilo of uranium, 1000 kilos of uranium ore are needed. Furthermore, it regularly happens that half can't even be released from the compound with other materials.

Despite the antipathy towards nuclear energy in the Netherlands, the Dutch are extremely active in the field of uranium enrichment. Since the 1970s, Twente has been the Dutch centre in this field. The area vested this position during the time that there was a lot of unemployment. The area of Twente has no appreciable seismic activity and is therefore suitable for plants, laboratories and centrifuges for uranium enrichment. Urenco is the country's showpiece when it comes to enrichment plants. The multi-dollar company, which is a-third owned by the Dutch government (the English government, EON and RWE each respectively have interests of 33.3%, 16.6% and 16.6%) has the capacity to supply 30 large nuclear power plants via its factory in Almelo.

9.4 Depleted uranium

Depleted uranium is used in so-called breeder reactors. A fast breeder can also partially use depleted material, by which the energy yield per kilo of uranium is sixty times higher. Nuclear power plants have large supplies of depleted uranium stored on their premises.

Breeder reactors split plutonium (P239) that usually comes from dismantled nuclear weapons. During the process, neutrons are left over that can be used to up-grade the depleted uranium to P239. In this way, the reactor meets its own energy requirement. It is from this somewhat perpetual-motion condition that the breeder reactor derives its name, and when the discharge of neutrons happens at high speed, the name 'fast breeder' is applicable. In ordinary nuclear reactors, the speed of neutrons is curbed. Water usually functions as the slowing agent as well as the cooling liquid. Apart from that, helium and sodium are also used as cooling agents.

9.5 Non-Proliferation Treaty

Political games are played internationally, even at nuclear energy level. Iran, according to the US, is a dangerous player and a thorn in the side of Western society. The US labelled Iran and North Korea as the two most prominent countries from 'the axis of evil'. Since then, Iran has thrown some irons in the fire and made a few provocative pronouncements. The fundamentalist country even launched a new banknote in 2007 upon which a nuclear sign is depicted. The US reciprocated by drawing up a list of companies that possibly work with Iran on its nuclear (weapon) programme. These enterprises may no longer do business with American companies.

According to Mohamed El-Baradei, director of IAEA, Iran is as yet only enriching uranium on an experimental basis. The first nuclear power plant will be in Bushehr and, according to the planning, become operational in 2008. Iran claims to have purely peaceful intentions with its enrichment of uranium. However the West, led by the US, fears for applications in the field of nuclear weapons. The United Nations has imposed sanctions on Iran, but the usefulness of these are seriously challenged. A counterproductive effect is probably greater.

The Non-Proliferation Treaty (NPT) is an agreement from 1968 between 189 countries to limit ownership of nuclear weapons. The treaty is based on three cornerstones: non-proliferation, disarmament and the right to use nuclear energy for peaceful means. The enrichment process of uranium is extraordinarily complicated. Before a percentage of four is reached, various enrichment steps have to be taken. The number of centrifuges passed through during the enrichment process is not made public. Secrecy of details should reduce the chance of nuclear weapon distribution. For these military armaments, 95% enriched uranium is needed. The International Atomic Energy Agency (IAEA) controls plants that enrich uranium by checking that they don't exceed the permitted limits (4%, for example).

9.6 Scarcity forces creativity

Uranium is transported by truck and is therefore not dependent on inflexible pipelines or other transportation shortcomings, which makes transportation of the commodity relatively simple. Between 2000 and 2007, the price of uranium sky-rocketed fifteen times. Shares in the Australian uranium miner Paladin rose in that same period by 34,000 percent. For investors, an interest in a uranium mine or miner is an excellent way to profit from this sort of development. In 2007 there was, incidentally, still no futures market for uranium. Transparency of pricing leaves a lot to be desired. Direct investment is therefore not realistic for most parties.

At the beginning of 2007, annual demand for uranium was about 170 million pounds. However, in a twelve month period no more than 110 million pounds was found, and that is only enough for 65% of the total requirement. For the time being, the remaining part of the uranium is extracted from the dismantling of Russian nuclear weapons. The American company Usec is the largest uranium enricher in the world and recycles scrapped Russian nuclear rockets, among other things. The Russians have concluded contracts with a number of countries to supply them with uranium derived from nuclear rockets until 2013. After the collapse of the Soviet Union, the largest part of the Russian nuclear arsenal came into the hands of the Ukraine. In 1996 the weapons were officially completely handed over to Russia, but because of administrative confusion it is unclear whether or not weapons were left in the Ukraine. This could give cause for uranium trading on the black market.

The second largest mine in the world belongs to the largest mining company in the world: Cameco. There is 232 million pounds of uranium in the ground at Cigar Lake in the Canadian province of Saskatchewan. At the beginning of 2007 this represented a value of about 14 billion dollars. The mine should have annually met 10% of worldwide demand, but there was a hitch when a dislodged boulder caused an underground landslip and the mine flooded with water. It is unclear whether or not the mine can still be used, but it is beyond question that there is a delay of at least a year. A part of the uranium had already been sold on the futures market but it could not be delivered as a result of physical shortage. Customers therefore had to seek their salvation elsewhere.

Nuclear power plants used 64,000 tons of uranium in 2001. The estimated extractable supply is 17 million tons. Building all sorts of extra plants will probably lead to more shortages. A big part of this problem can be overcome by recycling; this can happen by processing old fuel or by utilizing fast breeders. This form is recycling is, however, not danger-free.

If mankind wants more, other possibilities must be sought. Extracting uranium from sea water is one of the solutions. There should still be 4,500 million tons of uranium in the oceans; the trick is actually getting it out. If that succeeds, nuclear energy can to some continuing extent be labelled 'sustainable'.

Rich ore	20,000
Depleted ore	1,000
Granite	4
Sedimentary rock	2
Continental crust	3
Sea water	0.003

Figure 52: Typical uranium concentrations (averaged in ppu)

The production of uranium from sea water is still in its infancy and at the testing stage. Japan has already closed a testing plant because pumping up the water required more energy than the extracted uranium could ever provide. A technique that is now used a lot is the application of racks with absorbents being hung in ocean currents. A ship collects the absorbed elements, after which these are processed and prepared for further production. The performance of contemporary absorption materials is dependent on all sorts of factors, one of which is temperature. Because of a certain minimal heat, this technique can actually only be applied on the surface of oceans. But not to worry; sea water is subject to currents which automatically create new charges.

And it isn't only uranium that is caught by the absorbents; molybdenum, titanium and cobalt are also trapped. As soon as the prices of these products also start rising, total extraction-costs will greatly decrease. If the prices don't rise, attention will need to be given to extraction techniques that don't attract any excess elements.

The search continues; not only for new techniques, but also for alternatives for uranium. Plutonium of thorium could both also be used for the production of nuclear energy. The world actually contains three times more thorium than uranium. Germany is even considering starting a moon-mission in 2013. The moon is rich in helium-3 and the extraction of it could offer a new solution for nuclear fusion. Only 150 kilos of helium-3 has been found on earth, which makes it much too scarce to be able to do anything significant with. The moon-mission is still far from being well developed, but because of the supposed potential it is being much discussed by technicians and scientists. The big advantage of fusion processes with helium is that there is no radiation because hardly any neutrons are released. But helium-3 does have to be heated to about 450 million degrees. That sounds impossible, but scientists claim that it is achievable. That would offer a wonderful solution, as there might be enough helium-3 on the moon for a thousand years' worth of energy generation. Unfortunately, this technique can't be started for at least another few decades.

France, the country pre-eminent in regard to nuclear energy, is also doing tests with deuterium and tritium. Reality dictates that real commercial generation is still far off. India is already testing thorium techniques. This alternative element is suitable for nuclear power plants, but nuclear weapons cannot be made from it. This seems ideal and would be extremely useful for the situation in Iran. If Iran really is searching for peaceful solutions, it would at least avoid any pretence by using this technique. Of course, science still has to delve deeper into the material and the technique behind this substitute, which will undoubtedly be pursued.

CHAPTER 10:
Feasibility

10.1 Introduction

There are plenty of possibilities for the application of (alternative) energy sources. Willingness towards these is one thing, but economic feasibility is another and it must certainly not be underestimated, although these issues are closely linked. Complexity and high prices create extra risks. In order to have a good chance of success, the recommendation is not to strive for a whole range of objectives, but to focus on the most important aspects. It is, for example, important for a large part of electricity generation to be done on a sustainable basis. Preservation of fuels for transport is considerably less simple.

The feasibility of initiatives is therefore dependent on the investments man is prepared to make. Enormous amounts will have to be invested in the energy sector over the next few years. At a conventional level, 5,300 billion dollars will have to be invested in exploration and development of oil and gas fields over the next 25 years. During the same period an extra investment of 1,700 billion dollars is required just for the transportation of natural gas; and we haven't even started talking about investments needed for the building of all sorts of new electricity plants.

Budgets will therefore soon be used up, while money will still be needed for stimulating sustainability. For the time being, governments will have to take on a guiding role in the actual application of sustainable energy sources. Government can help guide society in a particular direction by imposing taxes, granting subsidies or setting obligations. Although even in this the world is dynamic. That means that what is applicable right now might not be applicable in the future.

Many paths can be taken to guarantee supply security and to bring about energy transition. One path will be more desirable than another; it is therefore essential to gain insight into the feasibility and usefulness of the various possibilities and suggestions. Apart from that, ways in which the objective can be reached differ. It is therefore crucial to make the right choice.

Within the framework of stimulation by governments, the difference between long and short-term objectives must not be lost sight of. Long-term and high-subsidy regularly lead to over-stimulation. In such cases, inefficiencies can lead to the desired result not being obtained. The introduction of green power failed in the Netherlands for similar reasons. Political and cultural change is possibly more important than technological or economic transformation. Rules and regulations must be drastically dealt with. There has to be a price tag on pollution (CO2 emission rights, for example), while sustainability has to be rewarded. All sorts of laws and rules can be created in the fiscal field in order to carry through the desired changes. Governments continually hesitate between stimulus on a voluntary basis and forcing the issue by means of rigid regulation. Should an environmentally-friendly car be subsidized (stimulus) or should a car that creates a lot of emission be more heavily taxed (determent policy)? The first option costs money, while the second initially results in a positive cash-flow for the government.

10.2 Differences in price and efficiency

Stimulus by the government is necessary as long as existing price differences are disadvantageous for clean energy sources. Mankind has a tendency to watch the pennies. The Energy Research Centre Netherlands (ECN) reports on energy prices and their dynamics. It seems that generating power by burning waste is the cheapest method at the moment (see figure 53).

	2007	(in respect of gas)	2020	(in respect of gas)
Gas-fired plants	0.06		0.06	
Waste incineration	0.055	(0.90 times)	0.05	(0.85 times)
Wind energy at sea	0.13	(2.10x)	0.08	(1.30x)
Wind energy on land	0.10	(1.60x)	0.08	(1.30x)
Solar energy	0.47	(7.80x)	0.30	(5.00x)

Figure 53: Cost-price of electricity (in euros) generated by different energy sources (compared to generation by burning natural gas) and the development over time (2007 and 2020)

At the beginning of 2007, the cost of a kilowatt hour of electricity generated by a gas-fired plant was 0.06 euro cents. The same amount of electricity generated by waste incineration at that time cost a fraction less, about 0.055 cents.

Gas-fired plants instead of coal-fired plants	10
Wind energy instead of coal-fired plants	50
Car running on ethanol instead of gasoline	100
Hybrid car instead of current gasoline car	250

Figure 54: Costs per ton of avoided CO2 emission (in euros)

This means that not all sources are equally efficient. It is advisable to focus, initially, on areas where the most can be achieved. It is evident that electricity generation emits 4 times as much CO2 gas as the use of private cars. Moreover, the costs involved in reducing electricity power plant emissions are quite a bit lower than with the mentioned cars. The price of a kilowatt of energy differs per type, but it is important to define which elements are included in this calculation. Is it purely production costs or is possible pollution as a result of production taken into account? Electricity generation by means of coal or gas creates pollution. This will create costs in the future which should actually already now be calculated in the cost-price in order to be able to compare it with clean (solar) energy. When external costs like damage to health and climate are taken into account, power from biomass is even cheaper than electricity generation from coal or gas. At least, that's what supporters say. These costs are not normally taken into account because they are not easy to calculate, but also because parties love to juggle figures in order to represent issues in a way that benefits them most.

10.3 Governmental policy

In order to stimulate energy transition and the use of sustainable energy, governments can implement various measures. Households and commercial organizations are not themselves continually prepared to take the initiative with regard to world improvement. Measures to protect our environment are often expensive and therefore do not always lend themselves to be used as spearheads. That is why rewards (subsidies) are coupled to certain actions, and certain blockades (taxes) are set up to prevent adverse effects. Governments must take a leading role in this process and they will have to steer market parties in the execution of their activities. Governments can directly influence execution or use their power via third parties, like the European Commission or supervisors.

10.3.1 Sustainable energy incentive schemes

The current subsidy system in the Netherlands is open to improvement. With the subsidy on 'green power', more consideration must be given to the actual development of electricity prices, and investors must have security over a period longer than ten years, according to a report that the Dutch Lower House drew up at the beginning of 2007. Minister Van der Hoeven of Economic Affairs expects to implement an improved subsidy scheme in 2008. Her predecessor, Joop Wijn, stopped the so-called Environmental Quality of Electricity Production subsidy on 18 August 2006 because the cost of it had got out of control and the environmental objective for 2011 would already be reached with the subsidies granted until then. The new regulation will be implemented with retroactive effect.

When making the afore-mentioned EQEP subsidy, a number of crucial mistakes were made. With subsidies for biomass-burning installations, insufficient consideration was given to the fact that these also have environmentally-unfriendly aspects. Using palm oil does not by definition provide less CO_2 emission than burning coal, for example. Burning biomass will in some cases create more problems than it prevents. Sustainability becomes an issue as soon as rain-forests are cut down for the production of biomass, crops for food production are used instead for energy products or when the quality of air around biomass power plants deteriorates. Furthermore, the granting of subsidies must also be linked to the actual energy price. This means that the

193

government's contribution can decrease as soon as the electricity price rises because alternative methods of production will then be more profitable.

The lack of subsidy regulation for green power is not good for the sustainable energy market in the Netherlands. Some projects (like wind farms) are not yet profitable. Knowledge must be increased, and that can best be done by on-the-job training. A number of production parks will therefore have to be started up.

The old EQEP subsidy was, according to the Dutch National Audit Office, not focussed enough on a reliable, clean and affordable sustainable energy supply. The new EQEP is called the Sustainable Energy Incentive Scheme (SEIS). This regulation covers the so-called non-remunerative costs of sustainable energy projects. It involves the difference between the costs of conventional power and those of sustainable power. Applicable to the SEIS is that the subsidy is dependent on the price of electricity, also during the period of the project. This was not the case with the EQEP as with that, the amount of the subsidy was fixed each year for projects that were starting up at the time. This sometimes resulted in excessive profits for companies, especially when prices rocketed. In addition, in the SEIS every category of sustainable generated power will be allocated a certain budget. The probable categories will primarily consist of combined heat and power systems, durable gas and durable electricity (biomass, solar energy, wind energy on land and wind energy at sea).

10.3.2 Small Fields policy

In order to secure the availability of energy, governments do not only need to take action with regard to new forms of energy. The conventional sources also require attention. The Small Fields Policy is a good example of securing the availability of natural gas. From the 'Oil and Gas in the Netherlands' report that Minister Van der Hoeven sent to the Lower House in the middle of 2007, it appears that Dutch natural gas extraction will drop by a quarter over the next few years. The reason for this is the depletion of small fields, and because there is a maximum annual production level imposed on the Groningen field. Extraction from small fields will drop by about 20 billion cubic metres over the next few years. That's a lot, especially knowing that the total annual production amounts to about 70 billion cubic metres.

The Small Fields Policy has always been focussed on stimulating extraction outside the

Groningen field, but it has not been working properly over the last few years. Little is being done to motivate companies to take on the development of very small fields. Reintroduction of the fiscal advantage, smaller governmental interest in the profits and changes in the concession policy would probably contribute towards getting extraction from small fields up to standard. The last contribution could even mean that existing development allocations could be withdrawn and then re-allocated. It is indeed highly likely that companies outside Europe applaud the development as at the moment the rights are only granted to European market parties.

10.4 Participation of developing countries

The Dutch government is therefore taking all sorts of measures to stimulate possible solutions. In order to cope with the problems in the field of energy, countries' governments will have to rally together behind important initiatives. But is it realistic to expect that China, India and other developing countries treat their environments in the same way as more developed regions? Is it fair to expect them to produce as sustainably as industrialized countries want to? The Western world has already sucked half of a number of natural sources completely dry. Upcoming countries have become the victims of this exploitation. The West is requiring that even poor countries produce clean energy, but can we really ask that of them? Is it ethical to think so? The Chinese, in any case, are stirring themselves nicely on this front. Oil company PetroChina published its first sustainability report, in which is stated that they used almost 20% less energy extracting oil and gas in 2006. In addition, they also saved 60 billion litres of water. Furthermore, improvements have been realized in the social sphere: health, social wellbeing, philanthropy and security. PetroChina's efforts have been rewarded with an international price.

On the other hand, the Chinese authorities reported in their climate plan that they want to prove themselves in the fight against climate change, but that willingness applies only as long as it is not at the detriment of the growth China is striving for. That again means that the realization of concrete objectives is hampered. The fact that China ratified the Kyoto Protocol, as opposed to the US, has everything to do with the fact that until 2012 the Chinese do not have to commit to emission ceilings. Within this period, the Chinese will surpass the Americans as the biggest polluters in the absolute sense. Relatively speaking per head of population, an American for the time being creates five times more pollution than an average Chinese person.

10.5 Poverty, food shortage and desertification

The problems surrounding poor countries are closely linked to commodities and their availability. Problems concerning the climate, like desertification, also play their part in poor countries in Africa. It is lucky that the world is trying to transform its energy portfolio to other energy sources, but this again encounters new problems. Demand for bio-fuels (see Chapter 8, section 8.6) is largely being met by using grains, sugar cane and palm oil, among other things. This, however, decreases the supply remaining for food consumption. The word-series, and the relationship and battle between the items, *'food'*, *'feed'* and *'fuel'* receive a lot of attention. Prices increase because of shortage and the poorest are unable to remain consumers. This makes the energy situation not only an environmental and economic matter, but also one of social significance. China has resolved no longer to produce bio-fuels that come from sources that could also be used for food.

	Soya Beans	Wheat	Maize	Sugar cane	Cole seed
Food for people	31 %	81	26	85	33
Food for animals	68	17	67	1	57
Bio-fuel	1	1	7	14	10
Total	100 %	100	100	100	100

Figure 55: Application of crops in percentages (Goldman Sachs, 2006; FD 2007)

Critics also claim that the Western world could solve the poverty problem, but that doesn't happen in practice because then the shortage on the commodities market would increase even further. Rich countries would be digging their own graves. So, on the one hand poor countries are ignored, and on the other, they have to contribute to solving the environmental problems caused mostly by the West. That is how the Africans, for example, experience the shocking consequences of our pollution. They are highly dependent on the climate as particularly agriculture and fishing largely determine the state of their economy. A large part of the African population lives in extremely dry regions, which makes them even more vulnerable to climate change; desertification, for example. Climate changes will not be the same, or occur to the same extent, everywhere on earth; in some areas the temperature will rise, while in others it will drop. More rainfall will fall in some parts, while other regions will suffer drought, and in places already subject to critical conditions, this could result in desertification. This would again lead to the worsening of current problems or to the creation of all sorts of new problems. Climate change is, therefore, not only an environmental problem, but also an economically-charged subject. Without any form of intervention, the gulf between rich and poor will only get bigger.

Governments will have to consider compensating neglected countries. That is actually quite simple; for example, by not producing any crops like maize, but producing jatropha and sugarcane instead. Reasons for a switch are highly valid, seeing as the mentioned products are the most efficient crops; furthermore, the profit (or a part of it) could end up at the place of production. Jatropha and sugarcane are best cultivated south of the equator, and that is the region where there is the most poverty. That would kill two birds with one stone. As long as Western countries want to be as independent as possible, they will not, unfortunately, enforce this sort of initiative.

10.6 The need for research

The subject of sustainability is relatively new; there are still many things to be discovered. But research takes a lot of time and knowledge is nowhere near the desired level. That also means that some businesses that are nowhere near as beneficial as they pretend to be are being set up and are slipping through the net.

And the use of catalytic converters could also do with being subjected to new research.

The metals platinum, palladium and rhodium are possibly of great value to the working of converters, but the process that precedes extraction could do with being scrutinized. Bringing the mentioned metals to the surface costs an extraordinary amount of energy. About 3 grams of platinum is needed to produce a soot filter for one of today's private cars. To produce these 3 grams of platinum, more than 120 kilos of fossil fuel is needed. That means that converters keep the air clean, whereas producing the converter ingredients results in a lot of CO_2 emission. Furthermore, in order to extract those 3 grams of platinum, one ton of sand, stone and grit has to be dug up. The material is dissolved in all sorts of acids, which strikes the landscape a severe blow. Nickel is extracted in a similar way. This metal is used in the batteries of some hybrid car engines.

Rhodium is the only metal that neutralizes nitrogen oxide (NOx). This exhaust gas causes acid rain and damages the ozone layer. Diesel engines in particular emit this gas, and it is exactly the transport sector which uses it that is showing the biggest growth, because of which the demand for rhodium is exploding. Because of the scarcity of this metal, the price shot up 1,500% between 2003 and 2007.

10.7 Energy-saving & Efficiency

The more pressing the situation becomes, the more mankind is realizing that we have to be more efficient with energy. This applies generally and involves savings, among other things, but it also involves efficiency levels of power plants. Levels of efficiency differ per production unit. The high-efficiency boiler that hangs in the cupboard at home produces an efficiency level of 90 to 95%. Compared to that, a gas-fired electricity plant gives a poorer performance as this averages out at 60%. The best coal-fired plant doesn't even reach 50%.

In addition to building new power plants, the old industrial park is regularly patched up. Unfortunately, a similar situation applies to that as to reconditioning car parts: the older a car gets and the more often it is refurbished, the greater the waste.

Efficiency crops up on all fronts within the energy sector. Bio-energy, for example, is not always as efficient as it should be. What's more, bio-energy in general is less efficient as a source of energy than fossil fuel. 7.5 tons of wood or straw is needed to produce 1 ton of synthetic fuel, whereas 1 ton of fuel can be produced from 1.3 tons of crude oil.

In spite of that, there is still a lot to be realized in the area of fossil fuel. Crude oil that gushes out of the ground contains energy that mankind readily utilizes. Even so, the viscous material first has to pass through all sorts of processes before it can be used and provide fuel for our cars. Through logistic activities, like burning off methane gas at extraction, transport to refineries, distilling processes whereby gasoline is made from petroleum and supply to the end-user, much of the original energy is lost. But it doesn't end with the converted form of energy that is used in cars. The engine is not as efficient as it should be either and wastes 70% of the basic material. Then the last bit is lost through the resistance of the tyres on the asphalt. The ultimate yield of the black gold extracted somewhere on this earth appears to be only 1%. Improvements in the field of efficiency could offer considerable savings.

Apart from all the initiatives to meet the problems surrounding energy, energy-saving and more efficient use of traditional (read: fossil) energy sources probably provide the most important contribution. The fact is, it meets efficiency-improvements, increases the industry's competitive power, reduces dependence on external energy suppliers and is good for the environment. In 25 years, the use of fossil fuels will still account for about 80% of the total. Petroleum will probably still represent 38% of the total use of all essential energy worldwide.

According to the *Tracking Industrial Energy Efficiency* research from the *International Energy Agency* (IEA), the global industry could be 18 to 26% more efficient with energy. Of course, then the best techniques available would have to be used everywhere. This would result in a reduction of both energy consumption (by about 6%) and CO_2 emission (about 10%). According to the *International Atomic Energy Agency* (IAEA), an improvement in efficiency would lead to an emission saving of at least 2 trillion tons of greenhouse gas, which is equal to 37% of current worldwide emissions. The reduction target can be reached in many ways, for which the use of sustainable sources would not even be needed.

These results are more significant than what most alternatives offer, and they are, moreover, easier in use, cheaper and faster to effect in general. A reduction of 20% would save the EU 100 billion euros in costs annually. This seems excellent and could raise the idea of using this amount for stimulating sustainable energy sources, but a great deal of money is needed to get the energy-saving process started. In order to increase the saving from 1 to 2%, it would cost the Netherlands alone about 3.5

billion euros a year. In 2007, McKinsey & Company calculated that the cost of achieving the environmental targets set by the European Union to 2020 is 1100 billion euros. The European Commission has drawn up an energy-efficiency plan that must be implemented by 2012. Every member state will have to make its own national plan. The measures relate to transport (mileage tax, toll gates), buildings and apparatus (refrigerators and water heaters). Statutory obligation that all houses must be provided with a so-called 'Energy Performance Certificate' took effect from 1 January 2008. This stamp is also jokingly called the 'house MOT'.

Purchasing saving-installations requires considerable investment. In the long-term the costs are often more than compensated for by savings in energy expenditure, but pre-finance often causes problems; psychological, for example.

In order to realize energy-saving and a more efficient use of our sources, we first need to work on awareness among the population. People often have no idea of all the uses energy is put to. Of the total amount of electricity needed for lighting, 10% is used for street lighting (lampposts). To be able to send 1 megabyte of information via internet, 200 grams of coal has to be stoked in a power plant; down-loading five books or DVDs via internet therefore requires a kilo of coal.

Awareness is an important step that has practical results. Some forms of energy-saving don't (or hardly) cost anything. Lowering the temperature of the thermostat in our homes already leads to a saving of 5%. Putting on a sweater instead of turning on the heating can therefore provide considerable saving. Other things that contribute to energy-saving are turning off the tap when we brush our teeth, drying the washing outside instead of in a dryer, and ensuring our cars have the correct tyre pressure. Soft tyres can increase gasoline usage by 3%.

Initiatives are being launched and measures taken on various fronts. From 2007, the American government hopes to save energy by bringing summer-time forward three weeks. In the future, winter-time will take effect from a later date and contribute towards pushing back energy consumption. There was a low-energy light bulb campaign in the Netherlands in 2007 following Australia who, in 2007, banned the use of ordinary light bulbs in favour of low-energy light bulbs. Minister Jacqueline Cramer of Environment (Ministry for Housing, Regional Development and the Environment) put forward the idea of copying the Australians. The savings the low-energy bulbs provide compared to the old-fashioned bulbs is staggering; one low-energy bulb uses an average of 70% less electricity than the traditional bulb. The biggest disadvantage was the purchase price, but when the significance of the low-energy bulb became known, the cabinet suddenly abolished the tax on cheap Chinese low-energy lamps, which means a low-energy bulb can now be bought without having to dig too deeply into the pockets.

CHAPTER 11:
Liberalization of the energy markets

11.1 Introduction

Until now this book has dealt particularly with energy products, their specific characteristics, pricing and attendant problems and the consequences they have on the energy markets. This chapter deals with the liberalization of the energy markets. This path was begun some time ago and it appears to be the right path leading to the solution of a number of problems. However, the transitional phase requires a government that will keep an eye on the progress and the processes, otherwise new problems will arise.

Energy markets are highly fragmented; each country or region has its own network that provides the transport (or supply) of energy. Due to the lack of couplings between these various networks (capacity limitations at interconnections), energy provision was organised purely locally in the past. Apart from that, the energy world contains other products, each of which has its own characteristics. Because of the reasons mentioned, we cannot talk of an energy market but of energy markets in the plural. Several energy markets have been increasingly integrating recently; this process is in full swing and will continue for quite some time as it involves expanding capacity for interconnectivity, harmonizing regulation of the mutually associated markets and further liberalization. Developments in local and national markets cannot be seen as separate from international energy markets, and vice versa. Therefore, both aspects are alternately dealt with in this book. In respect of local energy markets, this book is primarily focussed on the Netherlands.

11.2 Market power

Market power occurs in all sections of the energy sector. The state monopoly of Gasprom and the OPEC cartel are well-known examples. The specific characteristics of electricity can also promote market power; think of the limited possibility of storage, the fact that market demand is only to a limited degree influenced by the price, and the situation that means of production differ in marginal costs and flexibility. Market power is expressed, among other ways, in the withholding of capacity or manipulating high price levels. This is true for both national and cross-border market power. Three basic scenarios apply to cross-border market power, although it has to be said that the European Commission is increasingly getting it better under control. On the other hand, there is still a long way to go as the support of those who have it cannot be blindly expected in the attempt to get rid of market power.

The first scenario in which market power is expressed is the restriction of the import and export capacity that the market makes available. In the long-term, investment in the network is restricted; and in the short-term, the available capacity is too conservatively estimated. In 2007, German energy companies still had the function of producers and were TSOs (transmission system operators) at the same time without there having been unbundling from this activity.

The second scenario is to do with capacity that is allocated but not used. Concrete rules have been drawn up to avoid this phenomenon. This is also called the 'use it or lose it' principle; it means that unused capacity has to be offered to the market.

The third scenario refers to the practice of cross-border market power by parties that have production capacity on both sides of the border. For the Netherlands, that means that Electrabel can produce in both the Netherlands and in Belgium. E.ON has production capacity on both sides of the Dutch / German border. Both parties were subject to a malpractice investigation in the past, but the optimization of the separate portfolios in each country can be seen as normal. The fact that a foreign party in the Netherlands is not subject to the same scan as a native party doesn't make such investigations easy.

11.3 Liberalization

Energy markets have been governmentally-driven from way back. Energy was regarded as a primary necessity of life and because of that, energy companies were the property of the state. For the last few years people have been trying to break open the markets with the objective of transforming them into open and free markets with commercial enterprises. Liberalization stands for competition and freedom of choice. Energy consumers (households and industry) decide for themselves which energy supplier best meets their requirements. The competition that this creates between energy companies has to lead to optimal performances (an efficient market). The consumer can choose for the lowest price, or extra service or a combination of both. Governments and economists expect that competition will lead to more innovation (creativity) and clout. To this day there is an undesirable concentration in the energy markets; it is more the rule than the exception that only a few parties together hold a market share of 50% or more. All too often there is even talk of monopoly positions.

After a phased introduction, liberalization of the energy markets in the Netherlands was completed on 1 July 2004. It is a part of the basic principles of the European Union that covers free movement of goods, services, capital and people. Guidelines were laid down in the 'European Guidelines for Electricity' in 1996 and 'Guidelines for Natural Gas' were added in 1998. These guidelines set out which requirements an EU member state's national regulations have to satisfy in order to liberalise the markets for electricity and natural gas.

The European Commission's view determines the strength of the Dutch cabinet; ministers therefore regularly attune their policies to it. In June 2007, Neelie Kroes, European Commissioner for Competition, described how one European energy market could best be created. She referred to the thought prevalent within the European Commission: competition in the gas and electricity markets is not working well. She gave three reasons for that: firstly, national energy markets show too large concentrations and a lack of liquidity; secondly, there is a shortage of cross-border transport capacity; and finally, there is insufficient unbundling of network and trading activities. This results in consumers, like companies and households, not being given the desired (supply) security, affordable prices and sustainable energy that they have a right to. For the same reasons, new players in the local markets get insufficient access to the energy supply, networks and end-users. In order to improve a few things and to work in a European context, organisations issuing rules have to attune their policies to those of their colleagues in neighbouring countries. The electricity markets in the US and the United Kingdom were liberalised years before those in the EU, which is why both countries also have financial markets that are far further developed in the area of energy than those in European countries.

11.4 Governments

Governments are important players on the energy markets and they have to steer the liberalization process of the energy markets in the right direction. Transformation will take some doing; it won't take place without effort.

11.4.1 State Interests

Governments have had large interests in energy companies since way back because energy has always been regarded as a primary means of sustaining life. Liberalization is often linked with privatization, but that is not necessarily so. The West watches regretfully as Russia politicizes and monopolizes its commodity sources. The change from private to state-controlled companies happened at an earlier stage in many oil-rich countries in the Middle East. Much attention is given in the media to the mentioned regions, but the West is no stranger to such practices. We also see energy as being of national interest and various European governments hold large interests in energy companies. Under President Sarkozy, the French merged the companies *Suez* and *Gaz de France* during 2007 and then acquired 35 to 40% of the shares in the amalgamated product. Discussions have also begun about the possible merging of the (state-owned) nuclear energy company Areva, the industrial (nuclear) conglomerate Alstrom and the mining company Eramet. Areva is at the moment already 85% in the hands of the French state.

Other countries had similar influential share interests in 2007. The Italian government holds a 30% interest in the oil concern ENI and the Norwegians control about 65% of the merged result of *Norske Hydro* and *Statoil*. The Dutch government has a state interest of 50% in GasTerra and 100% in Gasunie and Gas Transport Services, while local and county authorities are large shareholders in energy companies like Essent and Nuon.

Governments play an important role in the energy-company arena of present-day Europe. Many energy companies try to create scale size and want to develop across country borders. As soon as take-overs are effective, governmental intervention regularly crops up. They try to hold on to their energy companies and avoid being swallowed up by foreign entities. The European court is taking Spain to the European Court of Justice because the country is interfering in the bid German E.On is making for

Spain's largest energy producer, Endesa. Spain is imposing conditions on the take-over, and that is totally against the rules.

Conflicting interests do not only occur internationally, they also happen at national level; people sometimes clash privately even within the government. The Finance and Economic Affairs departments have differing interests and therefore occasionally clash. Finance receives significant revenue from the sale of gas by GasTerra: this money is used to help finance the budget. In 2006 it amounted to about 8 billion euros. Economic Affairs has other interests and this department is trying to open up the energy market. They are responsible for the Independent Network Management Act, have to guarantee fair competition and hunt down parties trying to form cartels. GasTerra is seen by Economic Affairs as a party that does not meet the principles of a free market.

There are more conflicts going on in the cabinet. Environment (Ministry for Housing, Regional Development and the Environment) tries to propose and initiate many things in the field of sustainability and sustainable energy, but Economic Affairs has the last word as far as this subject is concerned. The department focuses especially on supply-security and cost-saving, and this regularly clashes with the clean and efficient objectives that Environment has in mind.

11.4.2 Choice, cost and quality

A large number of people on earth have to make do without energy. In South-east Asia, 1 billion people still do not have electricity. Governments must take care of their citizens. The Dutch energy policy is directed towards reliable, clean and affordable energy provision, and it is therefore important to the government that the supply-security or energy is maintained. It strives for the lowest possible market prices in order to provide households with this vital necessity. Besides this, the government also has to take the environment in which all this is happening into account. That means that it must always keep an eye on national interests, including employment. Governments have created various bodies in the area of legislation, regulation and supervision. In the Netherlands, DTe, part of the Dutch Competition Authority, is the watchdog for the energy markets. This body is responsible for the competitive position of energy producers and customers or consumers.

11.5 Unbundling

The European Commission considers unbundling vertically-integrated energy companies as essential because this sort of company has the natural tendency to protect its market from newcomers. They offer new parties access to their networks under discriminatory, unfavourable conditions. Scarcity, after all, results in the highest prices. Energy companies are now supposed to allow third parties into their networks; this is, however, not to their benefit and they prefer not to do it. Furthermore, energy companies do not eagerly invest in laying new transport systems as they then have to allow third parties to share in the new capacity. Capacity problems arise because of this underinvestment; artificially created scarcity.

People have been struggling with the unbundling of the Dutch energy markets since 1996. The third energy green paper of that same year from Hans Weijers, the Economic Affairs Minister at the time, already mentioned privatization of the energy sector. Annemarie Jorritsma held that ministerial post from 1998 to 2002 and she also had her say on the subject. At the beginning of 2004 the cabinet, on the initiative of the then Minister of Economic Affairs Laurens Jan Brinkhorst, came forward with a future vision for the Dutch energy markets. Energy companies would have to split their activities, whereby energy systems (gas-pipes and electricity grids) would be separate from the sale and supply of gas and electricity. Energy companies have long managed distribution networks themselves, while they were also responsible for supplying energy to consumers (private and commercial). In the previously regulated market, the government dictated the price and assigned suppliers.

The *Independent Network Management Act* (the so-called 'Unbundling Act') by which electricity and gas networks can be split from energy companies, was passed in the Netherlands in 2006. After the intended privatization of energy companies, the networks (electricity grids and gas pipelines) can still remain in the hands of the government, and are then still a natural monopoly. A maximum of 49% of the networks may be privatized. In October 2006, this unbundling became conditional via a motion from the Upper House. Foreign activities or alliances by or with Dutch energy companies must not jeopardize the public or the independent system operator. It can be expected in the near future that Dutch energy companies will become part of international concerns that will compete with each other on the European energy markets.

According to the cabinet, independent system operation is strictly essential in this, particularly because of the public interest in energy provision. On 7 June 2007, Minister Maria van der Hoeven of Economic Affairs decided that network companies and trading and/or production companies in the energy sector may no longer be part of one company. The resolution came into effect on 1 August 2007, from which time enterprises have 2½ years to become independent system operators.

Production, supply and trading of electricity and gas are placed under separate commercial companies. The current shareholders of the regional energy companies, local and regional authorities, could possibly sell their shares in the commercial enterprise after the split. The aim of unbundling is to create efficient, reliable and sustainable energy provision at as low as possible social cost. Consumer interest must be paramount. That is why the draft bill stipulates that control of the most important (regional) high-tension networks will be in the hands of TenneT, the company that now operates the national grid. This will be the backbone of the Dutch energy provision. Because of the centralization, TenneT can react more quickly, especially when necessary for supply security, and it is easier to supervise the quality of the system operator. A similar story applies for gas. The final piece of the liberalization was the unbundling of Gasunie into a network company (Gas Transport Services) and a trading concern (GasTerra) in 2005. The network company remained fully in the hands of the state, while only 50% of GasTerra is owned by the Dutch government. Oil companies Royal Dutch Shell and ExxonMobil each hold a quarter of the shares.

Liberalization stands for free pricing and aims for an as low as possible price via competition. Opponents of liberalization nevertheless argue that decontrolling the market will result in greater environmental problems, particularly because cheap coal and nuclear power plants will be used for this, which will again lead to high energy prices for the general public, who are charged prices based on the costs of expensive gas-fired plants.

Energy companies claim that they should be compensated for the unbundling because it involves a form of compulsory purchase. Their balance will be weakened by the loss of their primary assets and this will definitely not benefit the investment required in new plants and sustainable energy. But this argument is not balanced as the grids can be capitalized on. The proceeds can be used to expand and/or strengthen activities. Apart from differences of opinion between companies, countries also hold differing views about the unbundling of energy companies. In countries like Spain, England and

Denmark, unbundling is already a fact and is therefore no longer a hot potato. Germany and France in particular are having trouble with the plans, which is understandable considering which countries have the largest energy concerns (see figure 56).
Germany would very much like to see a distinction made between gas and electricity. They are more prepared to continue with electricity than they are for gas. The high-tension networks in Germany are not in the hands of one company as they are in the Netherlands, (TenneT), but are owned by the four energy giants, E.On, RWE, EnBW and Vattenfall.

		Turnover (2006)	Corporate value (2006)
EON	Germany	68	73
EDF	France	59	113
RWE	Germany	44	44
Suez *)	France	44	52
Enel	Italy	39	52
Gaz de France *)	France	28	34
Centrica	UK	24	21
Endesa	Spain	20	43
Vattenfall	Sweden	16	unknown
Iberdola/			
Sc.Power	Spain / UK	14	42
EDP	Portugal	10	15
Gas Natural	Spain	10	17
Essent	Netherlands	6	15
Nuon	Netherlands	5	12
Dong	Denmark	5	unknown
Statkraft	Norway	2	unknown

*) Gaz de France and Suez merged in 2007

Figure 56: Largest energy concerns in Europe (in billion euros) (FD, 2007).

Opening the energy markets will lead to parties merging or making acquisitions. Expanding scale size gives parties more purchasing power (low purchase prices) and ensures that the costs can be spread over several customers.

In the Netherlands, the intended merger between Nuon and Essent stuck out most. The two largest energy companies in the country wanted to merge, but there proved to be all sorts of snags attached. The NMa wanted to protect the home market from a monopoly position as the intended combination would gain a market share of 60%. The NMa therefore required that the combination (temporarily) dispose of or outsource two power plants the size of 1,900 megawatts and sell 1 million customers. The shares of both companies are for the most part in the hands of local and regional authorities who could not agree to the exchange ratio. Nuon would get 45% of the combination, whereas many people and Nuon itself thought that half better represented the relationship. What with one thing and another, the merger was eventually abandoned. The combination would have created an energy giant, but at European level the combined company could still have been labelled a Tom Thumb (see figure 56).

CHAPTER 12:
The financial markets

12.1 Physical delivery versus financial settlement

As well as the integration of various energy markets (from local to international), there is also integration of energy markets in the financial world.

Each product has its own markets and peculiarities, which also applies to the whole commodity sector. Gold is a typical example of a commodity of which little is extracted but in which there is a great deal of trade. Iron-ore is a product of which much is extracted but in which trade is extremely thin.

Energy markets have always chiefly been typified by physical delivery, but nowadays it is increasingly more a matter of financial products that are 'cash settlement' only. Tangible exchange of energy products remains essential for energy-requirement provision, but the underlying value of the goods-flow compared to the size of the cash-flow is becoming less significant.

The underlying trade in commodity markets and energy markets is the physical flow of goods or products. Invoicing of these reflects the underlying cash-flow, but the actual financial cash-flows are much bigger. The physical flow and the accompanying cash-flow are restricted because of capacity limitations and the availability ceiling of the products themselves. Virtual trade can create unlimited growth of cash-flow. Risks can be infinitely moved between involved parties my means of financial products. Trade is sometimes vehemently done in energy products by means of these instruments, but some involved parties will never see or use the underlying value. The reasons for this are that parties use the trade in a speculative sense, purely to make money; others cover their company's activities risk via specific financial products and manage their portfolio risk in that way. Derivatives (see Chapter 14) are excellent instruments for optimizing risk management. Cash-flows that involve these derived products increase spectacularly and are many times larger than cash-flows linked to the underlying value (the physical flow of products). Derivatives are being far more frequently applied in energy markets and this is an important expression of the integration of energy markets in the financial markets.

12.2 Exchanges and bilateral trade

Financial markets are not restricted to the exchange system. Most trade in financial products does not go through the exchange but 'over-the-counter' (OTC). This privately-negotiated, or bilateral, trade is generally more sizeable than exchange-regulated trade. Many professional parties use the OTC markets. Private parties are forced to use the central platform of exchanges. Nevertheless, even some exchanges are not accessible to them, especially if the traded products involve physical delivery.

With bilateral trade, two parties agree a transaction, but unlike exchange-regulated trade, a guaranteed settlement is lacking. Should one of the parties default, through bankruptcy for example, the other is left holding the baby and has nowhere to turn for help. Despite those involved generally being large and reputable parties, such situations regularly occur. The consequences go without saying. By carrying out direct trade, without the mediation of the exchange, parties do indeed save possible costs, but counterparty risk or credit risk is applicable. Settlement of transactions entered into via the exchange is guaranteed (*clearing*). Furthermore, an exchange guarantees transparent pricing and anonymous trading. The exchange will also never make public which (counter) parties are active in the market. On the other hand, OTC trading, contrary to exchange transactions, offers the possibility of creating specifically-tailored contracts. The conditions can be fully geared to the wishes of the involved parties. Only standardized contracts are traded on the exchange.

The relationship between the number of OTC deals and the amount of exchange-regulated transactions differs per product and over the time measured. Credit derivatives, for example, were solely developed by and for large parties and were, in the first instance, only traded bilaterally for many years. Nevertheless, the first credit derivative was listed on an exchange in 2007. The energy sector is also characterized by a significant portion of transactions that take place outside the exchange. This is linked to the history and the characteristics of the sector: commodity and energy markets have been characterized by bilateral trade from way back. This form of business is usual for large parties: governments, energy giants and energy-wasting industrial organisations regularly mutually agree long-term contracts.

12.3 Price development of commodities

Long before the application possibilities of gas and oil were discovered, trade was vehemently being done in commodities. Rice was the first commodity traded on the financial markets, but it was tulip bulbs that caused the first bizarre incident in the 17th century. 'Tulip mania' involved a veritable run on tulip bulbs. There was a craze in the former Republic of the Seven United Low Countries between 1630 and 1637; tulip bulbs were sold for unprecedentedly high prices. At its height, one bulb cost even more than a complete house alongside the Amsterdam canals.

	Price rises	Period
Coal	150 %	2005-2007
Natural gas	300	2002-2007
Oil	400	2002-2007
Uranium	1,600	2000-2007
Palladium	200 %	2004-2007
Platinum	300	2004-2007
Nickel	300	2006-2007
Rhodium	1,500	2003-2007

Figure 57: Price rises of commodities

There have been several price explosions over the last few years: in respect of commodity prices themselves (see figure 57), but also indirectly via investments in shares (see figure 58).

	Sector	Return	Period
Gazprom	Oil	1,200 %	2001-2005
Sibneft	Oil	2,100	2001-2005
Lukoil	Oil	3,100	1998-2005
Energy fuels	Uranium	4,200	2005-2006
Cameco	Uranium	27,500	2004-2007
Paladin	Uranium	34,000	2000-2006

Figure 58: Exchange gain shares with interests in the energy world

12.4 Foreign reserves and development of currencies

Interests and positions in commodities or energy products that are listed in a currency other than the domestic currency are not only liable to price risk but also to currency risk. Investors or producers will generally benefit when the asset in which they have an interest increases in value, but if, in the same period, the exchange rate of the currency in which the product is settled drops comparatively more sharply, then the result on balance will still be a negative one. The oil price went up from 10 dollars a barrel in 1998 to almost 100 dollars a barrel in 2007, but the value of the euro rose from 0.80 dollars in 2000 to 1.40 dollars in 2007. Because of the altered rate of exchange, the impact of the rise of the oil price was much bigger in America than it was in Europe. Currency risk is generally regarded as undesirable and that is why an investor, producer or buyer/consumer/client can choose to cover this risk, by means of derivatives, for example. On the other hand, they could decide to take the gamble and anticipate doubly favourable developments. This decision is dependent not only on the view of those involved, but also on their risk perception. In other words, what is the risk tolerance of this party, their shareholders and other interested parties?
The dollar has been regarded as a 'safe haven' since way back. As soon as the world was subjected to a politically-unstable situation in the past, like war, investors on mass took refuge in the dollar. Until recently, the currency was considered stable. Reality has shown, however, that the dollar is loosing ground in several respects compared to

217

the euro. In severe times, the euro is increasingly being seen as an alternative for the dollar. This has significant consequences for all sorts of countries' policies. By trading with other countries, including in oil and gas, they are paid in an agreed currency; often this is the dollar. When a country exports more than it imports, a trade surplus is created and the country's 'money supply' increases. Seeing as until the present day the dollar is usually chosen, this currency is the world's official 'reserve currency'.

Increasingly fewer governments extol the virtues of the dollar. Iran is the world's fourth largest oil producer and therefore exports huge quantities of the black gold. Trading in oil has been a dollar-related business since way back. All products and every transaction is priced and settled in dollars. At the end of 2006, Iran intimated that it would in future carry out its foreign transactions in euros. A representative also said that the country is planning to convert its foreign reserves to euros. Processes like this lead to sales pressure on the dollar and stimulate demand for the euro. The result is a shift of exchange rate, which starts a spiral effect and the price of the dollar ends up even further under pressure. Iran's action is therefore a powerful political charge. Nevertheless, it seems sensible for Iran to spread its reserves across several currencies. Countries diversify their currency portfolios by not only relying on the dollar. Iran is, incidentally, no longer alone as other countries recently played the same game. The United Arab Emirates also revealed plans to exchange a large part of its dollar reserves for euros. This diversification decreases their dollar dependency. The objective is to keep 10% of the reserves in euros; at the end of 2006 that was only 2% of the 25 billion dollars. Because of diversification, interest for the euro, the Japanese yen and the English pound is increasing. Central banks jointly manage 2,875 billion dollars worth of reserves in foreign currencies. The majority is invested in dollars; the euro is in second place. Only 4% (115 billion dollars) is invested in English pounds and the Japanese yen scores 3%.

Many Gulf States have linked their currencies to the dollar. In 2010 a number of them want to form a monetary union, which is why they have made certain agreements regarding the link with the dollar. The link has a historical basis: in the past, the Americans suggested offering military protection to countries that priced their oil in dollars. Due to the weakening of the dollar, certain countries are now inclined to abandon the link with the dollar. The Kuwaitis and Saudis had already decided to do this in 2007.

Even the Chinese yuan has a link with the dollar. Initially the yuan was only linked to the American dollar, but it is now also linked to the euro and the yen. At the end of 2006, the Americans claimed that China was keeping the yuan artificially low in order to export more. China's foreign currency reserves had then already passed the 1000 billion dollar limit. Estimates vary, but the consensus shows that 65 to 70% was held in dollar-related products, including foreign bonds. The counter hasn't stopped yet: in 2007 the Chinese reserves increased by 20 billion dollars a month.

China	1,202
Japan	890
Russia	360
Taiwan	266
South Korea	251
India	204
Eurozone	192
Brazil	144
Singapore	141
Hong Kong	136
United States	41

Figure 59: Countries with the largest currency reserves (in billion dollars) (FD, 2007)

12.5 Sovereign Wealth Funds

A few countries that previously had little influence in global economy are suddenly a force to be reckoned with due to all manner of developments in the energy sector. Oil and gas producing countries like Russia, Venezuela and a number of Arab states, earn a lot of money because of the rapidly-rising prices. Other countries are dependent on the supply of these energy sources and are increasing being forced to dance to these suppliers' tunes.

219

China is also beginning to increasingly stamp its mark on world politics. In 2006, the country had a balance of trade surplus of about 184 billion dollars, almost totally thanks to its trade with America. The rest of its international transactions showed more equilibrium. The *Gulf Cooperation Council*, the Persian Gulf region's equivalent of the European Union, ended up with a trade surplus of 239 billion dollars in 2006. According to the IMF, the oil-producing countries achieved a trade surplus with the rest of the world of 1,700 billion dollars between 2002 and 2007. The size of this sum is indeed hugely dependent on the oil price seeing as almost all their export is dependent on petroleum. More than half of this money ends up in the Middle East. This in turn stimulates consumer interest, which mainly results in increased consumption in Europe and Asia, from which the European economy then profits, and the circulation of money is in full swing.

The Americans also profit from increasing consumer interest in other countries. Japan and China finance America's national debt as they have large portfolios in American government bonds. The Chinese finance about 10% of the American deficit by purchasing government bonds, and therefore the US is hugely dependent on China. But oil-exporting countries also chip in. About 80% of the petrodollars ends up with their governments (central banks). They then use this money to invest worldwide. Between 2002 and 2005, more than 800 billion was invested in this way, mainly via Sovereign Wealth Funds (SWF). Norway, Russia and Saudi Arabia together invest 60% of the worldwide petrodollars; which is a good thing because the American national debt rises by 2 billion dollars daily. At the end of 2006, the total debt amounted to 8,600 billion dollars and in that same year America paid about 125 billion dollars in interest to foreign countries, or 310 million dollars a day.

12.6 Regulation & transparency

Until recently, the Sovereign Wealth Funds usually put their money in safe government bonds, but now their assets are continuing to increase they are looking for investments that offer more risk and higher expected potential. China, for example, is not only planning to diversify its foreign currency reserves by investing in a currency other than the dollar, but it will convert increasingly more of the reserves into commodities. The Chinese government already greatly invests in foreign oil and gas fields, and doesn't hesitate to increasingly apply a similar strategy to metals and other materials. Initially, according to several Chinese sources, it involves a fund of 200 billion dollars. The investments of such funds lay a serious foundation under the commodity prices.

The mentioned state-controlled institutions also perform many take-overs in the Western business world. Americans and Europeans experience this as extremely threatening. The Dutch Bank (DNB) proposed in its quarterly report of September 2007 that transparency of these funds must be increased, especially now that it appears that more than 30 countries already have a SWF. The joint assets of these funds amount to about 2,500 billion dollars, and that exceeds the value of all hedge funds put together. According to an earlier report from Morgan Stanley, this sum could increase to 12,000 billion dollars by 2015, and that would even exceed the world's total financial reserves.

United Arab Emirates	875
Singapore	430
Saudi Arabia	300
Norway	300
China	300
Russia	100
Kuwait	70
Australia	40
Alaska	35
Brunei	30
South Korea	20
Malaysia	18
Taiwan	15
Canada	13
Iran	11

Figure 60: Government-controlled investment funds (in billion dollars) (FD, 2007)

Developments on the financial markets described up till now mostly relate to international level, but the integration of energy markets and the financial world has also undergone all sorts of developments at national and regional level. Examples are: regulation (this and next section), market-linking (see 12.7) and new price mechanisms (see 12.8), although this last category can also have a global character.

12.6.1 Regulators

Governments regulate all sorts of sectors, for which purpose they create various specific agencies whose job it is to perform the task. The Dutch Bank (DNB) was just pulled in as regulator of the country's financial stability, but for the energy sector, DTe and AFM are especially important.

12.6.1.1 NMa and DTe

In the Netherlands, the implementation of the Electricity Act 1998 and the Gas Act, as well as regulation of compliance with them, was and is the task of the DTe (*Directie Toezicht Energie* – Energy regulation service), which is the responsibility of the Ministry of Economic affairs and is a part of the NMa (Netherlands Competition Authority). The mission of DTe is to make sure that the energy markets function as well as possible; this means, among other things, that access to the grids is guaranteed, that sufficient transparency exists and that the consumer is protected from possible misuse of suppliers' positions of power. In the past, for example, the DTe established that the surplus profits made by network companies come from too-high rates that have been fixed by the government.

The position of power is due to the size of concentration on the energy markets, which is high. And this does not only apply internationally, but also specifically for the Dutch situation. The three largest energy companies in the Netherlands (Essent, Nuon and Eneco) had a market share of about 80% at the beginning of 2007. This is indeed about 5% lower than two years before, but still extremely high. The slight drop in percentage is the result of liberalization of the market, which opens the field to new players. This process has to make the playing field more competitive and reduce the position of power held by the large players.

To be able to supply energy, energy suppliers have to have a permit from the regulator. DTe issues these licences after checks have been carried out, or if the intended supplier meets certain requirements. Different requirements are fixed for the supply of gas and for the supply of electricity, which results in there being two separate permits.

12.6.1.2 AFM
Energy exchanges are, of course, subject to legislation and regulation. In the Netherlands, the energy exchange Endex is subject to the regulation of the Authority of Financial Markets (AFM). Each exchange that lists products that have a term of longer than a few days has to have a licence from the AMF. Energy exchange APX Group is exempt from regulation by the AFM in the Netherlands because on its platform it only offers the Dutch market products that have a few days' duration. These products also only require physical delivery. Apart from this, Endex is also authorized to list financial instruments.

In the Netherlands, APX focuses primarily on the balancing market where market parties trade products in order to optimize their portfolios. APX has, incidentally, obtained a licence in England from the British equivalent of the ADM, the Financial Services Authority (FSA), which allows APX to offer a trading platform for long-term financial instruments there.

12.6.2 Chinese walls and hallmark institutions

As yet energy markets are neither fully developed nor fully transparent. Important information is often only known in closed circles and not made public. In order to avoid market-sensitive information being leaked, integrated energy giants should implement not only a legal separation but also a practical one between their network divisions and their commercial or delivery departments. Energy companies that both produce and supply electricity could take advantage of this combination. If they know that production is coming to a halt, whether intentionally or through technical defect at the plant, or if they have information about a competitor's transport contract, they can anticipate the situation by making transactions in the market. Their counterparties are not aware of the situation and have to contend with information deprivation. In Scandinavia more transparency of market parties is already being demanded because such information is deemed relevant to the market.

The concept of *Chinese Walls*, which is deeply rooted in the financial markets, has of yet left no real footprint in the Dutch energy markets. The knowledge of financial markets and competence in trade and risk management of many parties who participate in the energy sector are not comparable to the level of knowledge and competence of a derivatives-trading firm or a bank's dealing room.

At some energy companies, traders are responsible for managing the company's trading portfolio and can also make transactions on their own account (*propriety trading*). It is particularly the result achieved with this personal portfolio that is crucial at the end of the year for the size of the bonus the trader receives. It was not an exception for traders to make transactions on the so-called prop-book only to transfer the deal, without any hesitation, to the company book account as soon as it seemed that the pricing was developing to their disadvantage.

With the development of the energy markets it is advisable to also expect those involved in this area to attach themselves to a hallmark institute for financial parties, like the *Dutch Securities Institute* (DSI). Regulators will have to demand of employers that they affiliate themselves to such a body; while in turn the same employers may expect their employees to register with the same organization. Ethical trading and honest behaviour are important conditions that first have to be satisfied before the designation 'mature market' can be attributed.

12.7 Market coupling

Consolidation in the energy sector has recently been the order of the day and looks as if it will continue to be so for some time. Besides mergers and take-overs, the integration of energy markets in the financial markets has already been referred to. That also involves market coupling. The energy networks of various countries have been linked to each other in some way for years in order to cope with possible calamities, but the (cross-border) transport capacity leaves much to be desired. The networks of the Netherlands and Germany are certainly not adequately coupled at the moment, which is a shame as the need for international energy-flows continues to increase.

As soon as price differences appear, need for import exists in the most expensive country; and in the country where the price is lowest, the desire to export bubbles to the surface. The objective is to keep this up for as long as supply and demand are in balance. In other words: in an optimal situation, the physical flow of energy continues until the price differences are arbitrated away. Unfortunately, the transport capacity is generally insufficient for that, which results in the need only partially being met. The border capacity is not only limited in the physical sense but a large part of the existing volume has also already been sold via long-term contracts (contractual restriction). Apart from that, something else affects the Netherlands. The large-scale wind farms in Northern Germany flood the Netherlands with electricity: when the wind suddenly picks up, the Dutch national grid is put out of balance as the grid is not equal to the generation capacity produced by 16,000 wind turbines.

12.7.1 Trilateral Market Coupling (TLC)

Market coupling is the linking of networks and the organizing of a system to which exchanges and TSOs are connected. Regulations and clearing & settlement also have be geared to each other. By optimally using the transport capacity between countries, electricity is transported from the country where it is cheapest (lowest production costs) to the country where the price is highest. Free market system in optimal form. Germany and Luxemburg will also be joining the TLC project in 2009. Scandinavia and Great Britain are also expected to be coupled with this network; the NorNed and BritNed cables (see Chapter 4, section 4.3.3) will provide a significant contribution to the much-needed international transport capacity. Until that time, market fragmentation remains the energy world's biggest problem. Countries and regions have, after all, always only relied on their own local networks.

By implementing the market coupling of the Netherlands, Belgium and France, the spot markets in the field of electricity in these countries (APX, Belpex and Powernext) are linked together. Since Trilateral Market Coupling became effective on 21 November 2006, maximum available capacity is being better utilized. Import and export depends on the price differences between the Netherlands and its neighbours, but also on available capacity. When (limited) capacity is optimally utilized, a price difference can still occur as electricity prices do not only differ per region, but also from day to night. These so-called peak and off-peak loads differ per country.

12.7.2 The copper plate

The conclusions that can be drawn a year after the introduction of TLC are extremely positive. Because of TLC, the price differences between the participating countries have decreased, price levels have dropped and available transport capacity is being better utilized. The lower prices are particularly favourable for consumers, therefore also for the general public. That justifies the coupling and meets the government's requirements. Partly because of that, vehement attempts are being made to expand the market coupling and involve countries surrounding the Netherlands in the project. The objective is to create one Northwest European electricity market.

Several countries in Europe have picked up the market coupling initiative and have launched plans for introducing similar ideas. Scandinavia had already coupled its market in a similar way even before TLC came about. It is expected that, in time, the coagulated markets will again flow together. If this mission is successful, one large European electricity market (copper plate) will exist. Electricity will then increasingly be regarded as a commodity. Until recently, it could scarcely be transported over large distances.

12.7.3 The gas roundabout

Just like the coupling of the electricity grids and the accompanying power markets, the gas pipelines (and gas markets) of countries can also be coupled to each other. This process has already been started. It must be said here that some (existing) pipelines are already a few thousand kilometres long: these connect the various networks of several countries together. Even the Netherlands, or maybe especially the Netherlands, optimizes the coupling of its systems to those of surrounding countries. The countries involved in the project have agreed to supply gas to each other if one of the countries has a shortage. This contributes to the supply security of the individual countries and strengthens all of their positions. Collaboration is becoming increasingly more important because the gas position of European countries in relation to the rest of the world is continuing to weaken. Imports will become more sizeable and take place over greater distances. The position of the Netherlands will change drastically. If the country wants to hold onto the strong position it has now, significant changes will have to be made. The Netherlands will have to make considerable investments in the expansion of the network. Gas Transport Services (GTS) plays a major role in this. The independent natural gas system operator is responsible for the uninterrupted supply of gas in the national network. GTS has to ensure that there is always sufficient capacity available in order to guarantee a flexible, secure, viable and sustainable supply of gas.

Now that natural gas reserves in the Netherlands are running low, the government is trying to stimulate companies to import gas from foreign countries and store it in their empty fields so that effective use can be made of them, just as with the intricate network, and enable the Netherlands to continue to play a key role in the gas market in the future. Successful introduction of the Netherlands as (Western) Europe's 'gas roundabout' will cost a great deal of effort as countless conditions will have to be met. Geographically, the Netherlands is centrally situated and has good geological features. The network in the Netherlands is extremely well-branched, of high quality and logistically particularly interesting. Moreover, GTS has an excellent level of knowledge and a wealth of experience in the field of gas transport.

The Netherlands is increasingly being used for the transit of gas to, for example, the British market. In 2007, Gasunie announced that it was going to invest about 1.5 billion euros in its network in order to cope with the growing import flows. The money is to be used for laying 450km-long pipes and for compressor stations. More import possibilities also mean less dependence, and therefore more supply security. The government has also adapted the regulations so that 'Groningen' can ask higher prices for the transport of gas.

Apart from the mentioned advantages, there are also a number of issues to which much more attention needs to be paid. The more liberalized the market becomes, the more the chance of success. That chiefly means liberalization in the practical sense, and not only in word (regulation) but also in deed. This relates, among other things, to effective places of trade, transport, storage and the production and purchase of important things to do with gas. In addition, value-creating issues like gas conversion are significant. That means that there must be capacity available in the mentioned areas. Until recently, however, transport capacity and conversion capacity had often already been auctioned for the long term. The building of additional (transport) capacity (*Open Season*) and preferably also some level of over-capacity are therefore issues that are highly desirable. But an eye has to be kept on newcomers in the market; they must also be given a fair chance of opting for capacity. Until now that has only been so to a limited extent. During a so-called *Open Season*, GTS consults market parties in regard to their requirements in the area of future transmission capacity. *Open Season 2012* is chiefly aimed at market parties who want to contractually fix transport capacity at border points and at storage compounds.

The more market parties like GasTerra sell gas via the virtual TTF trading platform, the more form the idea of the gas roundabout will take. This can carry extra weight if it takes place via a central market place like APX. The more the liquidity on the platform increases, the easier it will be for parties to trade gas. In this case, flexibility seems to be the key. The easier it is for parties to store, import, export, buy, sell, buy more and sell more gas, the more likely it is that the gas roundabout will succeed. Small monopoly positions will then have to cease to exist; only then will the roundabout really stand a chance of being a real gas junction where everything comes together, and not end up as a fly-over. As yet, however, there is still a great deal to do in the areas of trade, conversion and transport.

12.8 Valuation, pricing and price mechanisms

12.8.1 Complexity

In free financial markets, prices are always determined by supply and demand. These two elements can be influenced by various factors, a number of which were extensively covered in Chapter 1, section 1.4. When these are examined, insight into the complexity of pricing on energy markets is gained. The large number of factors and the related risks make it extraordinarily difficult to price products properly. The price of natural gas is dependent, among other things, on the price of electricity, coal, crude oil, oil-related contracts and CO_2 emission rights. But storage, market accessibility, political games, liquidity and LNG prices also have repercussions for the price. It should be said here that *the* price of energy doesn't actually exist; nor does *the* price of oil, gas or coal because prices differ per region and quality.

The problem of correctly pricing energy products is made even more difficult by the non-transparency of many relevant issues. Doubt can, for example, often be cast on reserve figures, and exercising control of them is almost impossible as governments simply do not it. This is harmful for transparency in the market.

Dutch energy prices have more than doubled over the last ten years and are now among the highest in Europe. The average Dutch household paid about 2,300 euros on energy costs in 2006, whereas they paid about 1,000 euros in 1996. The average European's energy costs in 2006 were 1,730 euros. Only in Denmark and Italy in 2007 was the price of electricity more expensive than in the Netherlands, whereas gas in Denmark, Sweden and Germany was more expensive. There are various reasons for this. According to some people it is the result of liberalization and commercialization of the market. The energy companies claim that the duties imposed by the government on energy should be reduced. Final supply to households makes up only 10% of the energy rates; duties account for 30%, as do network tariffs (fixed by DTe) and wholesale prices (arrived at on the world market). That last factor has to do with the fact that oil prices have risen sharply, which also makes gas more expensive as the gas price is linked to the oil price. Because the Netherlands chiefly uses gas for the production of electricity, the price of electricity has also risen relatively sharply.

By liberalizing the energy markets it is expected that pricing will be reached in a free way, which it is often not in Europe. Electricity prices are sometimes more determined by monopoly positions and politics than by business economics. The largest energy company in Europe, the French EDF, which only at the end of 2005 became partially privatized with 70% of the shares remaining in the hands of the French government, had to promise, for example, not to increase the electricity price in France by more than inflation.

It deserves to be said that blame is very quickly laid at certain party's feet. In a free market, pricing is subject to volatility, which sometimes causes huge price changes. The acute shortage of production capacity, transport capacity and availability of mineral commodities force the price up. The free-market principle and simultaneous control of prices do not go together.

12.8.2 Production costs

The price of oil generally swings around the level of the most expensive marginal production costs in the industry. This last cost is determined by the cost-price of an extra barrel of oil at the world's most expensive place of production. The production of one barrel of oil at production locations in the Middle East, where oil is relatively easily produced, costs about 2 or 3 dollars. The cost of a barrel of oil produced in the North Pole region or made from tar sands from Canada, is tens of dollars. On balance, countries like Saudi Arabia receive a price that is comparable to the price paid for the most expensively produced oil.

A similar story applies to gas and electricity. The cost-price of electricity is determined by the production costs. These are dependent on, among other things, generation capacity, fuel prices, interconnection capacity, the weather and the price of CO_2 rights. Seeing as coal is quite a bit cheaper than gas, energy production in coal-fired plants is cheaper than in gas-fired plants. Because Germany has more coal-fired plants (and wind farms) than the Netherlands, the production costs of electricity are generally lower in Germany. In a country like the Netherlands, electricity prices are uniform. That means that electricity generated in coal-fired plants is sold at the same tariff as electricity generated in gas-fired plants. The ultimate price is further dependent on taxes and excise duties, which differ from country to country.

Netherlands	20.00
United States	12.00

Figure 61: Price of electricity (in €/MW*h) (2007)

12.8.3 Spare capacity

Prices in a free market are dependent on two factors: firstly, the relationship between production capacity and demand; and secondly, the availability of affordable, additional production capacity. Almost all cheap electricity-production locations are owned by the establishment. This group of energy companies produces at low cost because, to a large extent, their plants have generally already been written off. If this also involves coal-fired, nuclear fusion or hydropower plants, production can be carried out at even lower costs. At the beginning of 2007, these costs averaged out at about 20 euros per megawatt hour. Capacity built around this time was to result in costs of about three times as much: 60 euros per megawatt hour. In addition, establishment energy companies often have access to additional capacity in the form of gas-fired plants. These are much more flexible than coal-fired plants because they require a shorter change-up time. Gas-fired plants usually determine the prices in the market, whereby even electricity generated cheaply in coal-fired plants, for example, is sold at higher (gas-fired) prices. A retail price that represents many more times the production cost is not an exception. A solution to this problem could be the government obliging energy companies to hold on to a certain amount of spare capacity. Spare capacity is an important subject. It is applicable on all fronts, including OPEC, as similar methods to that described above also apply to the oil branch.

12.8.4 Indexation of the gas price

The gas price is often linked to the oil price. The gas price fixed in many European gas contracts is generally based on the price of North Sea oil (Brent). This price correlation has its roots in the Netherlands. After the Groningen-field find at the end of the 1960s, the economic value of gas had to be determined. At that time it was decided to base the gas price on the price of the alternatives that were being used on a large-scale. Until the moment that natural gas reserves were found in the north of the Netherlands, people mostly used heating and domestic fuel oils. This method of pricing was adopted by many neighbouring countries, where it is still a much-used method of determining the price. Yet there is the increasing inclination to process the market value of gas in privately-negotiated contracts. In this way, the so-called *gas-to-gas* market is created.

12.8.5 Benchmarks & indices

The achievements of financial products are often judged by a particular benchmark. Indices are often used as a benchmark. An index is a compiled portfolio which includes various products that, despite differences, share a common denominator. Think of a fruit basket. This generally contains a wide assortment of products but they all belong to the *fruit* category.

The components of an index can have a certain assessment, by which not all ingredients count equally in the scoring. Choosing to bring in an assessment factor can be justified: certain components are bigger than others, which makes the index a better reflection of the market. A price index reflects the price level of a specific group of products. An index reflects the price-level developments of the underlying group. The market can use an index as an indicator, which allows the development of the relevant product category to be followed. It is important that the market regularly asks itself whether or not an index is still representative of the market; because of the dynamics of the market, things can change suddenly. This applies to a large extent to the energy markets that occasionally show severe growing pains during the maturing process. Just like a child, these growing markets needs to be guided if they are not to go in the wrong direction.

12.8.5.1 A new oil benchmark

A new oil exchange sprang up in the Middle East on 1 May 2007. The *Dubai Mercantile Exchange* (DME) opened its doors in the United Arab Emirates. This strengthens Dubai's ambition to become the financial heart of the region. The Middle East appears to be the missing link in 24-hour worldwide trade. The time difference between the Far East and Europe is just a bit too big.

DME lists future contracts on oil and will be introducing options in the near future. The exchange distinguishes itself from other oil exchanges like NYMEX and ICE by having introduced a future contract that has crude oil from Oman as its underlying value. Oman, a neighbour of the United Arab Emirates, is not a member of OPEC; the oil that comes from there is representative of most oil in and around the Gulf. The most well-known oil futures and most important benchmarks worldwide are still based on *West Texas Intermediate* (WTI), which is produced in the US, and on Brent oil from the North Sea. The differences between these two oils and the majority of the reserves in the Middle East are essentially important. The composition of the bulk of the crude material from the desert is significantly different than the compositions of Brent and WTI. Most oil in the world is found in the Middle East, and seeing as the reserves in the West are running low, the relative significance of the Middle East continues to increase.

The Arab countries began with the easy-to-exploit fields where reasonably sweet, light oil is found, but most of the remaining reserves are to be found in the interior. In general, the oil in these regions is much sourer and heavier. It is therefore understandable that new benchmarks are being developed for this. DME's future contracts will contribute to increasing transparency in respect of pricing. Furthermore, with the arrival of these products, the market has a better resource for risk management.

12.8.5.2 An LNG benchmark

The development in Dubai has stimulated other countries: Qatar has begun a similar project in the field of liquefied natural gas. In addition to the physical flow of LNG, there is also need for financial trading of the product. At the beginning of 2008, Qatar opened a new exchange on which the first LNG contracts in the world are listed. The *International Mercantile Exchange* (IMEX) is a new energy platform on which the first exchange-listed spot-contracts for LNG are traded. The IMEX contract could probably become the leading worldwide benchmark for the price of gas (LNG). The contract will build on and rely on the position that Qatar holds on the international gas market. The Gulf state is now the most important player in LNG.

Because of the flexibility that LNG offers compared to gas, which is transported through pipelines, the IMEX contract will become attractive to suppliers who would otherwise be tied to a particular region; especially if prices in that region are uninviting. The presence of *spot* gas enables producers to arbitrate geographically.

12.8.6 Negative prices

According to economists, prices can never be negative, but this assertion has proved in practice not to be tenable in regard to the energy markets. Markets are perfect so arbitrage is not possible is another assumption that has proved to be incorrect. What appears to be economically and theoretically impossible is, practically speaking, sometimes only too real. The energy markets teach us that, too. Firstly, there is a great deal of arbitrage on the energy markets, which implies imperfection and, to a significant extent, even immaturity. The fragmentation and splintering could lead to a new imbalance. Price discrepancies exist because of the restricted coupling of regional networks, and these discrepancies can be profited from. This sort of situation is part and parcel of continuing change. The more the developments advance, the more the existing arbitrage possibilities will decrease and, in time, no longer even be significant.

A remarkable situation arose on the European gas market at the beginning of October 2006. The gas storage tanks in England were full and demand was low, chiefly because weather conditions were extraordinarily mild. At the same time, the tap to the new gas pipeline from the Norwegian Langeled field to the British coast was fully opened, and how high the pressure be could be turned up had to be tested. The pipeline was intended to provide England with a fifth of its total gas consumption, even in the cold winter months. All in all, more gas was transported through the pipe system than was used and, as is usual, the price fell. The system was out of balance because gas suppliers (producers) pumped more gas into the system than potential consumers wished to use. In such cases, suppliers have to pay a fine to the operator of the gas network (in this case the National Grid, the British equivalent of the Dutch Gas Transport Services), or they can choose to compensate traders for taking the excess gas. In this particular case they chose for the latter, which resulted in a negative gas retail price (minus 5 pence per therm).

**Chapter 13:
Risk Management**

13.1 Identification of risk

All parties involved in the energy markets are subject to risk. One of them is price risk. The price of energy can change both positively and negatively. Producers (energy companies) prefer to receive an as high as possible price for their energy, while consumers (large-scale industrial users, for example) wish to pay the lowest price possible, but neither party likes to be exposed to potential danger (exposure). Many parties wish to limit their risks. Those involved generally prefer a price (development) that is stable and, above all, easily predictable.

Risk management is increasingly becoming the centre of attention because of the extent to which parties take financial positions on their own account, on the one hand; and on the other, because of the volatility in pricing on energy markets.

In order to get a clear picture of market parties' exposure, we first have to know exactly what risks there are, and the magnitude of them, before we can even consider doing anything about them (acceptance or management). The essential order of risk management is to first identify, then measure, then manage. This following chapter is dedicated to management; identification and measurement are dealt with in this section.

13.2 Risk factors

During the process of risk identification, an involved party first has to decide which risks they are exposed to. Probably the most important is operational risk: this includes, among other things, technical issues like unforeseen maintenance as a result of hitches and defects. But just like operational risk, the financial risks are also extremely sizeable. These are further dealt with below.

13.2.1 Natural risk

Natural risk is the risk of the supply of energy being endangered as a result of natural disasters, like earthquakes, volcanic eruptions or hurricanes. Besides the operational damage they cause, the financial consequences can be huge. Taking out an insurance policy is one way to deal with this risk. Financial instruments, like catastrophe bonds or weather derivatives (see Chapter 14, section 14.3) are other options.

13.2.2 Market risk

Market risk, or price risk, is the risk that a market participant's result is negatively influenced by changes in the market price. After taking positions, the market risk of the portfolio can more specifically be described as the difference between the market-to-market value of a financial product or portfolio and the expected value. This difference changes due to price swings during the term of the position or during the period needed to undo the positions.

13.2.3 Liquidity risk

Professional parties usually take positions in financial markets. In order to manage their risks, they take positions with financial instruments. In so doing, it is essential to take the time needed to liquefy a portfolio into account as this liquidity period differs per instrument, per market and per time. On the currency market, trade can be done in the most liquid currencies at any time, but if a company wants to liquefy an OTC derivative it is not always possible to find a counterparty for the transaction in the short term, certainly not at the desired price. A period (liquidation period) is created during which the party is exposed to market risk. In special cases, like a financial crisis on financial markets, for example, the liquidity period is not the same as the duration that would normally be expected. The panic caused can then be so great that it is impossible to find a counterparty with whom to enter into a transaction.

13.2.4 Credit risk

Credit risk, also known as default risk or 'counterparty risk', can be described as the volatility of the result of a company caused by counterparty default (bankruptcy). Energy companies conclude contracts with other parties for significant amounts. If the counterparty defaults, the purchasing company is left with the consequences. This company's portfolio will no longer run smoothly and surpluses or deficits will arise that then have to be smoothed out in the market. But when the whole market has problems, the price against which the balance can be smoothed out becomes extraordinarily unfavourable.

With exchange-listed products, both parties are generally assured of settlement, even if one of the parties is in default. Transactions are guaranteed through clearing houses that take over the risk and do the honours if one party is in default. Of course, remuneration for this service is required.

13.2.5 Currency risk

Just like the majority of other commodities, many energy products are priced in dollars. The dollar exchange rate is essential for enterprises that report in a currency other than the dollar. Products are cheaper for them with a falling dollar, but if the dollar rises the opposite is true. Trading in energy products is therefore sensitive to exchange rates, which indeed applies to both producers and consumers. If necessary, involved parties can cover themselves on financial markets against the possible detrimental consequences of altered exchange rates.

13.2.6 Interest rate risk

Interest rate risk is the main risk in the financial world. The prices of almost all financial instruments are influenced by the level of interest rate. It has to be said, incidentally, that there are many types of interest rate; generally a global breakdown is made in money market interest and capital market interest rate. For simplicity, this division is typified as short and long interest and there is actually a measurable coherence between both rates. Large concerns are generally financed by both their own and borrowed capital; the borrowed capital can be regarded as interest-bearing capital (generally long-term) over which compensation has to be paid. As soon as the capital market interest rate rises, financing costs rise and the value of the company falls.

13.2.7 Transport risk

Transport risk includes capacity problems as well as risks related to physical trading (delivery or purchase risk). The actual delivery or purchase of products is sometimes a problem for energy companies because the available quantity of transport capacity is limited. Parties have to be able to use ships, pipelines or electricity grids; however, situations sometimes arise in which all capacity has been taken up for a particular length of time; or there may be capacity available but not at the desired price.

Apart from that, there are now increasingly more private market participants and enterprises who do not originally come from the energy sector; banks and other trading parties, for example. Physical delivery throws up a barrier for many of them because they do not have access to sources and often have absolutely no idea what to do with any delivered products. Large institutes like (merchant) banks attempt to solve this problem in a creative way, and they are becoming more successful by, for example, collaborating with energy companies or by building or acquiring production capacity themselves.

13.2.8 Geo-political risk

Geo-politics has been thoroughly covered in Chapter 5 and is actually the striving to achieve political objectives on the basis of geographically-grounded arguments. In other words: geo-politics engages in the domestic and foreign politics that countries implement on the basis of the combination of their geographical location and their financial-economic interests in regard to energy dependency.

Political risk is actually derived from the risk that countries bear. It is a form of international credit risk and relates to two things: on the one hand, the power of countries and their regimes; and on the other, the 'willingness' they display. Willingness is a political or policy component, while power refers to economic and financial interests.

Geo-politics comes down to the power play of superpowers. Expression of this power play varies from harassment and threat of cutting off the energy supply to the threat of war and real military action. Expropriation and sudden law and regulation changing play a negative role in the dependability of countries, the investment climate within their borders and the supply security of energy.

13.3 Measurement of risk

After the different types of risks have been identified, the magnitude of the various items has to be measured. This also forms a real part of risk management. Risk management can be done statically or dynamically. There are various methods and various names for the same methods of dynamic market risk management. The essence of it all is summarized in the application of *Value at Risk* (VaR). VaR is being increasingly applied because markets are becoming increasingly deregulated, the number of complex financial products is growing, the volatility of the markets is high and data is becoming available much faster. Because of the complexity of the energy markets, the fact that these are becoming more entwined with financial markets and a number of disasters in the energy world, the risk management of involved parties is tending towards quantification of the risk.

13.3.1 Value at Risk

The Value at Risk model was one of the first methods for quantifying market risk by means of probability calculation. This method of quantification is central to the application of dynamic risk management, whereby VaR is used to unequivocally express the risk on various levels. That could be for a product, the total portfolio, a department, an individual trader or the whole organization. The VaR concept further offers the company information that is relevant for measuring the performance, whereby the risk taken is taken into account. Furthermore, VaR can also be used for quantifying how much capital is needed for carrying out activities. Risks can be compared and consolidated with VaR.

A Value at Risk model can be described as a method of measuring market risk by establishing how much the value of a portfolio can change (drop) as a result of changes in the market prices of financial products.

13.3.2 Stress testing

VaR analysis can be done by using various methods, each of which has its own advantages and disadvantages. One disadvantage they all have is that they do no include *event risk* in the calculation because they work within certain security intervals. Exceptional but rigorous market changes (stress) are therefore left out of the equation. By means of so-called stress testing scenario-analysis, the models can be made complete; *(one time) event risk* can then be taken into account. Extreme situations are assumed to arise and the VaR is calculated on that basis. There have been more than enough extreme situations in the energy markets: the Enron scandal, the implosion of the Amaranth hedge fund and the misery surrounding Metalgeschellshaft are just a few striking examples.

CHAPTER 14:
Risk Management

14.1 Introduction

After the risk has been identified and quantified, the situation becomes clear and a decision can be made as to whether the exposure is acceptable or whether it would be better to reduce the risk exposure. Altering the level of risk run can be done with financial instruments. Derivatives are particularly suitable for this, which is why attention is paid to them in this chapter.

14.2 Derivatives

A derivative is a derived financial product because the pricing is derived from the price of the underlying value. Derivatives are contracts between two parties, in which certain mutual agreements are fixed. Examples of derived products are futures, options and swaps. All these products ensure a shift in the risk. They are therefore also instruments for passing risk on to someone else (or for taking it from them). Derivatives do not create value, but merely move it from one party to another. The appreciation that one party achieves is equal to the depreciation the counterparty suffers, which makes derivatives a *zero-sum game*.

Derivatives are contractual agreements and are set for a limited duration. The validity ends as soon as the contract expires (expiration). Settlement can be done by delivery of the underlying value (physical delivery: examples gasoline, grain and palm oil), but also by cash settlement, whereby the value difference is paid.

14.2.1 Futures

Future contracts are also referred to as forward contracts: exchange-listed *forwards* are also called *futures*. They are contractual agreements about a future delivery of a particular product. The buyer of a future has a purchase obligation, and the seller of a future has a delivery obligation. The specific product to which the agreement relates is included in the contract (the underlying value). This can vary from a certain amount of crude oil, for example, to natural gas, coal, soy oil or maize. The first oil futures were introduced in 1978.

The moment at which the obligations have to be settled is also included in the contract. Actually, everything is written down in the contract; everything except the price. This is fixed between the two counterparties (contracting parties) during their transaction at the exchange.

Futures offer buyers the big advantage of not directly having to invest in the products, but still being able to benefit from the price movement by buying a future contract. It is relative because buyers profit from the rising price movement of the underlying asset but do not (yet) have to store and save it.

There are, of course, also disadvantages to financial products. Futures are not the same as the underlying value; they are just contracts. That means that pricing of futures is not exactly the same as that of the underlying value. Sometimes the pricing of both products differs radically. The *spot price* is not the same as the future price (see section 14.4 about *forward curves*). Futures on financial values are available in various durations: some are for one month, for example, others for one year. That means that not only the date of delivery (or settlement) takes place at another time, but also that it actually relates to different financial products, possible also with totally different price developments. The price of a three-monthly future fell from 8,800 dollars to 6,400 dollars between May 2006 and December 2006. In this same period, the price of a five-year future rose from 2,500 dollars to 4,800 dollars. This caused the forward curve to change suddenly from a vigorous downwards line to a more level line.

Another example happened on the market for maize. The French *Matif Maize future* and the American *CBOT com future* hardly rose in value between 2005 and 2006, whereas the South African *Safex White Maize future* rose by 100% in the same period. After a market participant has decided he wants to take a certain indirect position in a particular underlying value, he then has to decide which specific individual commodity future he wants to trade in. The choice of contract is essentially important.

14.2.2 Options

An option is a right to buy (call-option) a particular financial value during a particular duration, or to sell (put-option) against a previously determined price. At the end of the contract's duration, the right expires and the option might have (intrinsic) value. If the option does have intrinsic value, the holder of the option contract will exercise his right. If the option no longer has any intrinsic value, it expires worthless and the right of the buyer definitely lapses.

The buyer of an option has a right; the seller (writer) has an obligation, for which he receives compensation (a premium). If the option expires worthless, the writer of the option can definitely pocket the premium he received. If, on the other hand, the option has value, he will have to discharge is obligation and he can deduct the premium from his eventual loss, which will make his result less unfavourable.

American-style options are physically settled, while *European-style* options are settled in cash. American-style options can be exercised during the duration, while European-style options can only be exercised at expiration.

A call-option is actually a postponed sale. When taking a position, it is already agreed that the buyer of the call has the right to buy a certain amount of a particular product in the future at the price agreed at the outset. This price is the maximum level against which the sale takes place. If the price of the underlying value drops in the meantime, the holder of the call-option would do better to buy the underlying value on the market at the lower price. In that case, he would not exercise his right, but would allow the option to expire worthless. The big advantage of a postponed sale is that initially no sizeable payment has to be made. The money can remain in the bank or be spent on something else. This offers financing advantage. The buyer of a put-option is at least assured of a minimum sale price. This guarantee is good for many companies and investors because they can manage their risks this way.

14.2.3 Swaps

Swaps more or less represent the game of 'musical chairs'. Swaps are contractual agreements for exchanging future money flows. Future cash flows or other obligations change 'owners' with this instrument. Here again, risk is shifted from one party to another and, on balance, a situation exists in which no value is created. By buying a swap, the buyer can participate in the underlying value without actually having it in his possession.

On the interest market, a swap can offer the following result. If party A has a loan and pays variable interest on it but would prefer to work with fixed interest, and party B has a loan with fixed interest but would prefer variable interest, both parties can swap their cash flows by entering into a swap-contract.

14.3 Weather derivatives

According to estimations, about 25% of world economy is dependent on the weather. The results of farmers, amusement parks, the hotel and catering industry with its outdoor cafés, ice-cream manufacturers, beer brewers, soft-drink companies, the tourism and aviation sectors, insurers and energy producers are all influenced by the weather. The mild winter weather of 2006 cost the Dutch energy company Nuon 100 million euros turnover in the fourth quarter. Because of the relatively high temperatures, their private and commercial clients used less gas. In that period, an average household spent 50 euros less on energy. The profits of the German insurer Allianz greatly increased in 2006, chiefly because of the relatively small number of damage claims as a result of natural disasters. The weather is an interesting factor, not least because it is difficult to predict and impossible to control. Events with the worst consequences and with the lowest probability of occurring are generally taken care of with insurance policies. The implications of floods, drought and storms are overcome that way. Weather situations that occur more often but of which the consequences are less severe, are often covered by weather derivatives.

Weather conditions have a huge influence on energy prices and, therefore, also on our economy. The uncertainty factor linked to this is what many people want to remove. Weather derivatives offer a solution and many energy companies make use of meteorological weather centres' services or even employ a meteorologist themselves. Statistics are enormously important for pricing weather derivatives. On the basis of historical figures, the current trend and seasonal patterns, an estimate is made of the scenarios that could be expected with the accompanying risks. The difference with standard derivatives is that the underlying value in the case of weather derivatives (temperature, rainfall or wind, for example) does not have any direct value for the prices of derived products.

The market for weather derivatives is exploding. This market started in 1997 when the market in the United States became liberalized. Strong growth is happening everywhere in standard products that have been traded on the exchange since 1999. The American option exchange, *Chicago Mercantile Exchange* (CME), has the most active platform. In the 2004-2005 season, 9.7 billion dollars' worth of products were sold. Between 2005 and 2006, that figure rose to 45.2 billion dollars.

Weather derivatives are extremely interesting from an investment point of view because this market manifests absolutely no correlation with stock exchanges. This category of products is expected to become a huge hype on exchanges. Speculators, arbitrators and hedgers will find everything that interests them in weather derivatives; from environment and climate aspects to a gambling instrument, and from a product with leverage function and chance of extremes to a subject from which the most thorough analyses can be made. The recent attention to the weather, environment and climate change contribute to the popularity of weather derivatives. Weather patterns appear to be changing and are becoming less predictable; fluctuations are increasing.

There are several forms of weather derivatives: from calls and puts to swaps, with underlying values from rainfall and wind to temperature. In other words, there is something for everyone.

Weather derivatives are derived products that are paid out as soon as the rainfall or the temperature has reached a particular level, or indeed if it doesn't. A rain contract, for example, can be concluded for 571.40 euros, whereby one party receives 100 euros from the other party for every day that there is more than one centimetre of rainfall,. This agreement is, of course, only for a limited period of time; a month, for example. There is, incidentally, only cash settlement with derived products. Delivery of the underlying value would, after all, be impossible.

It is important that a standard or benchmark exists for weather derivatives, on the basis of which measurements that relate to contracts can be done. Each contract can have its own control point where the final score is kept. If it rains, exactly how many millimetres of rain falls has to be determined. During the day, how many minutes the sun shines without being hindered by clouds has to be recorded. It is obvious that someone who has hedged against weather conditions and whose control point is 100km away may experience certain conditions while no significant results are registered at the control point. After all, weather is a geographic phenomenon and, as such, is extremely locality-related.

Catastrophe bonds are instruments that pay out when a particular disaster occurs. The buyer pays the seller a sort of insurance premium for this. If the doom scenario does not take place, the seller can definitely keep the received premium. Weather derivatives can help farmers to cover the risk they run with their crops. Almost 30% of all American oil production and 20% of gas production comes from the Gulf of Mexico. Of all American refining capacity, 50% is located along the Golf Coast, whereas a quarter of the oil import enters the country via harbours on the south coast between Texas and

Florida. There are also more than 400 offshore oil rigs in the US. The total number is more than 660. Because of this infrastructure, energy consumers, and particularly the Americans, are terrified of hurricanes. The damage from the storm in the Netherlands on 18 January 2007 brought the railways to a standstill. Trams were lifted off their rails, trucks were blown over and trees were uprooted. Six people were killed. The financial damage of that stormy day amounted to 160 million euros. Yet that was nothing compared to the havoc hurricane Katrina left in its wake in America in 2005. That hurricane cost 1,417 human lives. The costs of rebuilding were estimated at 125 billion dollars. Being covered against such disasters is essential.

14.4 Forward curves

A forward curve is a graphic reflection of the price of a forward contract set against the duration. The amount that has to be paid for a particular type of forward with a certain duration can be derived from such graphs. In that respect, the forward curve is comparable to the so-called *yield curve* for interest. The interest payment calculated with loans (like mortgages) varies as the term shortens or lengthens. If the payments remain the same, regardless of term, a flat curve exists. Generally there is a normal curve: a rising interest curve whereby the interest gets higher the longer the term is. The reverse situation is typified as an inverse interest structure. Similar conditions can be recognized in forward contracts in energy. Forward curve forms are not static and therefore always only apply for a particular period of time. The dynamics of the market bring about changes which can even reverse patterns. Moreover, curves can also manifest combinations of both elements: a rising curve that falls further along the graph, for example.

14.4.1 Contango

A market is *in contango* when the price of a long-term forward contract is higher than the price of a short-term forward contract. In other words: the market is *in contango* when the price of a forward contract is higher than the spot price, whereby the spot price is defined as the current price asked for the purchase of the physical product.
A seller of forward contracts has to finance the financial value and therefore misses out on the income from interest. Forward contracts on commodities have to provide for storage and insurance (*cost of carry*). The income that the underlying product generates (dividend for shares and coupon interest for bonds) is deducted from the price. Commodities do not pay out interest, dividend or the like, so, generally speaking, the future price should be higher than the spot price. Then it is a matter of *cash and carry*.

14.4.2 Backwardation

When the price of a forward contract is lower than the spot price and a forward contract becomes cheaper the longer the term is, we talk about *backwardation*. The forward curve then displays a falling line. A potato in the ground is then therefore cheaper than on the market. This situation presents itself when markets are confronted with scarcity. Uncertainty of availability is often reason for violent price fluctuations. Producers would very much like to remove this risk and therefore pay a sort of convenience premium: *convenience yield*.
Buyers of forward contracts in markets that are in backwardation profit not only from a rise in the underlying commodity (*spot return*), but also from the rolling-on of the instruments (*roll return*). For crude oil in the period 1989 to 2004, an annual *roll return* of 9% applied, whereas the *spot return* was only 6%.

14.4.3 Convenience yield

Generally speaking, commodity markets are in contango: this means that the future prices are higher than the spot prices. The longer the term of the forward contract, the larger the price difference. The rise can be traced back to the rise in costs. Goods have to be stored in a depot, which involves cost. That also applies to insuring the goods and the building. Interest also has to be looked at, chiefly because of pre-financing. The products have been bought and the money has been spent, so interest is no longer being received but lost.

When there is scarcity consumers are prepared to pay more for direct delivery. This can sometimes result in a reversed situation. The market then changes from being in contango to a situation of backwardation.

14.4.4 Curve trading

Energy company traders deal with optimizing the company's portfolio. This means that they have to manage the company's (purchase, sales and production) curve. The long-term patterns (annual basis) and the daily, hourly or even quarter-hourly requirements have to be in tune with the need that exists from the market, and with the need of the company's own production environment. This means that deficits have to be made good and surpluses have to be sold. The shorter the term, the more pressure there is to trade and the price results will increase accordingly.

14.5 Spread trading

A spread is a combination of two separate financial products. These can, of course, be traded separately, but if the intention is to set up both transactions or to trade in both it is easier to transact the total strategy directly. This saves costs in general, but more importantly, there is then no price risk. If both parts of the trade are done separately a time difference exists between both exercises. Because of this time difference, no matter how small, a change in the market can arise that could be to the traders advantage, but also to his disadvantage.

14.5.1 Crack spread

The refining margin made by oil companies is referred to in commerce by the term *crack spread*. Refining turns crude oil into ready-to-use end products, like gasoline and heating oil. The crack spread is the difference between the price of the crude oil and the price of the end product; gasoline, for example. The price of crude oil could be stable while the base price of gasoline rises, or vice versa. The reason for this is traceable to the availability of refineries. If the installations are unusable for a certain period of time, because of defect or maintenance for example, then capacity utilization is high and production capacity limited. This will cause the price to rise.

Refining margins are an important element for the eventual results that oil giants achieve. From January to May 2007, the price difference between crude oil and gasoline in the US increased by factor seven from 5 to 35 dollars. The reason again lay in the limited production capacity of refineries. If the shortfall is limited it can be met by importing products from Europe. The fact is that the continent of Europe has had over-capacity for years, and has been exporting oil to the US for years. As luck would have it, however, there were also all sorts of problems on the European labour market (unrest) at that time. For the first time since 1991, the American reserve of gasoline fell to below 195 million barrels, and that related to only a 3-week supply for motorists at that time.

Crack spreads can only be traded on a few energy exchanges. A market participant actually buys crude oil and simultaneously sells the refined product, or the other way around. In this way a speculator can anticipate a change in the price difference (the spread) while the refinery can use the instrument to cover the risk of adverse price changes.

14.5.2 Crush spread

A *crush spread* is for soybeans what a *crack spread* is for crude oil. With a crush spread, the refining products are soy flour and soy oil. Processing is subject to processes and so can, in due course, result in capacity problems.

14.5.3 Spark spread

A *spark spread* is actually the production margin of gas-fired power plants. Some energy companies stoke gas to heat the boilers which generate electricity. Most of the power plants in the Netherlands are of this type, whereas most plants worldwide are coal-fired. That means that companies with gas-fired plants buy in vast amounts of natural gas and then convert it to electricity, which is then offered on the market. Seeing as there is a time difference between the purchase of the gas or coal and the sale of the electricity, there is a risk. Because most market parties are averse to risk, they readily cover themselves against potential danger. The spark spread is traded as an instrument for risk management as it reflects the price difference between gas and electricity in an uncomplicated way. Furthermore, the conversion of one product into the over is taken into account.

14.5.4 Dark spread

The *dark spread* is comparable to the spark spread, except that gas is replaced by coal. If power plants are coal-fired, a dark spread can be chosen to cover the risk. The plant buys vast amounts of coal and sells the produced electricity. If the price of electricity falls and the price of coal rises, the power plant makes less profit. This situation can easily happen as the production of electricity has always been reasonably stable. Buying and supplying coal happens in fits and starts. This means that time differences arise between purchase, production and sale. In order to prevent these time differences being detrimental to the energy company, a dark spread can be set up. With this strategy speculators can try to profit from the price development of the product involved.

A dark spread is also called a *dirty spread* because electricity production by means of stoking coal releases a great deal of carbon dioxide. As a counterbalance, so-called *clean dark spreads* are also traded. These are 'ordinary' dark spreads with the inclusion of the required CO_2 rights.

14.6 Correlation

It was mentioned earlier in this book that there are several sorts of crude oils available, all with their own characteristics. That actually means that each sort is a separate product and can be found on the financial markets. The products each have their own price and display their own price development. The price of crude oil from the North Sea therefore generally displays a different price development than that of oil from the US. Nevertheless, prices in general display a reasonably similar pattern. Price results show a close relationship, and this phenomenon is reflected in the concept of correlation. If there is a positive connection between the price developments of two products, we talk about a positive correlation. The prices of Brent oil and WTI oil are positively correlated as, generally speaking, the prices of both products will (in the long term) rise when there is (geo) political tension, under-capacity or if oil supplies run low. The prices will both fall when a new fuel is found or when techniques have improved to such an extent that 90% can suddenly be extracted from oil sources instead of the current 30 to 40%. In other words: the products can to a large extent be used as substitutes.

When there is a negative connection and two prices move in different directions, we talk about negative correlation. An example of that is the price of sunglasses and umbrellas. People will pay more for an umbrella when it rains and less for a pair of sunglasses. As soon as the sun shines, the reverse is true. The prices of these two products are therefore negatively correlated.

It is important to realize that the mathematical calculations upon which the correlation is determined are based on the past; whereas it is exactly the future correlation that is important for decision-making. The calculated correlation should therefore not be seen as sacred, but as an aid for determining or estimating future correlation. Correlation is therefore a dynamic concept and must be seen and employed as such. The price correlation of two different products can never be completely (plus or minus) 1.00 (or 100%), and will therefore always fluctuate somewhere between minus one and plus one.

14.7 Cross margin

Spread trading appears in all sorts of forms and is definitely not restricted to the ready-to-use combinations described in the previous sections. Based on the story about correlation above, a participant in financial markets can choose to take advantage of the supposed positive correlation between the prices of two products. He can try to earn some money with it. As soon as a market participant has the notion that the difference (the spread) between the prices of two products is too small or too large and he feels the prices will develop in the direction he intended, he will buy the (supposed) most under-valued and simultaneously sell the (supposed) most over-valued.

Such constructions are often converted to forward contracts. The market risk is eliminated by the opposing positions. If the market in general falls or rises, by military entanglements or a financial crisis for example, the prices of both products will generally move in the same direction. They are then positively correlated, although it has to be said that correlations in situations of stress have a higher risk of ending up differently than was at first expected. If the price development does indeed go according to plan, the initiator will liquidate the positions at the desired moment. By entering into transactions that are opposed to the initial transactions, profit is locked in and the positive result can be realized.

The use of forward contracts has a big advantage: when two positions are taken with forward contracts, the initiator gets a discount on the capital that he has to guarantee (security or *margin*). Seeing as his forward positions are opposing and their prices also display a high positive correlation (example: +0.92), the market risk is particularly small. This is why the initiator of this sort of position gets a discount on the guarantee that he has to adhere to. Because of the opposing, or crossing, position, the generally-adhered to guarantee is also called the *cross margin*.

Institutional investors often try to profit from the negative correlation of energy products with other asset classes. It turned out in the past that the prices of commodities were negatively correlated with share and bond prices. By including both stocks and commodities in an investment portfolio, the investor spreads his risk. The result achieved by doing this is, in the long term, usually more favourable than by not taking this action.

SUMMARY & CONCLUSION

Energy controls an important part of our lives. Scarcity rules on the commodities market, which sends prices rocketing. The five largest economic blocs (the US, Europe and Japan, as well as newcomers China and Japan) all produce insufficient oil and gas to meet their own consumption needs and are, therefore, all dependent on import. Governments implement policies based on price, quality and supply security. Energy markets are interwoven both nationally and internationally; because of which geo-political interests increase, and that can be felt deep in all sectors of the markets. Sometimes the pressure mounts so high that it leads to military tension. Confrontations between the US and China can therefore no longer be excluded.

Politicizing and militarizing ownership of fossil fuels is an import consequence of scarcity. Many commodities are found in countries that have a politically-unstable climate, and the increasing importance of commodities creates a shift in the balance power. In addition, little is traded on many commodity markets, which results in pricing not being very transparent. This can be the cause of large price-swings or price differences between various parties. Moreover, illiquid markets and products are subject to the whims and fancies of speculators, and the strong concentration of suppliers is not good for the market either. One or a few parties can manipulate the (desired or intended) price. Fundamental issues like supply and demand are of secondary importance in a situation like this. Antitheses do not only occur in the commodity and energy markets, there is also discord between various governmental departments, between countries in general and between the rich West and the poor countries in the world.

Developments in the field of the environment are just as poignant. The climate is changing and the demand for control is increasing. Alternative energy sources have to offer a solution; the world can no longer shrink from energy transition. Need is high, but the transition process will take a few years, or maybe even decades. Acknowledgement and recognition come before energy transition and will give priority to the revised way of thinking. Governmental intervention with implementing the new policy is essential, as is the concluding of international agreements. It goes without saying that the necessary technological developments will cost a lot of money. For the time being, individual activities worsen the competitive position.

The problems surrounding energy and the environment are not temporary, but they do contain a number of characteristics that are. The current energy hype, just like every whim of fancy, brings anxiety and danger. The objective to have a clean, reliable and affordable energy supply in 2050 must not be overshadowed by too-strict ambitions for 2020. It is, after all, just an intermediate step. Apart from which, there is the risk that clean technology will be implemented before it is ready to be brought onto the market.

The market is hugely important as climate policy is nowhere without market processes. Statutory environmental standards are essential, as is a well-functioning fiscal policy. The problem is so vast and complex that taxes and subsidies alone are just not enough. Enormous investments are needed, but these will only be forthcoming when CO_2 reduction is worthwhile, economically speaking. Environmental policy will cost a lot of money in the short term. Sustainability will not be realized at the drop of a hat. Nuclear energy and carbon dioxide capture are not ideal instruments, but as far as sustainability is concerned, they have to be considered.

The problems on the energy markets are caused by the objectives mankind strives for. Everyone wants to advance, but what does that involve? What is progress actually? The answer to the second question lies in the question of whether or not prosperity is only measured in money. Economic developments involve heavy demands, for which a toll has to be paid. A number of parties are still acting dumb, but this hypocrisy will soon disappear. Research has shown that the economy has caused damage to the ecology since 1700, and it is not expected to be any different in the future. The solution to the problems requires intervention in all sorts of areas within society, and industry, the taxpayer, the energy-user, the motorist, the business-traveller, the holidaymaker and the consumer will all experience the consequences. We are leaving the world to our children, and we need to do that in such a way that we can ourselves lead satisfying lives without our descendents being saddled with the bill.

It is impossible that no drastic measures are needed. Radical change of thought is a bitter necessity. Everyone must head in the same direction, but we still have a long way to go as far as that is concerned. Energy markets are vast, involve a great many different issues and are extremely complex. No-one is all-wise and all-seeing; which is probably a good thing. But one thing is certain: time will tell. However, there will not be a quick change in the use of fuels. Thinking we can continue without oil, gas, coal and nuclear energy is proof of little understanding. Weapons against CO_2 emissions must not only be deployed in producing clean new cars, installing new power plants or new industrial installations; measures are also needed for existing and out-of-date production plants and vehicles. For cars we could think of fiscal measures, a solid traffic-jam policy, speed restrictions, traffic management, bio-fuel and getting rid of conflicting legislation like safety requirements.

The road we have to take is long and difficult. Sustainable energy sounds good, but production capacity is not automatically available. Rigorous actions, large investments and progress in technology are essentials. Now that urgency is more critical, it is essential that a number of scenarios are analysed and linked to probabilities. It is a matter of setting priorities and a long-term policy. Problems can only effectively be dealt with if we look further than the period of office of an incumbent cabinet. Future policy must take technological feasibility into account, and it must be affordable for producers and consumers. Correct choices can only be made when objective information is available. Debate is desirable, but it must quickly lead to the objective; problems do not solve themselves at the talks table. Fortunately there is hope. There are opportunities on many fronts and considerable amounts of money are available. That, together with a strong dose of will-power, should get us quite some way. Mankind is capable of achieving great things, especially when the pressure mounts.

The integration of energy markets in financial markets will be concluded. Energy companies will be increasingly driven because of cash-flows. Risk management will take on a more significant role and that will result in the increasing importance of derivatives within energy companies. It is highly likely that weather derivatives will become a real hype; and that will not remain restricted to applications for companies in the energy sector.

Increasingly more participants from the conventional financial world, like (merchant) banks and hedge funds, will enter the energy markets. They are experts in speculation and arbitrage, and it is expected that these parties will exchange knowledge with (former) utility companies. As a result of this cluster of knowledge, a real explosion can also be expected in the development of financial instruments, like structured products.

Because of integration, the volume of the capital flow and the increasing importance of regulation, legislation and transparency, it can be expected that energy companies' trading departments and the traders employed in them will be subordinate to a sort of hallmark institute. This sort of body will have to protect the branch's reputation from harm. The significance of the sector is enormous and is seen as being of paramount importance. The phenomenon of market power and the appearance of market abuse are issues that create a negative image of the sector. Those involved want to be proud of the sector's reputation and clear names where possible.

In conclusion, many developments are expected in the area of benchmarks and indices, fed particularly by the urgent need for transparency. New measures and standards will appear and the old indices will eventually be forced off the stage.

CONVERSION TABLES

CONVERSION TABLE FOR ENERGY

From: \ To:	TJ	Gcal	Mtoe	Mbtu	GW*h
TJ	1	238.8	$2.388*10^{-5}$	947.8	0.2778
Gcal	$4.1868*10^{-3}$	1	10^{-7}	3.968	$1.163*10^{-3}$
Mtoe	$4.1868*10^{4}$	10^{7}	1	$3.968*10^{7}$	11.630
Mbtu	$1.0551*10^{-3}$	0.252	$2.52*10^{-8}$	1	$2.931*10^{-4}$
GW*h	3.6	860	$8.6*10^{-5}$	3.412	1

Multiplication factors (whereby '^'refers to 'the power of')

CONVERSION TABLE FOR NATURAL GAS AND LNG

From: \ To:	1 bcm NG	1 bcf NG	1 mio te	1mio ton LNG	1 t. Btu	1 mio boe
1 bcm NG	1	35.3	0.90	0.73	36	6.29
1 bcf NG	0.028	1	0.026	0.021	1.03	0.18
1 mio te	1.111	39.2	1	0.805	40.4	7.33
1 mio ton LNG	1.38	48.7	1.23	1	52.0	8.68
1 t. Btu	0.28	0.98	0.025	0.02	1	0.17
1 mio boe	0.16	5.61	0.14	0.12	5.8	1

Multiplication factors

Whereby:
NG   = natural gas
bcm   = billion cubic metre
bcf   = billion cubic foot
te   = ton equivalent
t. Btu = trillion British thermal units
boe   = barrels of oil equivalent

CONVERSION TABLE FOR CRUDE OIL

To:	Tonne (metric)	Kilolitre	Barrels	US gallons
From:				
Tonne (metric)	1	1.165	7.33	307.86
Kilolitre	0.8581	1	6.2898	264.17
Barrels	0.1364	0.159	1	42
US gallons	0.00325	0.0038	0.0238	1

Multiplication factors based on average global gravity

LIST OF FIGURES

GLOSSARY

API

API is a measurement of the viscosity of liquids, like oil.

APX

APX is an energy exchange with platforms on which gas and electricity are traded. APX is particularly known for being a facilitator of the imbalance market.

Balancing regime

There must be a balance in energy networks (of gas and electricity, for example) between what is put in and what is taken out, otherwise problems arise. The service operator demands that parties in the energy market bear the responsibility for this balance. If they land in a situation of imbalance, they must rectify it quickly or be fined by the service operator.

Base load

Base load is the term used for the basic requirements of energy consumers.

Benchmark

Standard of reference used for measuring the relative strength of performance.

CO2

Carbon dioxide.

Commodity

Raw material. The concept of commodity is used in financial markets to refer to asset classes relating to raw materials.

Concession

The right to explore a particular area for the presence of oil or gas, and then to exploit the area..

Continental shelf

Geological undersea continuation of a continental region.

DTe

Directie Toezicht energie – Energy Regulation Service. The body is part of NMA (Netherlands Competition Authority) and is employed in ensuring energy markets function as well as possible.

Rollover
The closing of a position (in derivatives, for example) with a certain expiration date and the (often simultaneous) opening of an agreed position with a more distant exercise date.

EBN
Energie Beheer Nederland – Energy Management Netherlands is 100% owned by the Dutch state.

EC
The European Commission embodies and promotes the interests of the European Union. The Commission has its seat in Brussels.

ECN
The Energieonderzoek Centrum Nederland – Energy Research Centre - is the largest Dutch research centre in the field of energy.

Endex
European energy derivatives exchange, strongly aimed at the Benelux countries.

EnergieNed
EnergieNed, a federation of energy companies in the Netherlands, is the sector organization for all companies in the Netherlands involved in production, transport, trade or supply of gas, electricity and/or heating.

Energy Council
The Energy Council (or General Energy Council) is a Dutch governmental advisory body

ERGEG
European Regulators Group for Electricity and Gas: Coordinating organization of Europe's regulators in the field of gas and electricity.

EU
The European Union is a collaboration of 27 European countries. Collaboration takes place in the fields of politics, economy and law.

Eurohub
The Eurohub was an inter-connector in South Limburg which was set up as a gas trading place for various large international energy traders. It closed in 2006 and was the forerunner of TTF.

Exposure

The amount that is exposed to potential danger: the amount of risk.

Fade down

Reducing a power plant's production. The more a plant is faded down, the less production capacity is utilized. At total fade down, the plant will generate no production at all.

Fade up

The increasing of a power plant's production, as a result of which production capacity is better utilized.

FcFs (First come, First served)

The operator allots capacity to market participants on the *'first come, first served'* principle. In order of application and on a non-discriminatory basis, GTS sells 'firm' capacity in advance. If firm capacity is eventually not allocated or utilized, owners of 'interruptible' capacity may still utilize the unused capacity.

Firm capacity

Capacity sold in advance by TSO on a non-discriminatory basis and in order of application, whereby the buyer is assured that the bought capacity is really for him. This reservation gives security and makes 'firm' capacity more expensive then 'interruptible' capacity.

Fraction

Component of a mixture. The term fraction is chiefly used if the component can be separated from the mix by means of an isolating method, like refining through distillation or filtration.

GasTerra

Split commercial enterprise of the former Gasunie. GasTerra is 40% owned by EBN, 10% by the Dutch government, 25% by Shell and 25% by ExxonMobil.

Gas Transport Services (GTS)

GTS is the Dutch national transmission-system operator and a full subsidiary of Gasunie.

Gasunie

As trader and transporters, Netherlands Gasunie PLC monopolized the Dutch wholesale gas market from 1963 to 2005. The company was owned 25% by both Shell and ExxonMobil, 10% by the Dutch government and 40% by EBN.

From 2005 to date, Netherlands Gasunie PLC is a construction company and project developer for the Dutch gas sector. The company is now 100% owned by the government and is also 100% parent company of GTS.

GOS

The Netherlands has about 1,100 gas-capture plants. At a GOS, gas is injected into the national gas network or taken out of it. Bilateral trade only takes place at a GOS.

Groningen field

The largest continental gas field in Europe: it is spread out over a large part of the province of Groningen, but is also named after the town of Slochteren. The gas in the field is characterised by its low-calorie value (L-gas), and the field is characterised by low marginal production costs and its extreme flexibility in absorbing seasonal patterns (swing capacity).

GWEC

Global Wind Energy Council.

HHI-index

The Herfindahl Hirschmann Index combines the squared sum of all the market shares of all suppliers and is an indicator for market concentration. A monopolistic market has a score of one hundred squared (10,000). A market with an index between 1,800 and 10,000 is regarded as concentrated.

IAEA

The International Atomic Energy Agency is an United Nation's organization focused on scientific and technical collaboration in the field of nuclear technology and its peaceful use. In total, 136 countries are members of the institute, which is based in Vienna.

IEA

International Energy Agency set up by the Organization for Economic Cooperation and Development in 1974, to which 26 mainly Western countries are associated. The institute is actually an energy advice body for the associated countries. Its role is to coordinate problems in times of energy-source scarcity.

IMF

The International Monetary Fund is an institute that helps countries in financial need. Head Office of this 'crisis manager' is in Washington, USA. The IMF is a part of the United Nations and lends help under certain conditions. The IMF focuses on monetary collaboration and stability, monitoring economic growth, employment and exchange rate systems, and temporary financial help to correct deficits in the balance of payments.

Interruptible capacity

Switchable capacity that is sold when all the 'firm' capacity has been bought. The cheaper 'interruptible' capacity can, on a switchable basis, be utilized if 'firm' capacity remains unused.

IPCC

International Panel on Climate Change. Panel of the OECD.

Carbon dioxide

CO_2.

Quality conversion

The conversion of the calorific value of gas from high-calorie (H-gas) to low-calorie (L-gas): This is done by mixing H-gas with nitrogen or other gasses.

Kyoto Protocol

Climate treaty from 1997 signed in and named after the Japanese city of Kyoto. The treaty aims at reducing greenhouse gas emissions. Australia and the US, the biggest polluter in the world, have not signed.

Liberalization

There is talk of liberalization when a government lifts restrictions on access to a particular market and therefore allows competition. Liberalization of the energy markets involves making access possible for all parties who want to enter the market without discriminating against certain parties. The objective of liberalization is free pricing.

Light oil

Liquid oil, the viscosity of which is measured in API degrees.

Liquefaction

Converting natural gas into liquid form, resulting in the Liquefied Natural Gas that is transported in ships.

MNP

The Milieu- en Natuurplanbureau - Netherlands Environmental Assessment Agency – is an agency that was part of the Ministry of Health and Environment until 1 May 2005. The body now operates independently and is part of the Ministry of Housing, Regional Development and the Environment. The Director of the MNP is also an advisory member of the Scientific Council for Government Policy. The MNP's mission is to advice the government on political and social considerations regarding economic, ecological, environmental and cultural matters.

NAM

Nederlandse Aardolie Maaatschappij – the Netherlands Petroleum Association is an oil and gas producing company that has a large number of the Dutch licences. The NAM also has the licence for the exploitation of the Groningen Field. NAM is a joint venture between Shell and ExxonMobil

NWEA

The Netherlands Wind Energy Association promotes the interests of wind energy. Within the NWEA, all the organizations and companies that are active in the Netherlands in the field of wind energy work together.

NMa

Nederlandse Mededingingsautoriteit – Netherlands Competition Authority is the regulator of the free market in the Dutch economy and aims at preventing cartel formation and/or market power. It has set up separate bodies for sectors with specific problems; DTe is specifically focussed on the energy market.

Nominate

Determining, shortly before physical delivery, how much of the booked 'firm' capacity will be used. The un-nominated capacity is utilized by others as 'interruptible' capacity.

OECD

The Organization for Economic Cooperation and Development is a collaboration of 30 (chiefly Western) countries that discusses, studies and coordinates social and economic policy. The countries attempt to solve problems together and attune international policy.

Oil equivalents

Oil substitutes or products derived from oil. Generally gas is meant, which is then expressed in the same measure as oil: in barrels of 159 litres.

OTC

'Over the counter' refers to privately-negotiated trading. Transactions on the financial markets can be closed on a central trading platform, like an exchange, or they can be privately-negotiated, whereby parties make direct contact with each other.

Peak load

Peak-load pricing is a form of price differentiation, whereby a higher price is charged during peak times than during off-peak times. Peak-load pricing is intended to make better use of the total available volume of capacity. Consumers who have high price-elasticity (those who are price-sensitive) move their consumption to the period in which more capacity is available and prices are lower. It is part of an efficiently functioning market.

Privatization

The selling-off of government-owned enterprises.

Programme responsibility

Programme responsibility is the responsibility of consumers (except protected consumers) and licence holders to draw up introduction, transport and use of electricity programmes for the service operators, and to abide by these programmes. The entity responsible for the programme comes between the service operator and the supplier. This entity is responsible for purchasing electricity. Exit and entry must be equal: a difference is referred to as an imbalance, a situation that TenneT discourages by imposing a fine.

Regasification

Regasification is the process whereby Liquefied Natural Gas (LMG) is returned to gas form. This generally takes place (close to) import terminals.

Spare capacity

Spare capacity is available capacity that is not being used.

Senter Novem

A Dutch Ministry of Economic Affairs' agency focused on innovative issues.

Shipper

A company that transports gas in the national gas transport system based on contracts with the TSO.

Supercyclus theory

A theory that supposes that structural under-investment will eventually lead to supply and demand 'mismatch'.

Task Force Energy transition

An governmental advisory body set up by the Dutch Ministries of Economic Affairs and Housing, Regional Development and the Environment to make the Netherlands more sustainable.

TenneT

As a TSO and manager of the Dutch national transport system, TenneT is responsible for the 'motorways' of the electricity grid that links all regional and European grids together. In addition to service operation, TenneT guards the reliability and continuity of the Dutch electricity supply.

Teu
In the container shipping world, Teu stands for 'twenty-foot equivalent unit'. Teu is the unit of a container ship's capacity. Most containers worldwide are twenty or forty feet in length.

Title Transfer Facility (TTF)
TTF is a virtual network on which gas is traded in the Netherlands. GTS is actively involved in the setting-up of TTF.

TPA
Third Party Access relates to creating third party access to the infrastructural network by means of proceedings.

Transport Service Operator (TSO)
A Transport Service Operator, or TSO, is the organization/body whose task it is to manage/operate the energy transportation network. The TSO is generally a state-controlled company. TenneT is the TSO for electricity in the Netherlands and Gas Transport Services fulfils a similar function for gas.

UIOLI
'Use it or lose it' refers to the TSO's measure to avoid market parties buying more scarce transport capacity that they themselves need in order to keep it off the market.

ULCC
Ultra Large Crude Carriers: the largest vessels suitable for transporting oil.

VLCC
Very large Crude Carriers: the second-largest vessels suitable for transporting oil.

VOEG
The Dutch Free Trade Organization for Gas and Electricity is a collaboration between companies active in energy trading.

UN
The United Nations is an international organization set up in 1945 directly after World War 2. It is a global organization of governments working together in the field of international law, global security, maintaining human rights, developing world economy and research into social and cultural developments.

Volatiliteit

Volatility is another word for the amount of movement, usually of prices (the extent of price fluctuation). Volatility is a concept that is important for pricing of options.

World Bank

The World Bank is an organization that, just like the IMF, was set up after World War 2 in line with the Marshall Plan. It is an international organization that offers loans, gifts and technical support to help developing countries implement their plans for combating poverty. During the Cold War, the bank financed development projects to keep poor regions within the Western capitalist range of influence. The organization is a part of the United Nations and works according to the 'one dollar, one vote' principle, which means that control is divided in proportion to the money contributed.

Wobbe Index

Measure for the calorific value of gas.

WTO

The World Trade Organization is an inter-governmental organization with supranational characteristics. The body was set up in 1995 and is a continuing part of the GATT that was set up in Geneva in 1923. Its tasks are the promotion of international trade, solving trade conflicts and eliminating trade barriers.

Zeebrugge

Belgian sea port, which is also the physical hub for gas delivery in Belgium.

Sweet oil

Oil with a low sulphur level.

Sour oil

Oil with a high sulphur level.

Heavy oil

Extremely syrupy crude oil, the liquidity of which is measured in API degrees.